T0128273

Also by Pamela S. Alexander

Psyche's Poetry:
Beauty to Awaken the Soul

Initiation of the Soul

Myths and Fairy Tales as a Path of Awakening to Freedom and Wholeness

Pamela S. Alexander, PhD

BALBOA.PRESS

A DIVISION OF HAY HOUSE

Balboa Press books may be ordered through booksellers or by contacting:

Balboa Press
A Division of Hay House
1663 Liberty Drive
Bloomington, IN 47403
www.balboapress.com
1 (877) 407-4847

Because of the dynamic nature of the Internet, any web addresses or links contained in this book may have changed since publication and may no longer be valid. The views expressed in this work are solely those of the author and do not necessarily reflect the views of the publisher, and the publisher hereby disclaims any responsibility for them.

The author of this book does not dispense medical advice or prescribe the use of any technique as a form of treatment for physical, emotional, or medical problems without the advice of a physician, either directly or indirectly. The intent of the author is only to offer information of a general nature to help you in your quest for emotional and spiritual well-being. In the event you use any of the information in this book for yourself, which is your constitutional right, the author and the publisher assume no responsibility for your actions.

Cover photo by Michelle Lenhard
Cover painting by Pamela S. Alexander

Print information available on the last page.

ISBN: 978-1-9822-3798-1 (sc)
ISBN: 978-1-9822-3800-1 (hc)
ISBN: 978-1-9822-3799-8 (e)

Library of Congress Control Number: 2019917446

Balboa Press rev. date: 12/10/2019

Contents

Contents

Dedication

To Sophia, the Soul, and Unity.

Note to the Reader

*I*f you are interested in reading the fairy tales in their entirety, I recommend Ralph Manheim's translation of *Grimms' Tales for Young and Old*. The story of "Psyche and Eros" is a chapter in the larger work by Apuleius called *The Golden Asse: The Transformation of Lucius*. The chapter title in the book is "The Marriage of Cupid and Psyches." The version of "Beauty and the Beast" that I based this interpretation on is by Madame Leprince de Beaumont's, and an older version of the story is by Madame de Villeneuve.

*C*hildren are often raised by well-meaning parents who teach their child in much the same way they were taught. Rarely does anyone ever disagree with the important things they share, so the parents continue to believe they are right.

They name their baby and educate it about its body, thoughts, and emotions. They explain their family, religion, and society, as opposed to others. They create a story for the baby to live by. There is one small problem with the story... it simply isn't true.

Prologue

Once upon a time, there was a beautiful fairy tale princess who sat alone waiting for a handsome prince to come along and rescue her. Well, that's what you might think if you were in a patriarchal culture in which the rational, logical, literal mind-set was the predominant way of thinking, which of course we are.

Since the fairy tale obviously isn't meant to be taken literally, let's remove those glasses and put on ones with symbolic lenses instead. Now we can look at the story differently. The princess represents the soul. During the "waiting" phase of her initiatory process, she's not searching for solutions in the world, but is looking inside of herself. Real transformation doesn't come from outer changes, but inner ones. This princess is going against the culture's norms and beliefs; she's challenging inherited patterns of understanding about herself and the world, breaking the rules, and bravely following her heart.

The heroine's waiting is finished when she learns to take back her power, when she can face any adversity with courage, and once she discovers a truth inside of herself that's an unshakable *knowing* about her true identity. *Then* the prince arrives and it's time to act on what she has learned, which means to embody her truth in the world. The prince in this scenario represents the energy of doing or moving forward. When the couple marries, it represents a union of the unseen and the seen, or the form and formless, which is a movement out of duality and into a higher state of consciousness.

It's time for us to reclaim this courageous heroine from the pages of these old narratives as she shows us how to navigate our souls' journey through the terrain that we call life.

Many of us have categorized fairy tales as imaginal and dismissed them as irrelevant. They appear to be silly outdated stories that paint girls as passive victims and boys as rescuers. In many instances, we haven't even questioned that perspective. With our own personal stories, we have taken them to be solid, true, and unchangeable, without questioning them either. We have been conditioned by those who are caught in their own stories, and most of us don't see things any differently. What if fairy tales contain truth, and our personal stories aren't true?

The impulse we call life wants us to know and live the truth of who we are. Each of us has a unique version of what's possible for ourselves and our lives when we step out of the stories we've identified with, which is true freedom. This is what's really happening to us every day. We encounter people, situations, and have dreams, all with one purpose, which is to release us from the limited stories we have erroneously come to believe as who we are.

This is what stories, myths, fairy tales, religion, and dreams are really about. They are symbolically showing us how to wake up from the personal story we inherited and often have not questioned. Why are they symbolic? Because they speak in the language of the heart and soul, not the mind. Their agenda is to align the soul with a greater truth regarding its identity and free it from the old story.

The journey in a story is intended to facilitate an inner transformation, which will result in an outer change. This is how we can evolve into the next phase of being human to inhabit a new world. If we want to save this planet and ourselves, the stories say we need to transform ourselves, and they are showing us how. Imagine growing up in poverty and believing for your whole life that you were poor. Then one day, as an adult, someone tells you that your parents are royalty. You might wonder how on Earth could that happen? Babies switched in the hospital at birth? Well, not quite.

Our parents condition us from the time we are born and we usually accept what they tell us. Our self, family, culture, beliefs, and world are shaped and defined by others. In many instances, that's what we continue to believe. There often isn't any reason not to.

We might reject some beliefs as we get older—perhaps we leave their religion, embark on a career they disagree with, embrace more expansive views about gender, or date someone they don't like—but most of us stop there, unless we have a reason not to. Not believe the story of us, that is.

There is currently a resurgence of interest in personal stories: old stories, new ones, lived and unlived, what is and what's wanted. We are becoming more aware of our stories and whether those stories are the ones we want to live. We are deciding if we want new stories and how to live them.

Then there are the cultural stories that we live. Many of us share similar basic story lines, which are reflected in the cultural myths, fairy tales, and popular fiction, like *Harry Potter, Star Wars,* and *The Wizard of Oz.* The stories that resonate with large segments of the population contain symbolic information about the culture's state of consciousness.

Now imagine if hundreds of years ago a religion or society was being developed in which those seeking power wanted the people to believe the leaders had all the power. A time in which those in positions of authority wanted people to look to them for answers, to follow, and conform. But let's just say, there were others who saw what was happening and that the truth was being concealed to further the agendas of a few. Those others began telling fantastic stories around the fire at night. In order to conceal these stories from those who were in power, the tales appeared to be silly, imaginative, and nonsense. And the stories easily passed under the noses of those in charge and down through the centuries to us today.

The stories were collected from the fireside storytellers years ago when there was a concern that they might be lost or forgotten. The tales were written down and determined to be for children, but how to explain the horrific details of some stories? In a retelling of these versions, the gruesome parts were just omitted, and we ended up with watered-down remnants of the original stories.

Some people think fairy tales and myths are imaginative stories that are irrelevant to adults and life. Some scholars suggest classic fairy tales are detrimental to the perception of women and young girls, because they portray them as passive, weak victims waiting for the strong, handsome prince to save them. That perspective results from looking at these stories *literally.*

Fairy tales, like dreams, don't usually speak in a literal, logical, rational language, but rather utilize symbolism. When we view a story symbolically, as we are in this book, we can discern its deeper meaning in several ways. One perspective for these stories is as the soul's initiatory journey. The fairy-tale princess is not sitting around waiting to be rescued but is being initiated into higher consciousness. Her challenges with the stepmother, stepsisters, witch, and other contrary characters, are pushing her to the edge of her limits to help her break through the old beliefs that keep her from recognizing how powerful and capable she really is. This perspective reveals the deeper purpose and meaning of all we encounter in our own lives, which is to assist us in the expansion of our consciousness so that we might realize who we are. Since what we've been told isn't accurate, life initiates us in order to reveal the truth. These stories show us how to open our awareness to our own souls.

The soul isn't feminine, but it can be symbolically perceived as such when viewing spirit as masculine. This delineation helps us to understand the soul's journey, as depicted in the context of a story. The masculine and feminine characters represent qualities involved in the soul's development, which we master and integrate to embody a fuller expression of the truth of who we really are. A symbolic perspective can help us to understand the story's deeper meaning and how it relates to our own stories.

The Story's Characters

All of the characters in these stories can be perceived as aspects of us—for both men and women. The heroine may symbolize qualities often perceived as "feminine," and as the soul, while the masculine can represent "male" qualities such as spirit. These ways of being, delineated as male and female, are not truly about gender, but are frequently perceived as such. This way of interpreting a story helps us to see how they are personally relevant, and how we can integrate any unconscious qualities, which are those parts of ourselves that we have denied or repressed.

The predominant preference in many cultures is for masculine qualities, which often means that the things associated with the feminine are repressed or rejected. This may create an imbalance, which can result in many people as exhaustion, anger, and stress from too much "masculine" activity and not enough "feminine" rest, relaxation, and play. Our resources are being depleted at an alarming rate, personally and environmentally. We are often over-reliant on the intellect, literal and analytical thinking, while ignoring intuition, body awareness, heart, soul, and emotions. This limits our ability to generate creative solutions to our current crises. Our conditioning compels us to look outside ourselves for answers to personal questions. The experts tell us how much to sleep, what to eat, wear, believe, who we are, how to live, and where to find happiness.

Although, this set of qualities (masculine and feminine) may be judged, with one set as being better or worse than the other, neither has any inherent value. Many of these aspects, when combined, are required in order to be a fully functioning human. We can utilize rational and non-rational ways of perception, act and rest, in order to approach life in a balanced way. In the East, it is referred to as the "balance of yin and yang." This black and white symbol is contained in a circle, which represents wholeness. The qualities of male and female, when combined, give us access to a full range of capabilities.

In wholeness, we live in our natural state of joy and peace, which arises spontaneously by not rejecting emotions, thoughts, or others. When we embrace and accept all of the aspects we have judged and defined as being male or female, we don't project the so-called undesirable ones onto others. Then, we become open to all people, situations, and life without judgment or fear. We are able to tolerate differences and the world is a better place for everyone.

When we perceive all the characters in the fairy tales as parts of us, it widens our self-perspective, and this creates a more holistic view. We then acquire more compassion and understanding of others as well. The young women in these fairy tales are symbols of the soul. They are not waiting to be saved by a prince, but the soul is saving itself, as it becomes aware of the inner presence of spirit and unites with it. This leads to a conscious embodiment of the Self.

The Self

The Self is a unitary wholeness that accepts and contains everything. It is beyond judgment, opposites, and duality. It exists within a realization that there isn't any good or evil, separation, or positive and negative. When I refer to the Self, it contains the opposites, but they are not perceived as negative or positive, because there isn't any judgment. There is just an open acceptance of what is.

This Self is also not the fragmented self that is associated with the ego, which can be judgmental. The soul, that has forgotten what it is, has been conditioned to believe it is a separate individual that needs to be defended and protected. This egoic self is the worldly story that is defined as "me." I am these thoughts, emotions, and this body. I live here, I do this, I like this, and I don't like that. This happened to me and it was good, and that was bad. I want more of this and less of that. The list goes on and on. What you do is what you do, and what I do is what I do, and the two are not interdependent. This "I" isn't who the soul *really* is. This idea may be challenging to comprehend at this moment, but I hope it will become clearer.

When I write of the self with a lower case "s," I am referring to the ego construction that is the story we associate with "me." We could call it a false self, because the story isn't who we really are regardless of how much we might believe it is. Who we really are is an eternal presence that is always untouched by the story. Anything that changes isn't us. The intention of our personal stories is to awaken us to a greater truth of ourselves and the world.

The capital "S" Self may be perceived as an organizing principle or guiding force in one's life, a myth, or a fairy tale. It is considered the source of dreams and synchronicities, which are intended to draw the soul deeper into the truth of who and what it is. It is a vast, timeless, changeless presence of stillness and silence that exists within. It represents wholeness and the union of the soul and spirit, which in a fairy tale is symbolized by the marriage of the prince and princess. The realization of the Self is an indication that the soul has remembered who and what it is. The spirit that initially appears as separate is recognized as the soul and they are experienced as one.

The Initiation

The stories contained in this book are initiatory and show us how to overcome challenges in order to perceive ourselves differently and live in a new way. They demonstrate how to transform ourselves from identification with the ego and remember who we really are, which is the Self. The stories show us how to embody a power that is rooted in love and not fear. It's a power that isn't based on physical strength, war, manipulation, wealth, struggle, position, control, or dominance, but is rooted in the heart. These stories illustrate the challenges we encounter on the journey we call "life," and help us realize the presence that is our Self.

These stories illustrate a higher truth, which is that we are not the victims of our experiences or stories. Every experience and encounter, especially those that challenge us, are there to reveal more of ourselves to us. Life is meant to shape us and help us grow into the greater potential of who we can be. This is the initiation into higher consciousness so that we may embody the Self.

Consciousness is a term used to indicate awareness. When something is in the unconscious, we are typically unaware of it. When it becomes conscious, then we know it. The idea that things emerge from the unconscious, as something less than conscious, has been challenged. Why? Because the unconscious contains more wisdom than what we perceive with the conscious mind. The Self, for instance, in the unconscious, is in no way less conscious than we are, but could be perceived as superconscious. It knows much more about us and the world than we know. All we have to do is follow our dreams for a short time to discover that they contain a wisdom that is beyond us.

What is this consciousness that knows more than we do?

In perceiving these stories as offering insights into the culture and ourselves, from a psychological and spiritual perspective, we inevitably are faced with questions concerning spirituality, such as God, the universe, good and evil. If you find the word God offensive, then please substitute any term that fits with your belief system. The same goes with religion. Many of us live in a Christian culture and some of these stories have Christian motifs, so we will explore them symbolically as they relate to the stories.

There are some repeating themes in these stories. This commonality emphasizes their importance and can help to reinforce new behaviors, or ideas, that might be unfamiliar. I will repeat, each time these themes arise, what they mean or represent. It can be helpful to have these reminders, since they're easy to forget when we are in the midst of a challenge. Sometimes, just a mention can remind us how to handle such situations or of their deeper meanings. It also makes it a bit easier to jump around, or go back to one story, which you might do at a later date if you feel a story is particularly relevant to you. Although, I initially recommend going through the stories in order as they build on each other.

Each chapter begins with a brief overview of the story and then a fuller review in the interpretation. There are details in the symbolic interpretations that aren't in the initial story presented. The most complete versions of the stories, for those who are interested, are listed at the beginning of this book.

Let the Stories Guide You

The evolutionary impulse of life is toward an expansion and growth that doesn't in any way negate the necessity for being. In fact, it's the inner that feeds and shapes the outer. These stories, like our nightly dreams, guide us on this journey of knowing ourselves and embodying our fullest human potential. The template is inside as to what is possible for each of us. These stories show us how to access that inner wisdom and live freely.

When looking at these old familiar stories from a new symbolic perspective, we can be transformed by them like the heroines. We might notice how their experiences parallel those in our own lives and then we can utilize their insights to inform our understanding of ourselves. These courageous young souls in the following stories have broken a revolutionary trail to freedom for us. They walked the path to realize their strength, their inherent power, and embody their truth, which is wholeness. They can show us the way. All of us.

Introduction

Looking Inside

*M*y greatest curiosity as a child was with how things worked. I loved to use a butter knife to remove the screws from the backs or undersides of clocks, radios, an 8-track tape player, or whatever I could find, in order to look at the inner mechanisms. I even took apart my jewelry box with the dancing ballerina to see how she twirled and to watch the musical apparatus as it played. I remember the way in which the little cylinder turned, and the dainty notes emerged.

This fascination continued into adulthood and my first job out of college as a corporate designer. It was easy for me to learn how office politics worked and to "play the game," but my interest eventually waned. I left because I felt something was missing, although I didn't know what. After that, I drifted in and out of design jobs until I married at thirty. A year into our marriage, I had a mystical experience, an inner encounter with God, you might say. At the time I thought it was just an out-of-the-ordinary fainting spell, since the doctors couldn't explain what happened, but I later realized that it was spiritual.

This mystical encounter lasted only a few minutes, but it profoundly affected my life. I was focused on the material world, travel, career, marriage, and life, up until that moment, and then afterwards, there was a shift to the inner world of the soul, dreams, writing, poetry, journaling, and art. I didn't have any inclination toward any of these activities before that experience. I saw, in hindsight, that there were breadcrumbs along the path of my life that hinted at these hidden interests, but nothing was overt enough for me to be aware of it. One of these breadcrumbs was a book I'd had since childhood. Mr. Blumenthal gave it to me in the fourth grade and put a note in the front of the book that referred to drawings I gave to him.

Another breadcrumb came in my twenties, from a dream that I never forgot.

> *It's daytime. I am one of many people lying on the front deck of a cabin in a meadow. We are prisoners of the men sitting inside. In order to be released, we must stand up and catch a transistor that flies through the air, but this must be accomplished without anyone seeing. After a time of watching and waiting, I catch one, and am set free. I walk away from the cabin toward a forest. A silver Volvo station wagon pulls up and a woman gets out of the car with a girl of about two or three. The woman walks over to me with the girl in her arms. The little girl reaches for me. I take her into my arms and hug her. She clings to me like she's afraid I will let her go. I tell her, "We can't be together in this lifetime." As I hand her back to the woman, she cries and won't let go of me. The mother and I pry her fingers loose and they leave. I walk alone through the meadow and into the forest.*

This dream disturbed me at the time, since I planned to have a child and this dream suggested I wouldn't. I'd been brought up to believe in reincarnation, so this literal interpretation seemed plausible to me. I didn't understand the rest of the dream, or any of the others I began recording after that mystical experience. I was bothered by the images and themes that repeated and seriously questioned what they meant as I searched for answers.

The fascination I felt in childhood for clocks, radios, and my jewelry box, was reawakened and I became curious about the inner world of dreams, emotions, and psychology. My exploration of dreams and the dreaming world was with an open attitude, allowing the dreams to reveal what they wanted. I was endlessly enchanted with the inspired wisdom they contained, the synchronicities with waking life, and the practical information they offered about all aspects of my life. I felt like I had a direct channel to a wise source that spoke to every facet of my life with an intention to create greater wellbeing in all areas.

The dreams themselves were not all idyllic though, as they guided me through the shadow land of the unconscious. The dream themes were predominately about my gifts, reconnecting with the feminine, and my spirituality. I was encouraged to honor my heart through expressions in art, poetry, and writing. It became evident that I was to learn more about my inner feminine world of emotions, intuition, soul, and the body. I was attempting to get out of a habit of busyness and activity to create more balance, and night after night, the dreams tried to correct this imbalance. I'd been living in my head for so many years, it was as though I had to be retrained about how to listen to my body and reawaken to what I felt. I'd learned to ignore and dismissed all that was internal. And finally, spiritual ideas sprung up in dreams as they challenged my beliefs about the world and how it works.

It was an easy transition from the clocks, to dreams, and then to story. My first look was into the fairy tale of "Snow White and Rose Red," which drew me in completely. The dreams gave me a momentary snapshot of a specific subject, while the stories put the pictures together and revealed a much more complete journey. I discovered that they spoke to meaning and purpose, how to resolve challenges encountered along the way, and ultimately, what the destination was. The story's hidden meanings were concealed in symbols that were perfectly put together like the mechanisms of a clock. Each element was critical to the story as it contributed something to the whole.

I saw that life wasn't a series of random snapshots strung together and tossed into an album in chronological order. When I stepped back, as with the fairy tale, I saw that there was much more to the story than I initially realized. There was pattern, meaning, and purpose. All the characters in the story, or a life, contribute to the development of the heroine, or person. Jung saw that life had a path he called individuation and he believed the destination was wholeness.

My next deeper dive into story was *The Wizard of Oz*. I was stunned by the level of complexity in the symbols and couldn't fathom how anyone could possibly have the breadth of symbolic knowledge required to write it. Every element fit into the whole story with the utmost precision, like a jigsaw puzzle that doesn't have any extra or unnecessary parts. Then I read about how the author said the story just came to him. It made perfect sense that the story emerged from the collective unconscious, as have the other stories in this book.

These stories persisted for centuries, through times of tremendous oppression, right under the noses of the authorities, because they were seemingly meaningless. They were told and retold, because they spoke to something deep inside. These tales fed the soul and kept it alive from one year to the next, passed from generation to generation, until their hidden truths were revealed. Now these stories are ready to be lived consciously through us.

The Self

The Self is the creator of dreams with an intention to awaken the soul. Through all these years of dreamwork, I came to see that even the smallest fragment had meaning. I learned that dreams address every single aspect of life. They break apart old beliefs and paradigms that are erroneous, guide us toward a fuller embodiment of who we really are and can be, and teach us about the greater truths of life.

I discovered through my dreams that I was an artist and poet when I had no idea I even had any talent. The dreams guided me to reclaim the feminine qualities I had repressed and move into greater balance. I was able to reconnect with emotions that had long been dormant and become more physically active. I was guided to become vegetarian, to begin writing, and to find a new inner orientation for life.

I see both dreams and stories as containing an immensely abundant treasure that never stops flowing. We can revisit dreams and stories repeatedly over time and receive different meanings from each visit. They are here to guide and transform us so that we might live fuller lives, embody more of our Self, and learn greater truths about the world we inhabit. The general messages of the dreams are that life, and we, are so much more than we realize.

This book is an exploration of stories related to the initiation of the soul. The dreams suggest our challenges are initiatory, as they break down identifications that are incorrect in order the soul to realize a greater truth. We often don't even know what it means to live as the soul, since many of us were conditioned to live from our heads. The intention of these stories, and their interpretations, is to awaken us to our souls, its needs and desires, and to help us remember our truth.

One of the other messages of my above dream was that I had chosen masculine-oriented patriarchal achievement over the feminine, as most of the members of my family did. I had started to repress my feminine qualities when I was young. A girl of thirteen recently told me about her dream of being in the house of an old woman with dogs. The old woman was like a cat lady, but with dogs instead. She made the girl act like a dog.

I gave the girl a general sense of the dream's meaning, but later confided to her mother the deeper meaning of the loss of the feminine. This girl was normal and typical of other girls and her mother didn't see anything in her daughter to be concerned about.

I imagine you might be wondering what the dream means. Cats can be seen as feminine symbols. The old woman, who normally has cats, has dogs instead, and was forcing this girl to be a dog, which can be perceived as a symbol of the masculine. An old woman consciousness was active in this young girl, making her act more like a boy and causing her to suppress her feminine. Of course, dreams are multilayered, and have many meanings, so this is only one possible interpretation.

Repression

When anything is repressed, it goes into the unconscious and we no longer have access to it. Children learn, sometimes in very subtle ways, what qualities are desirable and undesirable. If the parents, for example, don't value the arts, then a child may pick up that message, and despite having talent in the area, can unconsciously repress it because of the parental belief. This child might grow up not even knowing he's artistic and may even believe he has no ability at all.

If a little boy is seen as too feminine, he can be labeled negatively by those around him. Certainly, this attitude is changing and evolving, but when we can embrace all gender qualities without judgment, then children will be able to express all of themselves and grow up without fear of rejection. Nor will they need to repress that which is currently considered unacceptable. What is perceived as negative is what is often repressed.

If, for example, our emotions are rejected because they are considered unacceptable by caregivers, then as an adult it can be difficult for us to feel. When emotions don't flow, the result may be depression. When this is the case, it is hard to love, feel sad, cry, allow anger, and ultimately to feel true joy. It isn't for us to judge what is right and wrong for anyone else, but only to become aware of ourselves. We don't want to look at others and say this or that person has too much of this or that quality or emotion, but only need to look inside ourselves and determine what is right for us. The intention here is to strip away the distinctions we have placed on certain feelings and embrace the full range of emotion.

Over a year after the conversation with the young girl above, I saw her mother again, and she told me about her own recurring childhood dream of being held hostage by men. All three of us dreamt of being held captive by the masculine. Another symbolic view of the dream is that the soul is captivated by the outer world of form. In the case of my dream, and the girl's mother, we weren't free due to an overreliance on our own masculine qualities and the repression of our feminine.

This dream theme appears in men as well, when their feminine qualities are relegated to the unconscious and repressed. This doesn't mean a man should act more feminine, but to be balanced, he would still have to access the qualities we describe as feminine, such as intuition, feeling, body awareness, and an ability to be. Men need these qualities as much as women do.

An example from a male client is a dream in which he was in line at a buffet. His wife turned to him and asked if he could put something on his tray for her, but he said there wasn't any room. He'd sampled everything on the buffet and his tray was full. He didn't have space for his wife, or the feminine, in his life because he didn't value the feminine. He didn't appreciate women or the qualities often attributed to them.

How do we discover what is repressed? Dreams, projections, judgements, emotional responses, and jealousy are a few of the possible paths to becoming aware of what we aren't conscious of. Becoming open to what arises strongly within us can alert us to deep desires we have repressed and to moving into greater balance.

Restoring Balance

The imbalance in masculine and feminine qualities is an issue for both men and women. When these qualities operate in harmony, life is lived more fully with access to many more capabilities. Let's say, for example, someone is faced with a health challenge. He collects as much information as he can from a variety of sources and is faced with the difficult decision of a course of action. Logically, he thinks one path is better, maybe one doctor has more education than another. But, for some reason, he can't explain, he feels drawn to another doctor. If he relies on logic, he will dismiss the other doctor because he doesn't value intuition as a way of knowing.

If this man listens to his inexplicable "feminine" feeling sense regarding the second doctor, his "masculine" qualities take over and he acts. Now is the time to take the logical path. He looks up the doctor's number, places the call, sets the appointment, and marks it on the calendar. This isn't to imply the intuitive feeling is always the right way to go, but it isn't dismissed as irrelevant. Maybe the second doctor has a good bedside manner and they will relate better than he would to the first doctor. Intuitive knowing takes that into account, which is information often not available in a logical decision process.

Defining qualities as masculine and feminine isn't to reinforce judgmental cultural ideals, but merely to have a conversation about the current situation for many of us in order to move beyond our limitations. The intention is to free ourselves from the preference for one quality over another because it's associated with gender. It isn't meant to, in any way, discount the rapidly transforming gender roles in our society, which is evidence of the current evolutionary impulse of humanity. This is an incredibly positive movement as those who are at the forefront of the blurring of gender lines are helping to break down our old, restricting ideas. They are pointing the way to a non-judgmental future in which we aren't so defined by gender or current beliefs regarding gender roles.

Aspects of the Heroine

In this book, we will view all of the characters in the stories—regardless of gender—as inner aspects of the heroine. We will also look at them as they relate to the heroine in an outer sense. In a Jungian view of dreams and fairy tales, all characters are parts of us. Swiss psychiatrist Carl Jung believed there is an innate impulse in the psyche toward wholeness and the Self—a transcendent center. The dreams and fairy tales address this psychic unfolding process Jung called *individuation*. The Self guides us as we integrate unconscious aspects of ourselves in order to experience this innate wholeness.

One of the repeating patterns in the stories in this book is of the father sacrificing his daughter. Psyche and Beauty's fathers sent them to be devoured by beasts and the Handless Maiden's father sold her to the devil. The sacrifice of other daughters was much subtler, such as with Cinderella, Sleeping Beauty, and Rapunzel. Sleeping Beauty's father, for example, valued her, but rejected another aspect of the feminine, which ultimately resulted in her sacrifice. Most of the daughters in these stories do not resist their fate and daughter sacrifices recur throughout fairy tales, myths, and dreams.

The sacrifice of the daughter refers to both the sacrifice of the soul and of the young feminine. This is also reflected in a few of the dreams mentioned earlier in this chapter. Dreams and any symbolic stories can be read in many ways. There isn't usually only one meaning attributed to them. The heroine may represent the soul and feminine qualities. The male can represent male qualities and spirit. Therefore, these stories are relevant to both men and women, because we all have soul and spirit. We are incarnations of the soul awakening to the Self and have access to all of the qualities associated with each gender.

The sacrifice of the feminine relates to us personally and reflects the predominant paradigm for many of us in which the feminine is suppressed in favor of the masculine. Some attributes of the feminine are being, stillness, feeling, emotion, the body, nature, the dark, the unknown and unseen, the unconscious, relating, the soul, and non-rational ways of knowing, including intuition. A few of the qualities associated with the masculine are striving, achievement, power, materialism, mind/intellect, ego, a literal perspective, spirit, the light, the known and seen, consciousness, and action. In our Western culture, both women and men have often preferred qualities associated with the masculine to those of the feminine.

When the feminine is sacrificed, it means she goes into the unconscious. The result is that we repress, or medicate, feelings, physical and mental illnesses increase, the needs of the body are ignored, the environment is contaminated, and money is considered more important than love or human life. We become dogmatic, individualistic, materialistic, competitive, focused on individuality at the expense of the collective, desire power and control over all that is perceived as other, and rational logical achievement is put before the heart. These are just a few of the culture's responses to this sacrifice and clearly, we are at a point of change.

Some of the young maidens in these stories willingly sacrifice themselves for their fathers. Why would they do this? Are they seeking their father's love and approval? Don't they realize their value? Do they believe they aren't as worthy as the masculine or their fathers?

The first story we will explore that follows this pattern of a heroine who willingly sacrifices herself is "The marriage of Cupid and Psyches."* *Psyche* is the Greek word for soul.

The story of "Psyche and Eros" has been examined by many scholars,[1] due to its archetypal nature and because it's perceived as being so relevant to us today. Sacred psychologist Jean Houston is one such scholar who stated that this story, which is estimated to date 500–600 B.C.E. comes from a time when many (male) spiritual teachers, such as Lao-Tse, Confucius, Zoroaster, Buddha, and Pythagoras were alive. She referred to it as a time, "of the rise of God-realized humans, of 'heaven dropping like dew' into the human psyche. ... The salvation figure in this story is no longer Pharaoh, or Priest-King; it is a human being, and a woman at that."[2]

Reclaiming the Feminine

These stories are like seeds planted in both the collective and personal psyche that teach us how to reclaim the feminine and awaken to the soul. The God-realized beings Houston refers to above were men, and therefore these stories with heroines may be thought of as compensatory. They balance out a male-dominated spirituality, which doesn't put much emphasis on strong competent women. The stories in this book are some of those that carried what wasn't seen, what was hidden, or repressed. We don't hear of many enlightened women from that time, possibly because they weren't valued, and in some instances their stories were erroneously interpreted. The beauty, wisdom, and power of the feminine was also in the unconscious. The women's stories didn't disappear though, they were camouflaged by misunderstandings, or concealed in fairy tales and stories that were usually dismissed as imaginal. The old stories are now being reviewed with fresh eyes to reveal new insights.

In the "Psyche and Eros" story, Psyche is described as so beautiful that people worship her as an incarnation of Aphrodite, which leads to the neglect of Aphrodite's temples. As a result, Aphrodite is upset with her. Psyche's beauty places her beyond the reach of mere mortals,

---

* The story appears as a chapter in the book *The Golden Asse* by Lucius Apuleius. The title of the chapter in his book is "The marriage of Cupid and Psyches." I will refer to the story from this point forward as "Psyche and Eros" and am using the Greek names of the gods and goddess.

which prompts her father to ask an Oracle what to do because she doesn't have any suitors and is miserable. The king is told to take Psyche to a mountaintop dressed in funeral attire and sacrifice her to a beastly serpent. Psyche's funeral procession makes their way to the top of the mountain believing she is being sacrificed to appease the gods. Her parents are beside themselves with grief and Psyche tells they that they lost her long ago, when everyone first began to worship her far and wide as the incarnation of Aphrodite.

Her parents don't value Psyche for herself because they appreciate the accolades her adoration brings to them. They and others don't *see* who *she* is. They don't begin to grieve until the literal sacrifice becomes clear. She tells them, they lost *her* long ago. The daughter—the young feminine—had already been sacrificed way before this moment.

This is the story of the soul that was sacrificed as it was replaced by the human egoic personality. Her journey will be to reclaim her divine inner truth.

The Divine Feminine

We will explore "Psyche and Eros" in greater detail in the next chapter as a pattern for many of the modern fairy tales in this book. This myth still contains the divine feminine goddess Aphrodite, who is behind Psyche's— the soul's—sacrifice and initiation. The myths were eventually replaced by fairy tales and the goddess disappeared from the story. The divine feminine survived even though the myths declined, because of people such as Jesus, the Gnostics, alchemists, fairy tale storytellers, and depth psychologists, to name a few of those responsible for attempting to keep the divine feminine alive through the centuries.

So, what happened to the goddess in the West? The divine feminine went into the unconscious. For most of us Lilith and Sophia disappeared from the story of Western Christianity.[3] Lilith, the feisty partner of Adam before Eve, refused to be subservient to him and so was replaced with the more docile Eve, biblically referred to as Adam's *helper*. Sophia, or Wisdom, was the consort of God at the beginning of the Creation. According to the Gnostics, she fell from heaven into matter. She's identified with psyche, the soul, which is invisible and permeates all things including the body. The medieval alchemists believed it was their job to set the soul free as did early Christian Gnostics. These two groups were a response to Christians who wanted to repress the feminine.

Sophia fell from heaven, Eve is described as having been the cause of the fall, Psyche fell from a mountaintop to be devoured by a monster, and Beauty was sacrificed by her father to the Beast. Jesus incarnated, according to Gnosticism, to *rescue* Sophia from matter, just as the prince rescues the princess. The deeper meaning here is that the soul is rescued from identification with the world of form by the Self, which we will see in the following stories.

The marriage in these stories represents an inner sacred union of the soul and spirit, which results in the embodiment of the Self. This leads to an entirely new way of living in wholeness. Myths and fairy tales are initiatory stories that show us how to transform our consciousness and realize the transpersonal center of ourselves. A non-personal divine love is the product of this union.

Fairy Tales

Mythic and fairy tale stories are personal and can also be perceived as cultural dreams. They show us what is happening in our society and how to resolve it. When we take personal action toward transformation of the patterns in the story, we influence the collective unconscious and world in a positive way.

This book is a compilation of stories that are interpreted to assist us on the journey we are all making to realize the true nature of the soul. We will symbolically explore the characters as parts of our own self in order to understand the story's deeper, personal meanings. When the symbolic essence is revealed, it can provide insights into our own journeys.

Let's briefly look at the fairy tales that have directly descended from "Psyche and Eros."

The "sacrifice the daughter" pattern appears in "Beauty and the Beast," which was published in 1740.[4] In this story, Beauty prefers to spend her time alone reading. She is beautiful and has suitors, but isn't interested in marriage, since she is content living with her father. He gets lost in the forest and ends up spending the night in a palace, which unbeknownst to him belongs to a Beast. At first, the Beast threatens to kill him, but then agrees to take his daughter instead. This initiatory story shows not only the transformation of Beauty, but also the Beast.

The Grimms' fairy tale, "The Girl Without Hands" (also known as "The Handless Maiden"), is dated slightly later than the twelfth century, "a time in European history when our present attitudes were being formulated in those deep places where the collective unconscious is generating the next step in its evolution."[5] In this story, the father unconsciously trades his daughter for wealth when he sacrifices her to the devil. She frees herself, chooses to leave her parents, and embarks on her own journey.

The beasts in "Psyche and Eros" and "Beauty and the Beast" turn out not to be the beasts they were thought to be. In "Psyche and Eros," the beast is really the god of love, and Beauty's beast turns out to be a handsome prince. What we are afraid of in the beginning—this sacrifice of the young feminine to a beastly masculine, which would end in her death—results in not only the soul coming to consciousness and into power, but also the masculine is transformed from beast to prince, or to the god of love.

The characters in these stories are changed by their journey. The defensive, angry, resentful masculine energy that can appear as a warrior, beast, or devil is changed by the heroine's ability to *see* and/or *love* him. She sees through the façade and the defensive armor he has worn to protect himself from the world. He isn't who she, or anyone else, thought he was, but turns out to be the exact opposite.

Aphrodite, the goddess of love, disappeared from the fairy tales as the initiator, and Eros, the god of love, isn't the husband of the soul anymore either. The initiator is the goddess of love (divine feminine) and the beast is really the god of love (divine masculine). Despite not being present in the fairy tales now, they are still active in our dreams and lives. The divine feminine, as Sophia, made her presence known to me a few years ago.

I was at a mission near San Antonio in the early evening on Christmas Eve speaking with the curator and a park ranger about the statue of a woman on the altar. I asked the Mexican American ranger who he believed she was, and he said, "Mother Mary." I told them that I thought the statue was Sophia, the divine feminine in the Book of Revelation with the stars on her cloak and the sun and moon beneath her feet. Neither of them, despite being Christian, had ever heard of her. As the three of us stood outside the deserted mission on the front lawn chatting, a small family emerged from the mission. Suddenly, the young girl walked over to us, placed her hand on the curators back to gently moved her aside, as she continued walking right through the middle of the three of us. Her mother was behind her and, obviously surprised at her daughter's behavior, which would typically be considered impolite, called out, "Sophia! What are you doing?" Her mother was apologizing for her daughter when I interrupted to explain that I was speaking about Sophia when her daughter walked into our midst. We were all speechless.

Sophia, and other aspects of the divine feminine, are still present and available to us. The more we open to them and become aware of them, the more they reveal themselves to us. On that day at the mission, Sophia obviously wanted me, and us, to know that she was real. She's an active force for us and the world today as she emerges from the unconscious into our awareness. We are her children and she cares about us as we evolve out of our old stories.

In some stories, the daughters are sent, consciously or unconsciously, to their deaths by their fathers and sacrificed in exchange for something the fathers' value more. What do we believe we gain from sacrificing the feminine, the inner life, and the soul? When the focus is on the outer world, materialism, the desire for more, and action, the feminine is often devalued, rejected, ignored, and sacrificed. These tales reveal the implications of pursuing masculine ideals at the expense of the feminine. The fathers are wounded; they can't, or don't, protect the young feminine and are willing to let their daughters perish for masculine achievement. The fathers think only of themselves, having their needs fulfilled, and surrender their own young feminine.

The Masculine and Feminine Today

Today, many of us are out of balance. When masculine ways are valued, and the feminine repressed, we see rampant materialism, the destruction of things considered feminine, such as the environment and the body, and the devaluation of the feminine, seen in myriad ways throughout the culture. In the family, this appears as women, mothers, wives, who are angry and exhausted from doing too much. We see working and the endless pursuit of more at the expense of being, playing, living, and taking time to breathe. For women internally, according to Jungian Marion Woodman, their "pseudo-masculinity ravages their femininity and castrates their creative spirit."[6]

As mentioned before, we all have masculine and feminine energy. We need to utilize all of the qualities associated with the different genders in a healthy way to be in harmony with ourselves, others, and our environment.

When balanced, the dance of masculine and feminine is one in which they take turns. Both energies work together in one person to create that which is new and bring it into the world. The feminine receives and the masculine acts. She opens to accept the universal seed of new creation through intuition. He acts to carry what is new into the world. Both are important to wellbeing.

The devaluation of the feminine has created a situation in which many women are disempowered, which may be, but isn't necessarily indicated by financial circumstances, work, living conditions, or appearances. After all these years of repression, women are searching for ways to reclaim their self-worth and embody a balanced feminine and masculine energy. While men are looking for ways to reacquaint themselves with their inner feminine qualities and seeking to integrate that with a healthy masculine. The search is within and these qualities can't be imparted to us by anyone. They may develop from experiences that challenge us to reveal our strength, wholeness, and soul.

Empowerment is when we consciously take our power back from the places we have given it away and find it *within* us. We will then feel free to follow our hearts, live the way we want to live, and won't care what others think. We are empowered when we fearlessly live from the heart. True harmony, peace, love, and joy emerge when we accept, realize, and balance masculine and feminine energies, uniting soul and spirit.

Finding Balance, Power, and Wholeness

Are these stories really about a father's sacrifice of his daughter? Or, as this book aims to illustrate, is the goddess of love initiating the soul? Are our challenges in life initiating us in the same manner as they did for Cinderella, Beauty, and Rapunzel? Are we being shown the way to greater consciousness through story and our life experiences? Are these stories helping us—both men and women—learn how to access all qualities in order to be whole? Are we here on this planet to discover that we are souls who have forgotten who we really are and to remember in order to share our gifts with a waiting world? Is life a journey to rescue our own souls that have been imprisoned in matter?

These stories don't just tell us what the problems are, but they reveal how to find our way back to balance, power, and wholeness. Through a symbolic initiatory lens, these young women's journeys change from being about fantasy to real life. Initially, they seem to be victims, sacrificed by inept fathers, or the patriarchy, and appear to be weak as they willingly agree to their own sacrifice, but this isn't the case. They may do this at the beginning, due to lack of awareness, or for whatever reason, but really it's time for the soul to leave old allegiances and embark on a new journey. Sometimes the journey is outer, sometimes inner, but usually it's both.

Psyche appeared to be sacrificed by her father, but Aphrodite influenced the Oracle that told him to sacrifice her and guided her son Eros's actions. The goddesses are not as obvious in the fairy tales as they were in the myths. In "The Handless Maiden," the heroine is attended by an angel, and Beauty has a comforting dream of a beautiful lady on the night she goes into the Beast's palace. Cinderella receives assistance from the birds and a tree. When we see these daughters interacting with any aspect of the divine feminine, we can be sure that a deeper transformation is under way.

The heroines are challenged in these initiatory journeys, which require sacrifice. They must make sacrifices, but they are not *the* sacrifice, meaning they don't die. When we sacrifice something, we make it sacred and holy. If we see the soul as having been sacrificed, then to perceive it as being made sacred and holy through that act, gives the story a much deeper meaning. The heroines all survive their initiations and their sacrifices give them a new perspective.

Separation

One sacrifice is that of separation. The daughters have to discover who they are when they aren't with their families, friends, and partners. How do they define themselves when not living their old stories, depending on material things, or identifying with elements of their past life? Discernment, which means understanding what to keep and what to release, or what is mine and what is yours, what has value and what doesn't, is a type of separation. This discernment can symbolically appear in the stories as a knife or cutting. Psyche has a knife in her hand to protect herself when she dared to look at her husband Eros, the Handless Maiden's hands were cut off, and Beauty's father severed a rose from the bush, which was the reason for her sacrifice. Separation appears through the dismemberment/mutilation of the Handless Maiden; the division between mind and body in Beauty as an intellectual; and the separation of Psyche and Eros, which was caused by his flight after being seen by Psyche. Many of the heroines leave their families or ancestral inheritance.

Each daughter encounters challenges when she leaves her parent's house and their beliefs. Every single one of them does. Some return, but many never do. They may respond differently to their tasks, but every difficulty is intended to assist in the soul's growth into the fullness of its potential.

We are to learn the truth of our own soul during this journey called life. These stories demonstrate how to navigate our inner realms in order to function effectively in the world. They show us how to successfully complete our initiations. We see how to unite the opposites, value the feminine and masculine, and achieve balance. These heroes and heroines don't take the journey alone and neither do we, since we are all helped and guided by unseen forces. Let's take a look at the fairy tales and see how these initiations can awaken us to our own souls.

CHAPTER

One

Psyche and Eros:
Uniting the Soul with
the God of Love

*T*here once lived a king and queen with three daughters. Psyche, the youngest and most beautiful, was worshiped throughout the land as the incarnation of Aphrodite in physical form, while the goddess of love herself was ignored. The public adoration of a mortal infuriated Aphrodite and so she asked her son Eros to punish Psyche with an arrow that would make her fall in love with the vilest man alive.

Psyche felt isolated by her beauty and disliked the attention. No mortal man was ever going marry her, since she was beyond their reach, while her sisters were married to kings. Her father was distressed by her situation and wanted to alleviate her suffering, and so he went to the Oracle to ask what they should do.

Apollo's Oracle said to dress Psyche for a funeral, take her to a mountaintop, and sacrifice her to a serpent—destroyer of the world. Her parents were horrified at the thought of losing her, but Psyche told them they should have mourned long ago when people began to worship her as the incarnation of Aphrodite. Soon after, her family and the townspeople, also dressed in funeral attire, accompanied her to the appointed location, and left her there to die.

Psyche wept as she sat alone on the mountain, but then a wind picked her up, and set her down in a lovely meadow below. There she felt calmed and fell asleep. When she awoke, Psyche saw an extravagant palace fit for a god. The enchantment of the place drew her in, and she soon found that all her needs were attended by invisible helpers. A bodiless voice told her that all she saw was hers. She rested, bathed, and ate.

On the first night, in the dark, her husband—whom she believed to be a serpent—climbed into bed with her. She was afraid, but he alleviated her fears as they tenderly consummated their marriage, and he instructed her never to look at him. Thereafter, Psyche's days were spent happily alone, and her husband visited every night.

Life passed this way for some time, until the night when Psyche's husband warned her that her sisters were out to harm her. He told her they would visit the mountaintop and instructed her to ignore their false mourning. Psyche agreed, but the next day as she thought about how alone she felt, she began to long for her sisters. That night, Psyche pleaded with her husband to let them come for a visit. She promised she wouldn't tell them anything, nor would she let them convince her to look at him.

As the sisters wailed on the mountaintop, they were lifted by the wind, and carried to the meadow below. When they saw Psyche and her life, they were overcome with jealousy and demanded to know about her husband. She lied to them *and quickly ushered them out. The sisters hatched a plot against her as they departed.*

That night, Psyche's husband issued her another warning: if her sisters convinced her to look at him, then the child she carried would be born a mortal instead of a god. The early days of her pregnancy passed uneventfully, until one morning when he informed her that her sisters would return that day. Before he departed, she reaffirmed her promise to not divulge their secret.

Once again, during their visit, the sisters asked Psyche about her husband. She told them a new story, since she had forgotten what she'd told them before. As they left, the sisters were perplexed as to why Psyche lied to them. Either she made him up, or she hadn't seen him, and he was a god. If he was, then her baby would be divine. The mere thought of this made them seethe with jealousy.

Later that day, Psyche's sisters returned and convinced her that she must kill her husband. When they reminded her about the Oracle's details of a serpent husband, Psyche asked them what she should do. They instructed her to conceal a knife and lantern by her bed, and then to sever her husband's head from his beastly body as he slept.

That night, Psyche did as the sisters suggested, however, when she illuminated her husband's face with the lantern, she saw none other than Eros—the god of love. Feeling overwhelmed by what she had done, Psyche turned the blade on herself, but it refused to cut her. A drop of hot oil from the lantern accidentally dripped onto Eros, awakening him. He saw Psyche with the lantern and flew to his mother Aphrodite's house in distress. Psyche attempted to throw herself into the river, but the waters set her back upon the riverbank.

She went to her sister's house, told her all that had transpired, but added that Eros had instructed Psyche to send her sister to him because he wanted to marry her instead. At that glorious news, her sister raced out of the house and to the mountaintop. She joyfully leapt, but alas, the wind wasn't there to carry her, and she plunged to her death. Psyche then went to deliver the same good news to her second sister, who then leapt to her death in the same manner.

Psyche searched far and wide for her wounded husband, but finally, at the suggestion of two of the goddesses she met, gave up and went to face Aphrodite's wrath. The goddess was merciless. She beat her and gave her four difficult tasks to complete in order to test her worth. Little did she expect that Psyche, who was pregnant with her grandchild, would ever survive.

The first task was to sort corn, barley, millet, poppy seed, chickpeas, lentils, and beans. Psyche, initially overwhelmed by the task, was assisted by the ants who completed it in the allotted time. Aphrodite was furious, knowing Eros must have helped her.

Psyche was given the second task, which was to collect wool from golden sheep. She again felt that she couldn't do it and planned to cast herself into the river. But a reed on the bank asked her not to and then was divinely inspired to tell her how to complete the task. Since the sun's heat angered the sheep, she needed to wait until it was cooler and the sheep drank from the river, and then she could gather the wool stuck in the briers. Aphrodite was unmoved by the successful completion of the task and gave Psyche yet another one.

In this test, she was to collect water in a crystal bottle from a black river that flowed from the top of a mountain down into the underworld. Psyche climbed the mountain, saw the dragons guarding the river, and decided to end her life. She was so scared that she became immobilized. Zeus's bird—the eagle—came to her aid and filled the bottle. Aphrodite knew Psyche couldn't have completed the task alone and demanded that she take a box to the Underworld to get beauty from Persephone.

Again, Psyche felt utterly defeated, and climbed to the top of a tower to jump. But the inspired tower asked her not to and proceeded to give detailed instructions on how to complete the final task. She was to take two barley cakes and two coins for the ferryman. Then she must pass by the *begging lame man, use one coin to cross the river, not let the man in the water get in the boat, and ignore the woman spinning. These are traps set by Aphrodite. The three-headed dogs guard the gate to Persephone's palace and may be distracted with one barley cake. Once inside, Psyche was to sit on the ground, accept only a piece of bread, ask that the box be filled with beauty, and then return. On the way back, Psyche should feed the last cake to the dog, give the coin to the ferryman, and come out the way she entered. The final critical step was to not look in the box.*

Psyche perfectly executed all the steps as instructed and emerged from the underworld with the box of beauty. However, she did not heed the final warning; she peered into the box, and upon doing so, fell into a death-like sleep. Eros—who was now healed—flew directly to his beloved wife. He wiped the sleep from her face, put it inside the box, and pierced her with an arrow to awaken her. Eros told her to take the box to Aphrodite and then he went to Zeus to ask to be wed to Psyche.

At their wedding, Psyche drank the nectar of immortality and became a goddess. Shortly thereafter, she gave birth to a baby named Pleasure.*

Introduction

The mythic story of "Psyche and Eros" is rich in symbolism and guidance for the spiritual journey to embody wholeness.**

Psyche is the Greek word for "soul" and Eros is a Greek word associated with love. The story details the steps of the soul's initiation, which prepares her to unite with the god of love and awaken to her divinity.

Initially, Psyche identifies with the ego, and as such, she feels overwhelmed each time she faces, what seems like, an insurmountable challenge. She falls into victim consciousness, doesn't feel up to the task, but then help unexpectedly arrives, and the task is completed. She develops new qualities from each test, comes to see that she isn't alone, and that her

---

* Full story in Apuleius's *The Golden Asse*.
** I changed the name of Cupid, as it was in the original story, to Eros, and for consistency, I used the Greek versions of the names for the gods and goddess.

needs are always fulfilled. She dares to break the rules repeatedly, which leads to greater empowerment and ultimately to freedom for her soul.

This story contains elements of later well-known fairy tales, such as "Beauty and the Beast," "Cinderella," and "Rapunzel." In repeating themes throughout time, myths and fairy tales inform us of cultural issues and how to resolve them. These stories echo the Gnostic and Christian stories of a feminine soul that fell into matter and forgot who she was, because she became identified with the world of form and ego. The soul's initiatory journey is to remember and embody its divine origins. Jesus and the Messiahs, in the Gnostic view, came to Earth to rescue the lost soul, in the way that Eros descends from Mt. Olympus in this story.

"Psyche and Eros" illustrates a common theme of union—separation— reunion in which a couple is together initially, separates, and then reunites in the end. In the Gnostic view, the soul and spirit are together in heaven, and separate when the soul falls into matter. The soul falling into matter symbolizes the soul's birth into the world, and its identification with the body, mind, and emotions as itself. While the soul and spirit are apart, the soul faces initiatory challenges, to release identification with the outer physical world and to remember the inner spiritual one. The culmination of the journey is the sacred marriage of soul and spirit. The marriage symbolizes the successful completion of the union—separation—reunion journey, and the soul's embodied remembrance of its truth as spirit.

The seeds for this book were planted as I contemplated the common story theme of the father's sacrifice of the daughter, which is the perspective I still held at the time I considered this topic for a paper in grad school. But then, I had an intuition that said, "It's not a sacrifice by the father, but an initiation by the Mother." My hair stood on end in that moment. I realized that the idea of an initiation, as opposed to a sacrifice, changes everything. The princess, or Psyche in this case, isn't a victim at all, but is being initiated by the divine feminine.

Aphrodite gives Psyche initiatory tasks to complete, and these challenges bring Psyche into her power and help her awaken to her divinity. What appears as a sacrifice by the father, is the beginning of an initiatory journey to ultimately unite with the god of love, which is a part of herself that she only gets a glimpse of during the initial union phase.

The goddess, as *the* initiator, who is present in this myth, disappears in later fairy tales, or changes form. This story illustrates the steps of the soul's initiation that concludes with the realization of its immortality. The embodiment of the transcendent divine within is the journey of the human soul into the fullness of its truth. We are all souls, regardless of gender, although it may appear as the feminine, Psyche, the heroine of the story.

The soul isn't really feminine. It's merely a way to speak about it to create a context for understanding. Nor is spirit masculine. The qualities perceived as feminine in the West are associated with the soul. Female is seen as relating to downward motion, inner life, the moon, emotion and feeling, nature, relatedness, earthiness, and the body. The male is an upward motion, and is associated with the outer life, separation, discernment, the sun, and the mind. These are merely a few of the attributes or designations we have culturally attached to each gender; it doesn't mean they are true, nor does it imply judgment.

In this myth, Aphrodite is so angry with the mortal world that she descends to the bottom of the sea, which is a symbol of the unconscious. We don't have obvious powerful goddess images in the West, as is reflected in the later fairy tales. This loss impacts the community. When love abandons us, with Aphrodite in the unconscious and Eros hidden in his mother's house nursing his wounds, it's a calamity. Aphrodite left the world when people stopped valuing her, which parallels our current situation. Although, love is on the rise, along with a growing awareness of the goddess, and valuing of the feminine in general, however we are still in dire need of a greater understanding, awareness, and embodiment of love.

This highlights the importance of this tale to our own lives. We need to continue to shift our perception of the feminine as being *less than* the masculine, and love as a mere emotion. These stories emphasize the importance of not rejecting certain qualities because they are perceived as inferior or gender based. The love that seems to have abandoned us, is merely waiting to be rediscovered. It's still here and available, but it's hidden behind form. Psyche, as the soul, reclaims her divine identity, which is what we need to do as well.

Aphrodite: Goddess of Love

People all over the world worship Psyche instead of Aphrodite. They hail her, a mere mortal, as a beauty to be revered and increasingly ignore the goddess. This story illustrates a shift in focus from the divine feminine to the earthly, the soul to the world-created identity, the depth to the surface, and the unseen to the seen. It's not only one woman that is honored as the beauty of the goddess in manifest form, but she represents a societal ideal which looks to superficial physical beauty and doesn't see the inner natural beauty everyone contains, which is associated with the inner divine feminine.

Aphrodite is the Mother of all the world. The Divine Feminine from the very beginning of time. She's angry with a world that doesn't remember her. The good Mother is unseen in the story and the angry, vengeful feminine replaces her. People pray to Psyche and worship her as though she is Aphrodite. The goddess of love reminds us that the girl is a mortal and will die. The people are worshiping a temporary image that *will* come to an end, as opposed to her which is the imperishable one.

Aphrodite enlists the aid of her son, Eros, who is notorious for creating trouble in relationships and breaks the rules of the culture. He abuses his power and goes unpunished for the chaos he creates, because everyone is afraid he will shoot them with his arrow, make them fall in love, and then they will break their vows. He's an immature masculine who doesn't think about the implications of his actions, nor does he have any compassion. Aphrodite asks him to use his arrows to get revenge for her by making Psyche fall in love with the ugliest man alive.

That is the power of love, isn't it? It makes us do things that are irrational and fall in love with those who may not align with our expectations. We don't always conform to what the culture says is right and can go to great lengths in the name of love when it has us in its grip. Since Psyche is a good girl, who normally follows the rules and conforms, Eros then has a quality she will need to cultivate in order to become free. She too must learn that she doesn't need to follow the rules of others, even the goddess.

The Goddess in the Unconscious

The news about Psyche as the reason why her temples have been neglected causes Aphrodite to angrily descend to the bottom of the sea, which is a place where her power is still acknowledged. They know who she is and still pay homage to her as a queen, but the sea symbolizes the unconscious, and that's where they reside. The other gods and goddesses remember her, and continue to value her, but the mortals don't. We have forgotten her too.

When Aphrodite goes into hiding, true love is no longer in the world. The idea of a divine inner love is cast aside and a superficial temporary love takes its place. The notion that love is an inherent quality of matter, and the soul, is lost. Aphrodite created the world and everything in it. She pervades all that exists. Her loss means we lack an of awareness of soul love, which infuses all of creation. Man worships a mortal outside and misses the immortal love inside.

This doesn't mean love is now absent, but that we have grown unaware of the fullness of its powerful presence. All that occurs is at the behest of love, organizing events, regardless of appearances. When something is in the unconscious, it isn't gone, we just aren't aware of it.

When the goddess of love is in the unconscious, there is a general disregard for love, which is dismissed as an emotion. When we get caught up in love, it can make us feel as though we are out of control and powerless. Those we love can activate us in profound ways others can't. That is its power. It can take us to the heights of bliss and to the depths of despair. It has an ability to draw us together and separate us in ways that nothing else can.

If we are in a loving relationship, it can offer us a rare opportunity to see what keeps us from divine love. It reveals our blocks—the sensitive places—in order for us to heal them and to release any patterns that keep us from knowing our true nature. Our fears are activated by love so that we may see them and to expand more fully into the embodiment of an ever-deepening love.

Psyche represents the human soul in physical form. She believes she's a powerless mortal and a victim of circumstances, which makes her life unbearable. She didn't do anything to deserve the adoration as Aphrodite incarnate, nor does she want it. Psyche's beauty renders her undesirable and untouchable to mortal men, which causes her to feel isolated and unhappy. Her future certainly looks bleak.

Psyche Blamed

Aphrodite blames Psyche for her neglect, because Psyche replaces her as the object of focus for humans. In an alternate reading, if we see all the characters in the story as aspects of the heroine, then Psyche's inner divinity is being ignored, is unknown, projected outside of her, and she's afraid of it. She doesn't realize the significance of what's inside of her but believes and sees herself as a mere mortal. Therefore, the goddess's anger scares Psyche, since she's unaware of her true nature. The truth of the soul wants to be known and can be through an initiation, for Psyche and for us.

If Aphrodite had retained her old position of being worshipped and living on the top of Mount Olympus with the other deities, then nothing would have changed. These Olympian gods and goddesses are challenging to humans and can wreak havoc in their lives, since they have the power. Just like the Christian God up in heaven, apart from us, the goddess was removed from the world. She's separate from, and above, humans, which is what happens to Psyche when she's elevated above mortals.

The purpose of Aphrodite plunging into the unconscious, or the sea, is so that she may come to consciousness in humans, or the soul. The divine has been projected out, which means that now the divine has to be discovered within. Jesus said, "I and my Father are One." In the East, they call this "enlightenment." The soul brings the goddess of love to consciousness while in human form to unite with the god of love. The soul must remember her truth.

Psyche's father is distraught that his daughter is so unhappy and doesn't have any suitors. He goes to the Oracle of Apollo to pray and make an offering to the gods in order to find a husband for Psyche. The response is not what he expects. The Oracle tells him to dress her for a funeral, take her to a mountaintop, and sacrifice her to a beastly serpent husband—a destroyer of the world.

The feminine soul is being brought to consciousness through what appears to be a sacrifice. The heroine must sacrifice her identity as a powerless victim, who is a member of a worldly family, so that she may see herself as something more. What appears to be a rejection and devaluation of the feminine in the culture is actually occurring to help facilitate a greater awareness of the soul. This doesn't mean that we should continue to perpetuate this belief, but to understand it, so that we might transform our current relationship to the feminine, the soul, and become aware of the part that patriarchal thinking is playing in that loss of awareness.

This is about Psyche and us. For many of us, if it isn't personal in terms of feeling unvalued, then it may be at a soul level. The soul has been sacrificed at the altar of the material. Things that soothe, honor, and value the soul are excluded from life and other things are attended to instead. What does the soul need? It's nourished by creativity, poetry, being, rest and relaxation, nature, beauty, music, art, love, and time, and space, to breathe.

Psyche's Sacrifice

Psyche is a mortal and is unhappy about her beauty that separates her from others and elevates her to a status where she is untouchable, unapproachable, and unreal. As a result, she doesn't have any marriage suitors. That means she will remain stuck in her parent's house as a child, and not develop, evolve, or grow. Her unique self is unable to come to the fore in this situation.

The king doesn't know what to do and goes to the Oracle who tells him to sacrifice her. Psyche's father needs someone else—with access to deeper knowledge—to solve his problem. What the Oracle is suggesting is for the old version of Psyche to die—the one who is worshiped far and wide as Aphrodite herself—but the parents don't want to let *her* go. They may not want a normal daughter, since the association with Aphrodite elevates them as well. They weep at the thought of losing her.

Psyche tells her parents, as they proceed to her funeral, that *she* died long ago. Her parents are happy to have such a beautiful daughter and don't realize that she doesn't have her own identity apart from everyone's projections. She died long ago because she is playing a role and not living her truth. The patriarchy, as her father, sacrificed the young feminine long ago when they accepted the role she was playing in the culture—a role that wasn't authentic. Her sense of self was set by the outer world, as others told her who she was and what had value. This outer identification resulted in an inner loss of connection to her truth.

When we put our attention on, and value, surface beauty, material goods, and egoic gain, the soul is ignored. The mind's preoccupation with separation, as a way to classify and determine value, must be seen and transformed. The stories we live, and identify with, can serve to unite or separate us. In this case, the old story is one in which the young feminine complies with masculine superficial ideals, at the expense of her true self being seen and valued. The soul went into the unconscious a long time ago.

The young feminine soul is making its way back into consciousness through us. This is the plight of the soul, which has been overlooked as we have been conditioned to focus our attention on, and develop a preference for, the material. The evolution of the soul's story has both personal and collective implications for all of us—men and women. We are in the midst of a transformational revolution as we shift from the head to the heart, or the soul.

In reading the story as if all characters represent aspects of the main character, the heroine's truth is out of alignment with the old masculine view, since the true young feminine is rejected in order to receive love and approval. She must leave the outdated consciousness that values her surface beauty and that doesn't see or appreciate her inner self. The heroine has to do something radically different, since a major shift is needed out of the parental consciousness. She will leave the old behind and plunge into the unknown to find a new masculine that can see, value, and respect her. Psyche is sacrificed to a bridegroom who is not an ordinary mortal, but a wild and destructive serpent.

As the funeral procession makes its way to the mountaintop, and Psyche's parents lament, she tells them to stop carrying on and just sacrifice her to the husband who is the destroyer of worlds. Now that phrase should make our ears perk up. What does that mean? Again, as we look symbolically versus literally, he will facilitate the destruction of the world that she identifies with. She believes that she is the story of Psyche which she has been told—a powerless victimized mortal who is isolated and worshiped far and wide. Her husband will decimate her current worldview. Let's face it, she really doesn't have a choice. It's either stay where she is and stagnate or die to the old Psyche. Even if her parents are reluctant, she isn't.

Her parents and the townspeople take her to the mountaintop, which is an upward movement. This is where the gods reside, not literally, and is an opportunity to explore the spiritual. She's in a place where she can connect to the inner stillness, silence, and peace. Everyone leaves her there, but she doesn't feel any peace at the moment. She's terrified of what she believes to be her impending death. It feels like a death because what she faces is unknown. She's in that between space, as she leaves her old life behind and surrenders to fate. My dreams, and those of others I work with, repeatedly tell us, "what you fear, isn't what you think it is." There's something else going on that you can't understand yet.

A New Consciousness

Psyche is alone and frightened on the mountaintop as she wonders what's going to happen to her. Now it is best to sit, calm down, connect to inner peace, and surrender to the unknown. Once we find our way through the fear and chaos to peace, the energy shifts. The best way to do this is to accept what is and then peace naturally arises. A gentle wind comes, picks her up, and carries her to a meadow below. This suggests a downward movement from the head into the body, mountaintop to valley, bringing spirit into the physical. The wind sets her in a meadow of flowers, where she feels calm and falls asleep.

We may think all kinds of fearful thoughts when we are in the unknown and "in our heads." Our minds can conjure up all kinds of crazy scenarios that elicit fear. But when we move out of the head, connect with spirit, and shift into the body, the mind quiets, and we can relax. When we trust and surrender ourselves to fate, we discover peace.

She's refreshed when she awakens, as Psyche realizes she didn't die.

Psyche has fallen into paradise. This is a movement from the outer world to the inner. What does she discover inside, once the fear has passed? She sees a palace of such astonishing beauty that it can only belong to a god. She has left her father's outer world home to take up residence in a new inner dwelling that's more beautiful than anything she's ever seen before. This is a new vision, a direct experience of what's possible for her life. This is an unfamiliar level of opulence and beauty, a heaven on earth, the realm of the gods. Inside the palace, she discovers invisible helpers who attend to her every need and desire. *All her wishes are filled easily and effortlessly in this new state of consciousness.*

We can get a new vision of what's possible from life or dreams. It may be a glimpse of something we haven't seen before, or the seemingly magical fulfillment of a wish. We could get an indication that something we were quite worried about will turn out much better than we expected. This can take many forms, from the mundane to the magnificent. Visions can be of specific situations or new versions of ourselves. It may be a glimpse of who we really are, or insights into what we are capable of, when we live from the heart and not the head.

A New Masculine

She is frightened on that first night as her new husband comes to her in the dark. Eventually, he calms Psyche and tells her that all of her desires will be fulfilled. *This is the moment that she shifts from her father's house, where she can't have what she wants, to a palace fit for a god, where she can have anything she wants, and everything is possible.* Psyche goes from being miserable and unhappy with her family, to thinking she's going to die, and then ends up in an incredible life. There aren't any limits on what is possible, well, maybe just one little thing: she's not allowed to ever look at him, but other than that…

Her father thought he was sacrificing her to a beastly husband—a fierce and wild serpent—but things don't turn out the way either of them thought. What was she sacrificed to? A husband who loves her and gives her everything she wants. The father represents an old masculine based in limitation, and this is the new masculine, although, we don't know much about him yet.

The old fear-based masculine conforms to cultural beliefs and ideals. He's afraid of the new masculine and thinks the feminine isn't safe, because the beast will devour her. That belief must be transformed. This new masculine is still somewhat in the dark of the heroine's unconscious, since he remains hidden. The father is the one who sacrificed his daughter, which means he's really the beast who dressed her in funeral clothes and walked her to what he believed was her death. The erroneous view of the new masculine, as a beast, must be seen through to the truth.

What is your masculine like? How does he interact with you and treat your feminine? Look at the men in dreams and life to determine the quality of the inner masculine in your life. Is there anything you are afraid to admit, look at, or see—either in yourself or those around you? Is anything being hidden?

Psyche's, or the human soul's, apparent sacrifice to the imagined beastly masculine is really a transition for the soul away from the old worldly masculine. The beastly masculine is rejected by the culture, since he views the feminine differently. He's a troublemaker for the old order, because he doesn't follow their rules. He's a disrupter and does what he pleases without regard for what others think.

Relationships can feel immensely threatening to our sense of self, but when approached consciously, they can be transformative. They bring our fears to consciousness in order to achieve greater awareness. Romantic partnerships in particular, because we are so emotionally engaged, have the power to lead us to huge shifts in consciousness and eventually, to freedom. Dreams are doing this as well, but relationships often can emotionally activate us deeply, for long periods of time, as they push unconscious content to the surface.

Psyche's husband is in the unconscious because she's not consciously ready to know his real identity. She's unable at this point to sustain the level of consciousness required to bring him to awareness. Remember, it was only moments ago that she thought she was a powerless victim. She's just getting used to a masculine that values and wants to be with her, and who won't sacrifice her. This is a new life and a new state of consciousness. She goes from isolated, alone, and unable to have what she wants with her parents, to an adoring husband and anything she desires. Although, she may have gained a mate at night, she remains at home by herself during the day, which means this won't be the ultimate answer for her. She will need to have an inner shift to accept the full range of options that are open to her. He's the "destroyer of the world," which means her old conception of who she thinks she is, thought she was, how she lived, and ultimately, how the world works, are changing.

Transitions

These shifts from an old view to a new are facilitated for us through dreams and life. We are constantly being guided to expand into a new state of consciousness, if we approach both with an intentional openness. All of our experiences and encounters are assisting us in this transformation. The initiation is happening every day in every way and we can see our own life stories symbolically in the same way we perceive this story.

When we encounter challenges in any area of life, we can open ourselves to them and be curious about what they are trying to show us. When we are emotionally activated, it is often an indication that we need to look more deeply at a situation. We are always being guided to greater consciousness and each situation is a vehicle to deliver that to us. Just as the father was willing to sacrifice Psyche, we can inquire into our own experiences and dreams to see if we are sacrificing some aspect of our own soul at the hands of commerce, busyness, or the solar principle.

With her masculine in the unconscious, Psyche is taken care of like a child, as long as she follows the rules. This is an unequal partnership. If she doesn't listen to him, then things can't remain as they are. As stated above, this is acceptable at the moment as she continues to grow in awareness. Her ego isn't strong enough yet to hold the increase in consciousness that will happen when she sees who he really is. This is a limitation that she will have to transcend in order to eventually be his equal. She's living in a conditioned belief system that says he can determine what happens and she has to comply with his wishes.

When we accept that we aren't children anymore, and the power in us isn't destructive, we can adopt a new approach to life. We may transform our interpretation of what happens to us and see it is as a direct result of our state of consciousness. If we are victims, then everything just happens *to* us, leaving us passive and helpless. But when we realize that we have the power to change our lives by shifting our consciousness, then our fate is no longer in the hands of others. This is a part of our initiatory journeys. When her husband is brought fully to consciousness and seen, Psyche and he will change. But Psyche accepts her husband's terms for the relationship and doesn't question them . . . well, not initially.

Deceitful Sisters

Then one morning, her husband warns Psyche that her deceitful sisters are scheming and that they will be going to the mountaintop, to cry and pretend to mourn her loss. If she's persuaded by them, then they will ruin the life that Psyche and he enjoy. He tells her that she's pregnant, and further, that if she follows her sisters' suggestions, she will give birth to a mortal instead of an immortal baby.

The baby represents the birth of a new unified state of consciousness for the soul. If it is born and is a mortal human, then Psyche will not have fully embodied the truth of her being, but if she succeeds—becomes enlightened—then the child will be divine.

Psyche initially agrees to not be swayed by the sounds of her sisters falsely wailing on the mountain, but during the day, she begins to feel lonely when she thinks that she might have visitors. That evening she pleads with him to let her see them. He eventually relents but makes her promise not to reveal their marital arrangement. Some things still must remain hidden he says, and now it's from her sisters as well.

The wind carries the women from the mountaintop to Psyche waiting below. The sisters are overcome with jealousy when they see the riches surrounding Psyche and realize how much her husband must love her. They represent the part of her that feels inadequate and believes she doesn't deserve this level of good and abundance. This means she hasn't really accepted it as her own yet. The sisters need to become conscious as a part of Psyche. They are significant for her growth because there are two of them, which makes them twice as important to an expansion of consciousness.

A sense of inadequacy can compel us to look and search for something more than what we have and what we are. The feeling of not being enough is an opportunity to explore what we feel and reach for greater consciousness right where we are. Life mirrors what we believe. So, we have to face this feeling, and sense it as deeply and with as much presence as we can. This feeling has possibly been with us for a very long time and may be uncomfortable to feel. Sometimes, it has even been passed down from previous generations.

Psyche's sisters represent an aspect of the wounded feminine that is jealous and petty. They believe Psyche's gain is their loss. This is poverty consciousness and a limited way of thinking that's based on there being a finite quality to the material world. And again, since it's what's believed, it's what's seen. It's as though there is only a certain amount of love and abundance, certainly not enough to go around. Of course, that's not true. The sisters see Psyche's life as so much better and resent their own lives by comparison. They feel what they have isn't as good or enough.

The sisters must have received the message that they weren't enough throughout their lives. How could they not feel that way growing up in the shadow of Psyche? Imagine having a sister who is worshiped far and wide as the incarnation of a goddess. That couldn't have been easy. Regardless of how pretty they are in their own right, they would have been unseen with her around, and therefore invisible. What's unseen and ignored goes into the unconscious. They are the shadow, meaning they carry her projection of what's rejected. Like maybe she's the good and kind sister, while they are the mean and selfish sisters.

Sisters as Psyche

As the shadow side of Psyche, her sisters are critical, destructive, lack consciousness, have closed hearts, and a fear of the unknown. Although, they aren't as naïve as Psyche. They are the feminine with an old masculine consciousness of thinking, judging, and are oriented by the intellect. The sisters are a destructive energy, since they doubt the good that comes and don't trust life. They can't see that whatever happens will be beneficial, which means they are stuck in fear and judgment. This can appear as a sabotaging aspect of the heroine, who creates unnecessary drama and issues for herself. Some perceive the shadow as negative, but it's positive when evolving to greater consciousness, as we'll see.

Doubling in a dream means that which is doubled is significant to the growth of consciousness and to the realization of the Self. It highlights an aspect of an outdated story that is critical to freedom. There are two sisters here and in many other stories as well. Why are they so critical? They sometimes cause the heroine to carry out an important act that leads her to greater awareness of herself. Since they are often selfish, they also represent the balance that the heroine requires to shift from being a self-sacrificing passive victim. She can't just go along with everything she's told but must "selfishly" stand up for herself at times.

The three sisters together contain the opposites, indicating that Psyche vacillates between believing that what she has is good, and then believing that there isn't enough. She deserves a wonderful life, which conflicts with, who is she to have all that she's been given? Sometimes she is selfish and other times a servant. She feels guilty for having so much when her sisters don't. One part is conscious and the other in the unconscious. Both sides will have to be acknowledged and brought together consciously as parts of Psyche. There is a positive side to the sisters. They serve her as they compel her to shift out of complacency with what is and move forward. The sisters are the part of Psyche that's willing to ask for, and take, exactly what they want. If they hadn't come along, she might have remained hidden in a palace with a husband who only visits her under the cover of darkness.

Dishonesty

Initially, Psyche isn't honest with her sisters when they ask about her situation, nor is she being truthful with herself. She doesn't admit that her husband is keeping her in the dark about who he is. He isn't being open and honest with her or his mother either. Their living situation is a secret, which he's keeping from Aphrodite, for obvious reasons since she'd go ballistic. Psyche overlooks these things because she finally has a husband, but she isn't seeing clearly. A healthy masculine still remains in the unconscious.

Her sisters eventually catch Psyche lying to them and hatch a plot that they hope will result in her death. After several visits, they convince Psyche that her husband has an ulterior motive, as they do, of which Psyche is unaware. They cause her to doubt what she has, to distrust the situation, and persuade her to defy her husband's wishes. They tell her to look and *see* who he really is, and to kill this "beast" before he kills her. She must be willing to look at what she fears, which is the unknown, and not run away, or avoid it.

The sisters tell Psyche to shed light on her husband and cut off his serpent head while he sleeps. Here we have a conflict between what is and what's wanted, between the head and heart, or love and fear.

When a conflict appears, if we feel like a victim, we may choose stay and fight or run away. When we are triggered or feel like we have no choice in the matter, we can revert to survival mode. This isn't to be judged as a bad thing but is an opportunity to accept the feelings that might have been ignored in the past. When we witness the feeling and open to its wisdom, we are transformed.

We want to explore our level of honesty with ourselves and others. Is there incongruence between our private and public selves? Are we agreeing to any situations that keeps us from growing? Or avoiding taking responsibility, standing up for ourselves, and going after what we really want? Are there any areas where we are acting like a child or repeating outdated patterns because we are afraid? Whatever the current situation is, it must be accepted, and then open to it to learn what it is revealing. Any beliefs that need to evolve, must be changed inside first, and then the outer world shift will follow. If the beliefs aren't changed first, the situation may just repeat again.

Old Masculine Consciousness

The sisters are caught in the old masculine consciousness, believing that power comes from wielding a knife, and wanting to kill that which is perceived as a threat. Either Psyche or the beast, it's the same approach— which is an outdated way of thinking. They tell Psyche to use a knife to cut off his head; to kill that which is feared. The light of consciousness must shine on what is in the dark, and then the knife can be utilized to separate, in this case, that which is true from the untrue. The mind needs to be separated from the body, by cutting off the head. The fear-based thoughts need to be examined to discover what's true.

When our fears get activated by a situation, we can look to see what our interpretation is of what's happening. What are we telling ourselves?

What's the narrative? Our inner dialogue? Psyche's might go something like, "My sisters are right, he must be hiding something terrible. What other possible reason could there be for him to not let me see him? What's he concealing from me? I must know. It has to be horrible." What's she so afraid of? Her sisters say he's a beast and will kill her, which means she's afraid that what's inside of her is unsafe.

Psyche is meek and mild, just going along with her husband, until the sisters show up. They serve her by getting her to act and to look at the truth of her inner masculine.

Why is the masculine portrayed as a frightening beast? The fear of the new masculine killing the young emerging feminine is a projection of the old father's consciousness. He was the one who didn't see who she really was and was willing to send her to her death. This is a carryover of the past unconscious father's sacrifice onto the present situation. When Psyche left her father's house, she departed from her youth. Now, she is transitioning into the next stage of growth for the emerging feminine, which means she needs more power and a new masculine energy to succeed. The idea that she needs to be afraid of her inner masculine energy, because it's out of control, animalistic, instinctual, and not to be trusted, must change. Besides, how will she unite with it or integrate it if she's petrified of it?

We want to explore what we believe about our own power? And our instinctual power? What does it mean to be empowered and to stand fully in our truth? Are we comfortable or afraid of it? Do we even know how strong we really are? What's the extent of our capabilities? The quick responses aren't always the deepest answers. When we spend time with these questions, they can lead to a better understanding of ourselves.

The sisters tell Psyche not to trust what is, what she can't see, and the unknown. She needs to take control of the situation, according to them. What's hidden in her? Her instinctual masculine energy isn't compelling her to move forward or do anything for herself, until the sisters appear and tell her to what to do, which is to act on her own behalf. Their motives aren't good, but the outcome is. This is an illustration of how good comes out of what may appear to be bad. She looks at her husband and that causes everything to change. She grows. The old Psyche as a helpless passive victim, who just goes along with whatever she's told, is changing.

We can explore what causes us to make changes in our lives. Do we require drama and trauma? Or can we make true changes, not just a lateral move or job change, but transformative shifts that are compelled by our inspiration instead of fear? What inner transformation needs to occur now?

Break the Rules

Her sisters are a voice that's demanding to be heard. They talk her into acting and not remaining passive. They want her to peer into the unconscious to look at her fear. As she transforms her fear of the inner masculine as a destructive beast, she must break the rules and look. She's afraid of her primal instinctual power, which she identifies as masculine, and believes could kill her.

What we are afraid of inside ourselves, we project onto others and the world, in order to see it. Psyche projects her fear of her power onto the other, which in this case is her husband. Her knowing is projected onto her sisters, which is why she listens to them. Her unconscious fear of herself is carried by the idea that there is an outer destructive serpent.

She's afraid of being consumed by the power inside of herself. In a sense, it's a valid fear. The human Psyche is being transformed as the old version of herself dies. Who she thinks she is, is changing. Indeed, she died to her childhood when she was taken to the mountaintop. She's no longer living in her parental consciousness, or the old masculine, but is still afraid of being a victim, which means there is still power being projected outside of her. Her father didn't stand up for, or protect her, but sacrificed her.

How does Psyche transform the masculine in her psyche from a beast? Not by violence, despite the sisters' suggestion to kill him. That's a masculine approach, that comes from the mind, and not a feminine response. She kills the idea that he is a beast by *shining a light in the darkness and looking.* She dares to break the rules and looks in order to bring him to consciousness. Once she sees he isn't a beast, the possibility is created for a new masculine to emerge.

The belief that Psyche should be afraid of her power is transformed. Her fear of her inner power changes to love, just because she looks inside. She has the courage to look at what she was afraid of and discovers love is there. The power within isn't an angry, harmful, destructive, patriarchal, devouring, beastly energy, but is love-based. The masculine inside of her, which she was afraid of, is Eros—the god of love.

When we dare to *look* inside the darkness of the unknown within ourselves, and face our fear, we discover the love that compels all things.

If this is true, then why do the actions of others seem unkind at times and not loving? Our superficial judgments keep us deciding from one event to the next as to whether something is good or bad. When we see through what happens, to the deeper truth, we can see the love that's behind all events. I know this may seem radical and unrealistic, but it's true. Most of us have had a glimpse of this when something happened, which we had initially perceived as bad, but after a little time passed, we realized it was a good thing and in our best interest.

We don't need to wait for time to pass to discover the good in events. When we patiently sit with them after they happen, they will eventually reveal the deeper truth to us. But what if we can just trust that events are always happening for our own conscious development, to reveal the greater truth of love, and remove all that keeps us from seeing it? These revelations are the wisdom inherent in our life experiences, dreams, and the world around us. We have an ability to perceive the hidden meaning of challenging events.

Unseen

Psyche isn't seen by her parents or others, nor can she see the masculine, or perceive the motives of her sisters. She's afraid of Eros because her father didn't protect her. There are parallels between the inner and outer masculine and the fear was of them both. The sisters tell Psyche to use the knife and lantern to see the beast and sever his head from his serpent body.

The knife symbolizes discernment and separation. She needs to shine the light of consciousness on the situation and cut away that which is erroneous to reveal the truth. Her sisters tell her to cut off her husband's head, which is to challenge the masculine thinking function that creates the fears of what's unseen to begin with. She has to shed the light on her relationship to the masculine and see it for what it really is. Despite her husband telling her not to, she dares to defy him and looks. She could have run away in fear and avoided that moment, but she doesn't. She stays and that takes courage. The strength comes from breaking the rules, discovering the world didn't come to an end, and that her fears were unfounded. She was willing to see what was *really* there. When she saw the god of love, she fell even more in love with her husband. She saw the truth of what was inside of her.

Eros didn't want Psyche to look at him because a mortal can't look at a god and live, or let's just say, remain asleep, or unconscious. Initially, her ego wasn't strong enough to hold that consciousness, but once the sisters came along, then she was. Psyche was asleep because she agreed not to look too closely at their situation and challenge him. Why didn't he want her to know the truth? Why did he want her to remain unconscious where his true identity was concerned? As long as she remains in that consciousness, it means she's beneath him, unaware of her inner truth, hidden, dependent, and afraid of her own power. He doesn't want his jealous mother to find out that he's living with the woman she hates either. Aphrodite would be furious with him, so he hides Psyche away.

Eros and Psyche live in sheltered seclusion and avoid being fully engaged with the world. It's not that much different from her father's house as her inner masculine keeps her subservient, maintaining the status quo, and unconscious. But something deeper is coming into awareness.

Once Psyche sees Eros—the divine masculine that was asleep inside herself—she wants to kill herself, but the knife won't comply. The ego is obliterated momentarily by the light of the divine presence, which means "she" ceases to exist, or let's say her old story ceases. She *sees* and her sense of self expands. She's no longer the compliant young woman who does as she's told but dares to defy a perceived authority figure. She shines the light of consciousness and discovers that the god of love is her inner partner.

When we look inside ourselves and remain conscious, we will discover the god of love within us as well. The mind shuts off and the old story dissolves in the light of truth. We aren't who we thought we were. The love and fulfillment that we have been seeking out in the world is inside of us, if we can sustain the gaze. It takes time for some of us to accept that we could be that wonderful. It often requires a transformation of our own consciousness in order to embody this expanded awareness. Psyche will show us how to do exactly that.

Eros Awakens

Psyche accidentally spills a drop of hot oil from the lantern on Eros and burns him, which causes him to wake up. Oil is utilized to anoint and bless something in a sacred religious ceremony. The oil serves to elevate this action to make it sacred. That which is within us is sacred and holy.

The god of love, asleep in Psyche's consciousness, awakens. This is a momentous occasion. Psyche's consciousness isn't strong enough to sustain the truth of her own inner situation, and as a result, Eros flies away.

She's unaware of her own value or truth, and follows what her sisters, parents, and Eros tell her. She isn't standing in her own power, nor does she know about her own wisdom or divinity. She'll have to discover the truth of who she is as the soul, since she must see herself as an equal to unite with spirit—the god of love. The inner sacred marriage only can occur in equal partners, and she's not there yet.

Eros leaves, meaning he goes back into the unconscious, because Psyche can't maintain that level of awareness regarding the divinity of the inner masculine and love. The realization is so contrary to her sense of self that she can't accept her own inner truth, which is so beyond her realm of understanding that she can't comprehend the magnitude of it. Her inner divine masculine must be brought to consciousness and sustained, in order for him to not run away when seen.

Where did Eros go to hide? He went to his mother's house. On one hand, it can be perceived as a regression of sorts, even for a god, due to his enmeshment with his mother. He kept Psyche hidden from Aphrodite, because of her feelings about Psyche. Psyche is dealing with the father issue, while Eros heals his immaturity. He reverts to childhood, a place where he was taken care of, didn't have to be responsible, felt safe, and didn't have to be an adult, which was what was happening with Psyche as well. The masculine wants to remain a momma's boy and doesn't want to grow up. He's been living a double life, one with Psyche, and one with his mother.

On the other hand, this is a time for Psyche to grow in her own power, and the masculine, mortal or divine, remains hidden as her consciousness evolves and she learns more about the truth of who she really is. This means the transformation is happening inside and this part of the journey isn't occurring in the outer world.

This is a time to explore our own caretaking of others and desire to being cared for. The places within us that might still be living in a childhood consciousness and where we are not yet standing fully in our power. Any time someone has to ability to say or do something that brings us down, or elevates us, we have given power away. Any area of life in which we believe our well-being rests outside ourselves, is a situation in which we have projected our power onto an outer source. The foundation that we stand on must be moved from impermanent external sources to an inner permanent one. The journey reveals all the places where we give our power away and will challenge us to retrieve them.

Eros's hot oil burn is a result of Psyche's apparent betrayal. He flees from being seen by Psyche to Aphrodite's house to nurse his wounds. Eros is an immature masculine who has to grow into his power and stand up to his controlling mother. He must stop controlling the situation with Psyche as well. Her husband needs to transform himself from a rebellious boy consciousness—disrupting the lives of others and creating chaos—to a responsible man (or god) who can stand on his own. He defied Aphrodite when he fell in love with Psyche, and Psyche rebels against him by looking. They both need to mature in order to be reunited.

The inner masculine evolves from a patriarchal father, to a beast, to the god of love, but then he disappears from consciousness. None of the masculine figures really see or value the young feminine soul in her empowered fullness. Psyche's inner masculine is being transformed in her own psyche. Eros is immature and has to stop thinking only of himself and what he wants. He needs to become aware of how his actions affect others.

Transforming the Feminine

Eros and Psyche work on the feminine in two ways. Eros is healing the controlling regressive mother, and Psyche is opening to the divine feminine. The two are actually tied together as we will see. Eros is the aspect of Psyche that serves the inner mother and is unhealthy. Aphrodite wants Eros to remain a boy and serve her. She won't let him be an independent thinking and acting son, while he's afraid to openly challenge her authority, and so, their relationship remains incestuous. Neither Aphrodite nor Psyche want to let go of the young immature masculine.

Aphrodite is upset with Psyche during most of the story, even though it isn't her fault that the people worship her. She doesn't like it any more than Aphrodite does. Psyche's beliefs around the divine feminine are transforming in her consciousness as well. There's a separation in her consciousness between Aphrodite, Eros, and herself. These three will have to be integrated for Psyche to realize the full truth of her being.

The old feminine resents the young feminine taking her place. She doesn't want to give up her position of superiority, which means that she's in the unconscious too. Psyche must overcome her desire to remain a helpless dependent child projecting her power outside of herself and discover that power within. She isn't a victim of Aphrodite, the beast, her parents, life, her beauty, her sisters, or Eros. Her challenges will bring all of this to her awareness.

Psyche repeatedly judges her situations and falls into fight or flight mode. Her despair over losing Eros makes her want to throw herself into the river. She doesn't feel good, is convinced that her situation is hopeless, and wants the feeling to end. The only solution she can come up with is to end her life. She feels like a helpless victim whenever something challenging happens, which is what she feels at this point. She forgets she's the one who looked at Eros in the first place and set all of this in motion.

We may feel helpless at times and fall into victim consciousness, but if we bring as much presence to the feelings as we possibly can and just sit with them, they usually dissipate. When we open fully to the moment and what's constellated in us, breathe with it, and allow it, then we don't have to feel like a victim of an emotion, a situation, or life. We can just be with and accept what is. Psyche's reaction to her situation is acceptable and there isn't any reason to judge it, since it's all good.

Searching for Eros

When Psyche begins her search for Eros, she feels overwhelmed and wants to drown herself in the river. The God Pan sees her and intervenes. He encourages her not to and suggests that she seek out and appeal to Eros. Pan is associated with the goat. He wanders in the woods and hills, protects flocks, and frolics with the nymphs. He's an earthy God, representing an integrated instinctual awareness, because he is half animal and half man. Psyche decides to take Pan's advice to continue looking for Eros instead of killing herself.

Pan represents the emergence of an earth-based deity into Psyche's awareness. He instinctively knows what to do. This is the beginning of a different kind of consciousness in Psyche that's rooted in nature and spirit. Nature knows what to do and doesn't have the mind to interfere with thoughts of this or that. Flowers know how to grow and bloom. Birds know where to migrate and caterpillars know how to become butterflies. We also have an innate instinctual knowing that many of us aren't familiar with, but it's there and available.

When we face challenges, instead of falling into victim consciousness and drowning in the river of emotions, we can connect to our inner wisdom and learn what we can do.

Instead of beginning her search for Eros, Psyche decides to visit her sisters to retaliate. Their scheming doesn't turn out quite the way they planned. Psyche goes to her first sister's house, tells her Eros wants to marry her, the sister runs to the mountaintop and leaps, only to discover too late that the wind isn't there to carry her down to the meadow, and she dies. Psyche then visits her second sister and the situation repeats.

Both sisters must perish in Psyche's consciousness because they intended to kill her. If they are not killed, they will try again to get rid of her. If they had managed to kill her, then she would've end up as a cynical, judgmental, jealous woman who lived with a constant sense of inadequacy. Thank heavens the sisters were the ones to go. This means their consciousness—this part of Psyche—has been cleansed from the soul and she can continue her journey.

As Psyche searches for Eros, he lies in tremendous anguish barely clinging to life from the wound inflicted by the oil, or was it Psyche's betrayal that's causing him to suffer so miserably? Word reaches Aphrodite in the depths of the sea that the world is in turmoil, since both she and Eros are deep in the unconscious. There isn't any love or joy on Earth, since they left. There's a general disregard for love without Aphrodite and Eros to tend and inspire it in the people.

When there isn't any love in the world, the people suffer. We need love to be present and active in our lives to thrive. It must be cultivated, embodied, and flow freely to be lived.

Aphrodite returns home and sees Eros. She expresses her anger to him for betraying her with Psyche, who is the reason she was at the bottom of the sea, or in the unconscious, in the first place. Since Eros took Psyche, of all people, as his wife, she's even more humiliated. She threatens to find another son to replace him and strip him of his godly qualities. Although, it's only a threat, since what she really wants is vengeance on Psyche.

Meanwhile, Psyche continues to search for her husband. She speaks to two goddesses in her wanderings, but both refuse to help for fear of upsetting Aphrodite. They are quite familiar with the goddess' wrath and are unwilling to incur it for Psyche's sake. Psyche sinks even further into despair, as she realizes the only way out of her predicament is, as one goddess suggests, to face Aphrodite directly.

Tasks

Well, facing Aphrodite's anger is an unpleasant prospect. Almost as uncomfortable as dealing with our own anger over feeling ignored, rejected, not valued, not enough, overlooked, you name it. It definitely is a daunting task to feel the power of this emotion inside and to find a way to channel the energy until we can handle it. Those I know who have gone through this, male and female, myself included, were stunned and surprised by its magnitude. A tremendous amount of presence and awareness are required through this phase, but it does make us stronger.

Different options are available for working with this energy, and each person has to find what works for them. There is meditation, yoga, sitting to witness the emotion, exercise (only when it's too much to handle and not to repress it), scribbling with crayon pastels on a newsprint pad, and journaling, are a few of the effective methods available. There is always therapy, if you feel overwhelmed. You'll know where you are on the journey when you get to this stage. The good news is, it does pass. The intensity of the anger will greatly diminish as you repeatedly bring presence to it.

Dreams, during this phase, can be of meeting wild animals. Initially, we may be afraid of them. What are a pack of wild dogs doing wandering through the house? But there they are, wanting to get to know and relate to us. There may be snakes in the grass as we walk barefoot, or out of control animals, grabbing a hold of us and not letting go. Eventually, it should develop into a more harmonious relationship where you have less fear of them.

Anger in dreams can also appear as fire, which may be raging out of control or even as smoke without a flame. Situations in dreams may also trigger anger. The intention of which is to help us reduce the power contained in the repressed emotions. When we sit with the feelings from the dream, we can transform them and don't have face them as frequently in the world. There needs to be caution exercised to not take this anger out on others, but to resolve it.

When we sit with the anger long enough, we often will get to the tears and grief behind it. A feeling of inadequacy may be constellated by a situation and brought forth for us to feel an emotion that is still lingering from childhood. As we feel it all the way through, we transform it. I perceive it as having tea with a visitor or as sitting with an upset child. There's no need to rush the feeling in order to get rid of the discomfort. We just want to feel it for as long as it's present and be patient with ourselves.

The sadness often comes from an old feeling of neglect, or not being loved and accepted, that went unfelt in our younger years.

The people whose actions cause us to feel ignored, or neglected now, are merely here to help us transform the anger, or any feeling, that was buried in the past. They can do things that make us feel different emotions, so that we may see and heal them. Presence to whatever is felt, and acceptance of the feeling, will result in reduced emotions and drama.

Psyche's Value

Aphrodite gives Psyche tasks to prove the worth of her mortal daughter-in-law or kill her. Psyche needs to discover her inner worth and when she does, her old version of herself as a helpless victim will naturally perish.

There are multiple people who willingly participated in actions that could have resulted in Psyche's death. Her father thought he was sacrificing her to a dragon and her sisters wanted her dead. Psyche repeatedly thinks of killing herself and Aphrodite gives her tasks that may result in her death. She must feel vulnerable and afraid and believe the world is an unsafe place. Who can she trust? She's been abandoned by everyone, including her own husband. No doubt she feels alone and miserable. Who wouldn't?

We can find ourselves preoccupied with our own demise during these death phases. We may feel overwhelmed and think about how to end the discomfort. There is often a mistake in understanding during these challenging phases of a transformation. Our culture, having lost touch with symbolism, and knowledge of the initiatory journey, means we often think literally. The feeling of death and dying during the journey, means an old part of us has come to an end. If you feel overwhelmed during this stage, seek help. The feeling *will* eventually subside as the emotions are transformed.

The introspection, questions, and focus at this time should be around what needs to be released. What part of me is no longer serving me? What aspect has outlived its usefulness? What situations need to change? The fairy tales can often shed light on these questions. See where you are on the journey and what the story, dreams, and your life, say about the next step.

First Task: Sorting and Discernment

Many things transpire when Psyche leaves her father's house. She thought she would be sacrificed to a beast and wasn't. She believed she would be married to a serpent who was going to kill her, which didn't happen. She saw her husband was the god of love, decided to kill herself, but couldn't and lost him. Psyche realized her sisters didn't love or care for her. They also didn't have her best interests at heart and wanted her dead. She killed them. Her sense of who she is, and her world, have radically changed. Who she was when she left her father's house isn't who she is when she finally meets Aphrodite. She must look inside and sort through what's happened to her. Who is she now?

It's important to reflect on who we are as we go through these transformations. We want to acknowledge our efforts and the positive changes coming about through our own initiations. When we engage consciously with life, we will see ourselves and events differently. Who are you now?

Aphrodite is angry and vengeful. In the first task, she orders Psyche to separate different pulses and grains into piles. Psyche is overwhelmed by the magnitude of the task and is overcome with feelings of despair. She reverts to her old helpless victim role and doesn't know how to even approach such a daunting task. How does one sort a mountain of grains, beans, and lentils?

Well, she can't do it alone and help arrives from the natural world again. First it was Pan and now it's the ants.

The Ants

The ants assist her in completion of this first task by demonstrating that the way to approach such an overwhelming job is to join with others and take care of one small item at a time. The way to accomplish seemingly impossible projects is by breaking them down into manageable parts. The key is to do even a little bit every day. Ants work together as a community, which could mean that your project is just a piece of a larger whole. The community with which your efforts are connected may be seen or unseen.

As a victim, Psyche believes she can't deal with the situation in front of her. When she isn't in victim mode, she may see that the task is a large one and therefore, in order to accomplish it and to not feel overwhelmed, she must break it down into manageable pieces she can complete.

The ants unite the opposites. The large task is contrasted with the details necessary to get it done. The big picture, or goal, and the small steps that are required for completion, are brought together in this test. The goal must be kept in mind as the steps are executed. This is one positive aspect of discernment, and separation—breaking down a big task into smaller parts.

When we face a daunting task, we need to see what the manageable steps are that will help us to reach the goal. As we persist, we build the strength, patience, and stamina that are required to take a project through to its conclusion. We learn to stay with something until we reach the desired outcome, and don't give up in the middle, because we can't see the results yet. This is important since some desires may take years to manifest and we have to be able to stay with them, even when the end isn't in sight, and still maintain faith in ourselves.

Psyche utilizes masculine energy in this task. Separation is male energy, like with a knife, the mind breaks a big task into smaller steps, to make a project manageable. Once Psyche completes it, she learns that she can resolve issues that may at first seem insurmountable. She has what it takes to do so and sees a new aspect of herself emerge. She experiences herself as stronger and more competent. This is a success. The ants represent an instinctual natural aspect of her psyche that knows what to do and how to complete this kind of task.

She resolves this challenge with help from this new part of herself that is brought to consciousness as a result of the task. Assistance can arrive either way, from the outside as actual help or from the inside as inspiration, and sometimes both.

Second Task: Gathering Fleece

The successful completion of the first task leads Psyche to the second, in which she has to gather wool from some angry golden sheep. Since these tasks must be completed within a specified time frame, she can't ponder them for long, which heightens her anxiety. This when instinct, or intuition, is necessary to solve something we haven't encountered before. The mind doesn't have a precedent to determine what to do, so we have to rely on another part of us.

Once Psyche hears the second task, she leaves Aphrodite intending to kill herself again. This time she plans to cast herself off a cliff and into the river. Since the river is water, and water is a symbol for emotion, she's going to drown herself in her emotions. This means she's overcome by her feelings. She's afraid she won't be able to complete the task and is immobilized by emotion. If we look at the process of how her emotions get activated, we discover it's actually her *thoughts* about what she has to do that activate her emotional response.

This plays out as such. Aphrodite tells her to collect the golden fleece. Psyche thinks to herself that there isn't any way she can do that, because she isn't capable of such a difficult and dangerous undertaking. She's going to fail and possibly even die. Then the emotions set in and constellate a vicious cycle of ever-deepening despair and fear-based thoughts. They feed on each other until she sinks into inaction. Can't do it, doomed, no way out, it's over, etc. A helpless, hopeless situation, and feeling miserable, she must end it all by casting herself into the river.

Psyche is overwhelmed by the task, and like Aphrodite, wants to plunge into the water of the unconscious. This means she either loses time wallowing in emotion and not working to get the task done, or she adopts a victim role and refuses to work toward greater consciousness.

The Reed

This time it's a reed from the riverbed that is divinely inspired to speak to Psyche and tell her how to complete the task. There's an interesting story of the reed that's connected with Pan. He was chasing a nymph, who in trying to escape, pleaded with the River God to help her. He answered her request by turning her into a reed. The reed tells Psyche that she can safely complete the task by waiting until the sheep's anger has died down with the passing of the noonday sun and after they get a drink from the river. Then she can easily gather wool that's stuck in the briers. Pan is known to sleep during the heat of the day and is not be disturbed either, just like the sheep. This reed then knows the way around the wrath of the god and the sheep.

We think of sheep as passive, docile followers. Yet in this story they're angry and aggressive. The sun is a masculine energy of going and doing. When we are out of balance and doing too much, it can constellate aggression. The way to accomplish this task is to let the sun's hottest phase pass, meaning to let the anger cool down, or take a break from activity and rest.

This task reveals the conflict of opposites between being passively docile (like sheep) and angrily aggressive, which must be tempered, before we act. When we passively follow others, and do what they tell us, or want us to do, we are not free or empowered. We may not be listening to what we want or need if we let others decide what's right for us. If we put their needs and desires before our own, we may end up ignoring our own feelings and needs altogether. Then, this can result in feelings of neglect, fatigue, and anger, about passively going along. This can also happen when we are focused on what we must do, should do, or need to do, and don't feel like we have any choices or the time to take a break. When we don't feel free to do what we really want, it can appear as though the restrictions are imposed from the outside. If our anger gets triggered, we need to sit and wait until it passes, then act. If we act when angry, we may be destructive, or at least be out of balance.

Victim Consciousness

Psyche feels like a victim, since Aphrodite is angry with her and making her complete these daunting tasks. Initially, Psyche wants to kill herself and is passive and then, the anger comes up when the sheep appear. Once the anger subsides, then she can do what needs to be done. She didn't get angry when she faced the first task, but when the time comes to complete the second task, now she's angry. It appears as though the sheep are the ones who are angry, but the sheep represent aspects of Psyche as much as the sisters did.

Anger is a step in the right direction. When in helpless victim mode, it's as though there isn't any energy available to complete a task. But when anger shows up, there is energy that can compel us to act, although it's not always effective action because it's unbalanced. That's why it's important to wait for the heat of it to pass.

When we feel victimized, we may be at the mercy of fight-or-flight emotions, vacillating between helplessness and aggression. This can happen when the situation appears to be someone else's, or no one else's, fault. As we feel our emotions, whatever they are, and witness them, without reacting, we break the pattern of reacting or blaming others. This creates an inner stability over time, so the actions of others and situations don't make us feel like a victim, which frees us.

It would be easy to blame Aphrodite for Psyche's challenges, but we have to remember, this is an initiation; these tasks are meant to make Psyche stronger and more resilient. These tasks will strip away all her false self-beliefs so she can discover the truth of who she really is. Our challenges are intending to do the same for us. What daunting tasks are you facing? Are you being passive or aggressive? Feeling like a victim or blaming someone else for your situation? Or are you taking responsibility for your life, for the life you desire, and moving forward, knowing that all these challenges are to assist you in reaching the outcome you want?

This task will help to free Psyche from the emotional swings, from passive to aggressive, that impair her ability to act with clarity and balance. This releases her even more from her sister's consciousness of judging everything as good or bad, which causes extreme emotional fluctuations. If Psyche realizes each task is to bring her greater consciousness and that she isn't a victim, then her response will be different. She will feel more empowered, if she accepts that each experience happens for her benefit and growth. She isn't a victim in any situation but has been *chosen* by the goddess and god of love to realize her true nature. This is such a gift and a blessing. In the same way, our experiences, regardless of how they appear, are meant to assist us in embodying more clarity in consciousness.

All of nature, within and without, conspires to help us achieve greater wisdom about ourselves and life. Our mindset, rooted in duality, has the tendency to judge everything. Each moment is either what we want, or it isn't. We often ricochet from one pole to the other, from one experience to another.

It may sound simple and easy, to sit with whatever is felt and witness it, but can be quite daunting. We can feel swept away by extreme emotions like anger and helplessness, to such an extent that we feel it's beyond our control, like the sheep in the heat. It's helpful to find a non-destructive channel for the energy until it is more manageable. The feeling of helplessness, of not being able to do anything about a situation, constellates these emotions, and can trigger fear and frustration, which may result in a fight-or-flight, anger or victim, response.

When emotions come up, we can feel them fully and deeply while anchored in stillness. Wait until the noon-day sun, or the heat of the anger passes, and the sheep become calm. Do not act in the throes of anger.

Witness it. Then collect the wool, that has such value. The task may be completed easily, once the anger passes.

Psyche initially thought this was an impossible task, but then the reed conveyed to her how simple it could be. The simplicity of the solution arises when we sit with the anger and it passes, then the answer comes. Psyche was guided to the right action by the part of her that knew what to do.

The reed lives at the river's edge, a place that is in between land and water. It bridges the two. We are learning how to link the inner and outer dualities, or opposites. It lives in the water and knows how to thrive in that environment, which is the opposite of the fiery sun. Water may be perceived as a feminine soul element and fire as associated with spirit and the masculine. The navigation of these two further brings together these opposites.

Third Task: Water from the River

Psyche completes the second task having to do with fire and then Aphrodite gives her a third that involves water. In this test, Psyche has to collect water from a river of terrifying black water that flows from high on a mountaintop down to the swamps that feed the river of the underworld. This task unites the above and below. The above is the abode of the gods, heaven, spirit, divine consciousness, and immortality. The below is the underworld, unconscious, death, humans, and the swamps. We are moving from a place of separation to union. We have this idea that heaven is up in the sky, somewhere else, apart from us. We are uniting this opposite, or duality, as well.

Psyche has to contain these terrible waters in a vessel. Fear can lead to stagnation and eventual death. Psyche must face her fear of death, but here we are also talking about the death of who she thinks she is. We shouldn't let that lull us into thinking that because it isn't necessarily literal that it is somehow easier than death itself. We are so attached to our identity being a particular way that it can sometimes be very hard to let go of an old version of ourselves. Both versions of death can feel daunting.

As Psyche faces challenges, her old sense of herself as a powerless victim is dying. At the same time, the new baby—a new version of herself—grows inside her as she moves toward greater consciousness. She is transforming as a soul, from the physically based, powerless, helpless, victim, version of herself that she was identified with into a more empowered spiritually oriented self. A fear-based sense of self changes when the fear is seen, felt, and realized for what it is. It's just another emotion, albeit a very strong one, that must be understood as nothing more than that. Psyche is learning that she is so much more, and so much stronger, than she has ever known herself to be.

What continues to live when the body dies? The soul survives the death of the physical form, and Psyche's body is a vessel for the union of soul and spirit. What does she bring together within herself? We as souls, and vessels, bring spirit to consciousness through the physical. The soul incarnates to remember spirit and unite with the god of love. This union is of the above and below so then they are One. It's a realization that the inner and outer are One as well. It is all one seamless reality.

More of Psyche's unconscious fear is brought to consciousness in this task. The known and unknown are brought together. She must let go of who she thinks she is and open to not knowing the truth of who she really is. Psyche learns, through the tasks, how to bring out the power and skills that were inside her all along. These abilities are being drawn forward and into her conscious awareness. She has to discover her own power and how to use it effectively so that she can see through her fear of the death of her old self to the light of truth that it conceals.

Psyche has to learn how to feel the power of the emotions without being swayed by them from a center of peace, which is her greater truth. The emotions come and go, but what remains untouched and unaffected by these feelings, is the inner stillness and silence. As she achieves a greater ability to ground herself in that and witness her thoughts, emotions, challenges, and events as they pass, she gets stronger. Her inner power grows, and she can utilize it without it coming from a place of ego. She needs to reside in the heart and have that as the filter for her actions. Then, she will not seek power or control over others or events.

Psyche goes to the mountaintop and is terrified by what she sees. There are dragons guarding the water, and so, she decides to end it all right then and there, by flinging herself off of the mountain. There isn't any way that little old her is a match for those big fierce dragons. Psyche again falls into victimhood and becomes paralyzed by the situation she faces. It feels totally overwhelming. She just stands there. When we don't know what to do, we shouldn't do anything. Get quiet, turn within, and ask for an answer.

The Eagle

The eagle, Zeus's bird, sees Eros's wife, takes pity on her, and completes this third task for her. It flies high, which gives it an expansive vision to help it more easily find food. The energy of this bird is exactly what Psyche needs in this moment to see more clearly, get a greater perspective, and act decisively. The eagle is a powerful bird and a wonderful ally. The eagle unites the sky and earth. It shows Psyche how to do this by helping her see beyond the small limiting story of herself to a bigger picture of who she is and what she's capable of.

When the story we tell about ourselves is good, we feel good. When the story we tell about ourselves is bad, we feel bad. When we don't tell any story, everything is okay. We aren't the story. The story changes and whatever changes can't be who we really are. We are what persists as the story changes. We are beyond the story. We are the essence in which the story unfolds.

We are the still and silent presence that witnesses the story, but we are not the story itself. The stillness and silence are unaffected by the story. It exists before our stories are born and will exist after our stories die. That is the stability and ground that Psyche is being guided to root in by Aphrodite. That ground is unaffected by any story that unfolds for her, or as her. Her fear of death, either herself or the story, has to be seen through. The death of the story is the death of the ego, which is the story we have been told since birth about who we are, which is untrue.

The more we can witness the passing, transitory emotions, the greater the stillness and silence get. Acceptance of the emotions and what's happening leads to an unshakable stability and a rootedness in the depths within.

We can contain the dreaded water from the river of death, when we have a more expansive vision. The fear-based emotions are contained when we see beyond the details of something to the wisdom inherent in the experience. A different perspective is achieved when we unite the above and below, the wisdom of the experience with the experience itself. The opposites come together as we understand that our challenges occur to help us realize our true nature. Every situation we encounter peels back the layers of erroneous beliefs, old feelings, and illusory ideas to reveal a deeper truth. When we take the time to sit with what happens and reflect on it, its wisdom and the deeper meaning is revealed. This helps us to see the good, not only in all situations, but also in the wider world, since everything that occurs is for our benefit, personally and collectively.

Love compels us to act in particular ways that offer healing and awareness through every experience. It's love that makes us do what we do in order to reveal greater love. When we are open to the inherent wisdom of life, we can transform ourselves through each experience, and possibly, if we are persistent enough, even get a glimpse of the love which is hidden in it.

The third task tests her ability to see more clearly. Is Psyche able to demonstrate intelligence beyond that normally conceived as human? This is wisdom embodied. Can she see what to do and act on her knowing? Does she see more of who she really is?

When Psyche returns to Aphrodite, the goddess is furious and knows once again, that there isn't any way Psyche could complete the task on her own. She's obviously getting help from someone and assumes that it must be her son. Aphrodite tells Psyche the details of her final task—a descent to the land of the dead.

Fourth Task: Beauty and the Underworld

The fourth task is for Psyche to go to the underworld and get a box of beauty from Persephone, goddess of the underworld. Psyche, overwhelmed by the task, decides to climb a tower intending to jump. The divinely inspired tower intercedes and asks why she's going to kill herself right before finishing the final task—when the destination is within her reach. It then explains how to get the box of beauty from Persephone.

She's instructed to get two coins for the ferryman and two barley cakes for the journey. There is a particular location where Psyche will be able to enter the underworld. She's told to pass by the begging lame man and ignore him. The ferryman will take one of the coins to cross the river and she's not to allow the man in the river to get into the boat. Next she must not interact with the woman who is spinning. Those that request her help are traps set by Aphrodite. Psyche is to give one cake to the three-headed dog that guards the gate to Persephone's palace, which will distract it as she gains entrance. Inside, she's to sit on the ground, only accept a piece of bread from the goddess, and ask Persephone for the beauty. Then take the box and leave, give the second cake to the dog, the coin to the ferryman, and exit the way she entered. The final warning to Psyche was to not look in the box.

The tower is a man-made building that is sturdy, strong, and has deep foundations. It represents the stillness and strength created in the soul as we endure the experiences of life with awareness. This ongoing practice results in a greater perspective. The tower can be perceived as linking heaven and earth, a central axis to root in as she prepares to descend to the underworld. This center is critical so that she can face all the fears that arise there.

The tower offers a higher and wider perspective, like the eagle. The eagle is instinctual, while the tower represents a developed or acquired vision. Psyche goes into the tower intending to kill herself, but once *inside* the tower she finds out what to do: understanding how to establish an embodied awareness of the connection between the inner and the outer, in addition to the above and below.

This again represents a part of the heroine. Initially, she was overwhelmed, and felt like killing herself, but once she climbed the steps of the tower and connected with the Source inside her, she found the solution to the task at hand. She has both sides still active, but this answer to something she has never encountered before and has no precedent to solve, is found within. Once she no longer feels helpless, she begins to follow the steps to descend to the underworld.

When Psyche goes to the underworld this symbolizes the unseen, or inner realm, and the unconscious. She will journey through an unknown world of fear and death. The other outer-oriented tasks prepared her for this daunting inner one.

Her ongoing attempts to establish stability in the face of tumultuous emotions and death are critical to the successful completion of this task. Otherwise, she will be unable to survive the descent to the underworld. In the same way, our experiences are empowering us and have prepared us for our journeys as well.

Don't Help Others

The tower strongly emphasizes that she must not stop to help anyone who asks. The repeated requests she receives are a trap set by Aphrodite. These are tests. She must stay *focused* on the task at hand to complete it and *not get distracted*. This was a lesson from a previous task. When asked for help, she'll have to ignore her desire to assist, which was an issue for her initially with her sisters. She didn't have the ability to discern her sisters' motives and was naïve. This is her test to see if she has learned that lesson. Can she see the truth, stay on course, and get the box of beauty? If she can't, she won't emerge alive. This is serious business.

What do you need to do now? What does your descent look like? Are you prone to helping others and lose track of where you are, where you are going, or the bigger picture? Do you need to stop assisting others and take care of yourself? This can feel like selfishness, but it isn't. Keep your eyes on the prize.

Don't get distracted, she's warned, by the greedy masculine, who is consumed with "not enough-ness," a sense of inadequacy, or needing to be more. Let go of the attachments to what is temporary and perishable. Remember that value isn't determined by the outer world, how much we have, what we do, or who we are. We are fundamentally enough exactly as we are in this moment. Getting more of anything from the world will not change who we are, which is one of the things this journey will reveal.

The tower told Psyche not to help the man decomposing in the river of emotions: let that which is dying, die. It may be tempting to hold on to that which we perceive of as stabilizing forces in our lives. We may find ourselves clinging to what's clearly deteriorating. It can be challenging to let go, not only of outdated versions of ourselves, but also all that goes along with the old life. It may be time to leave the job and we know it, but we're still struggling to depart.

Do not help the lame man who can't walk on his own. These are all the old wounded dead or dying masculine energies. Don't resurrect them. These may be parts of us or relationships that are finished. Don't get caught in the desire to save them. We can have compassion and love for those who have been with us but are now leaving. When feeling compelled to hold on, acknowledge the desire to yourself to keep them in your life, take a breath, and release. The fear of being alone or in the unknown can keep us where we are. Just continue feeling the emotions that are constellated and keep the focus inside on the stillness that is who you really are. Remember the outer will change. The old masculine energies will leave, old things will go, in order to make space for the new. But, don't hold on to hope—a desire for this phase to be over and onto a different future—be present to the fullness of the moment, and stay grounded.

Follow the Inner

Psyche is told to follow the laws of the inner world and that means to not judge what happens as good or bad. She must understand that the experience of each person is designed for their own growth. This is where compassion can trip us up. Oh, we feel so sorry for them with their sadness and struggle. They often are aware of just how to draw us in and tug on our heartstrings. We might just offer a little helping hand instead of doing what we need to do. We might see exactly where they are headed and want to give the slightest bit of guidance.

But, if we are moving on, and they are remaining in the same old patterns, we have to stay focused and not get distracted. Don't reach out a steadying hand, remember you can't drop even one of those barley cakes, which will be needed later. Psyche is guided not to get caught in her old ways of seeing someone as the victim or being a victim herself. These dying energies in the underworld represent the parts of her that may be clinging to life. These are beliefs of not enough, inadequacy, helplessness, or powerlessness. The parts of her that may have wallowed and decomposed in emotion, and are just reaching out to her, if only for a hand up. The aspect of her that was lame and felt she was unable to complete a task is departing. She must let it all go. *She isn't a victim and they aren't either.* Right? They're learning their lessons just like she did.

Psyche is guided to let the fates weave their web and not to interfere in their work. This means she must surrender and not try to control anything. She has to allow what's unfolding to play out as it will. It's so incredibly tempting to try to manipulate things into remaining as they have been or to try to force things change before it's time, in order to get out of the discomfort of not knowing. We may only know one thing, which is the next step, and might have to surrender knowing how we are going to reach a goal. There may be a desire to see what's coming before we take the leap into the unknown, but often we can't get even a glimmer of what's around the corner. Trust is the key.

Don't get distracted by thoughts, like the dog with three heads, which symbolizes being too much in the head. Dogs represent a masculine energy. Don't get angry about what's happening as what you have known falls apart. Keep a level head and distract the dog by feeding it the cake.

A dog with three heads would indicate confusion about what to do and which way to go. The mind and thinking can lead to uncertainty over too many options, which can activate feelings of anger and frustration. This is the old Psyche. She needs to remember what she learned from the tower and not fall into a feeling of being overwhelmed.

We don't want to get caught up in thinking about what's going to happen. When it's unknown, we may feel compelled to seek any answer to alleviate the discomfort of not knowing. Distract this part of yourself by grounding in the inner calm and go straight across the threshold into Persephone's house. Psyche has all she needs to succeed on her journey to the underworld, as do we. She must pay her way as she goes and obey its laws.

Psyche makes the descent and reaches Persephone. She doesn't eat what's offered, as she was told. Don't get caught indulging on this part of the journey, take what's needed and move on. Don't get stuck in the inner world by eating too much. We can become enamored with the unconscious and what's discovered there. The tower told Psyche to ingest only what's absolutely necessary to sustain herself, get the beauty, and leave. Don't linger overlong as an avoidance mechanism. Psyche is being tested all along the way to see if she embodies what the other tasks taught her and if she can follow her inner guidance.

Psyche is embodying a new way of being. The energy associated with it is competent, strong, and focused. She's becoming aware of a greater stability and sense of herself, who she is and what she can achieve. The power that she has within herself is being embodied. This experience reveals to her how competent she is.

This is the time to reflect on the truths that have been revealed, to embody them, and make them true for us. This is necessary to transform ourselves in the world. We need to review what life has shown to us, about ourselves and about the greater truth of reality, and see if we are making the necessary adjustments based on what we have learned.

New Aspects of the Heroine

The eagle and tower, as aspects of the heroine, are newly emerging parts of her that can provide answers. This means Psyche is learning how to utilize her intuition to find solutions to problems without a history. Thinking is based on what is already known. This is how thinking of a lot of options can create confusion and uncertainty. Intuition arises from a deeper inner source of wisdom that has an eagle-type of vision with a wider perspective. When it comes from intuition, you *just know* it's the right thing to do.

Remember how we reflected upon Psyche's inner dialogue and how it landed her in victim consciousness? Well now the self-talk has changed to things like, "I know what to do. I can do this. I am capable and confident. I have all of the answers that I need and I am strong enough to complete this task."

The underworld is the unconscious and Psyche goes into the unconscious to see the goddess who presides over the dead and is associated with *rebirth*. Persephone is the goddess of spring and when she emerges from the underworld, the barrenness of winter is transformed into the beauty of spring. Her emergence represents a renewal and transformation of the land from a wasteland to abundance. Psyche meets Persephone, the goddess of beauty, to link her with the goddess of love. The divine feminine traits of inner beauty and divine love are aspects of the soul. When the inner truth of herself is seen, the outer world is transformed. That is the rebirth we are talking about. Heaven is discovered right here on earth.

Seeing and Reunion

The tower's final instruction to Psyche was to not look in the box. Psyche believed she had to follow the rules, which we saw with her husband and Aphrodite. But Psyche must break the rules repeatedly throughout her journey, by daring to look and see what's true. She looked at Eros when she's told not to. She saw her sisters, even though Eros warned her about their harmful intentions. And finally, as she emerges from the underworld, she disobeys once again, and dares to open the box. She doesn't listen and wants just a little of that beauty ointment for herself. She thinks it'll take just a dab to win Eros back.

This is an indication that there is a residual trace of inadequacy. If she believes that she *needs* anything to be "enough," then she's still not seeing the full beauty of herself as whole and complete. It's one more rule that she's been told she must follow, and which must be broken in order for her to see the truth of herself. She has to step into her full power, see herself as equal to the goddess, and realize that no one has authority over her. Psyche must understand that she's not less than or more than anyone else. She doesn't have to listen to, or adhere to, any of their rules anymore, since she's not subservient to them. No one has the power to dictate anything to her now. Psyche doesn't need to follow any limitations placed on her by others. The beauty ointment belongs to her as much as anyone else. She's earned the right to open the box, to do, and take what *she* wants.

Psyche didn't do anything wrong and nothing that happened was her fault. She was born beautiful and others worshiped her, which she found distressing. Her parents sacrificed her. Eros took her in and kept her hidden. She could have stayed in the dark with him, but was unconscious, and they weren't equals. None of the other characters were operating with Psyche's best interests at heart. They were all looking out for themselves. Although, all of their actions created greater consciousness for her. The old Psyche dies when she emerges from the underworld—the unconscious.

When Psyche dares to look into the box of beauty, she falls into a death-like sleep. This might be interpreted as a death or regression, but it isn't. It may be perceived as Eros rescuing Psyche, but that's not the case either. Eros emerges from hiding and nursing his wounds in his mother's house only *after* Psyche dares to look. The old suffering victim dies in order for the new healed masculine—as the god of love—to emerge fully and permanently in her consciousness. He clears the sleep from her eyes, she wakes up, and *sees* the god of love.

Psyche wasn't *allowed* to look at Eros before, because he was a god and she was a human. When she dares to look, she sees the truth of her equality. The old mortal Psyche dies, which is the death of the ego. When she looks within, she sees the truth of the beauty within—her wholeness—and is transformed. The outer mirrors the inner. She awakens to the god of love inside herself. When, and only when, she realizes her own truth, is she able to look and truly *see* who he is. The sacred marriage can only happen between equal partners.

Psyche is resurrected. She awakens, to herself as the soul and to the god of love inside of her. As within, so without. She unites with the him as her inner partner and gives birth to a new version of herself. The baby in the story, is sometimes called "Pleasure," and sometimes "Bliss," but either way it is a new immortal soul that emerges from her initiatory journey.

Psyche and Eros go to Mt. Olympus and their marriage is witnessed by all of the gods and goddesses. Zeus gives Psyche the nectar of immortality to drink and she becomes a goddess. This is the transformation of the soul into its rightful power and place in the cosmos.

We will find within ourselves, when we *dare to look*, the truth, wholeness, and beauty of who we are. We are the soul and the god of love resides inside of us. We can resurrect our awareness of the inner divine and discover we are not who we thought we were. We, as souls, have always been so much more than we ever dreamed. The tasks we encounter in our lives, just like Psyche's, will reveal the truth. Once we *know* the truth, and can *see*, we will never be the same again.

CHAPTER

Two

Beauty and the Beast:
Rediscovering Power
and Abundance

O *nce upon a time there was a wealthy merchant who lived in the city with his three daughters and three sons. The sisters were jealous of Beauty because she was much kinder and prettier than them. They liked going to parties and hobnobbing with the rich, while Beauty was the sweet sister who liked to stay at home and read. All were happy until their father lost his wealth and the whole family had to move from the city to their country home.*

This disturbed the two sisters immensely, but Beauty eventually got used to living in the country and doing housework. She grew healthier, stronger, and happier as time went by. Occasionally a suitor offered to marry Beauty, but she chose to stay home with her father. Her sisters were bored in the country, since they didn't do anything, but spent their days making fun of her.

One day, after living in the country for some time, the father, a merchant, received a letter telling him that his ship had come in. The two sisters were elated at the possibility of returning to the city and asked him for new dresses. Beauty didn't really want anything, but asked her father to bring her a rose, because she didn't want her sisters to feel bad.

The father traveled to the docks, but didn't find the expected riches there, and on his way home he got lost in the forest during a storm. The strong winds and pelting rains repeatedly forced him off his horse. He was petrified as he wandered alone through the dark forest, listening to the howling wolves. After hours of frightening sounds, and a distressing search for something familiar, he saw a palace lit from top to bottom.

He put his horse in the barn, gave him some hay, and went inside. There wasn't anyone there, but in front of the fireplace with a burning fire he saw dinner was prepared. He sat and waited for hours for the owner to appear, but when no one came, he ate, and then fell asleep in one of the bedrooms.

In the morning, there were clean clothes laid out for him along with a small breakfast. He thanked the fairies of the empty house and went for his horse. As he walked to the stable, he saw the roses, and clipped one for Beauty.

He was startled by a deafening roar and the menacing appearance of a Beast. The Beast was angry with the father for stealing a rose and told him that he was ungrateful, since all his needs had been met. The Beast then threatened to kill him, so the father confessed that his daughter had asked him for the flower. The Beast decided he would take Beauty in his place and said to fill a trunk with gold and anything else he wanted before he left.

His horse knew the way home. When he arrived, the father told his family what happened with the ship, the Beast, and the rose. The sisters blamed Beauty for what had happened. In response, she insisted that she take her father's place and concealed her emotions because she didn't want anyone to feel bad for her.

Beauty and her father returned to the Beast's palace in three months. They were eating at a table prepared for them when the Beast came into the room. Beauty was frightened of his ugliness, but that night dreamt of a lady who said that everything would turn out well. She told her father her dream at breakfast and then he left for home.

She cried when he went, but then regained her composure and explored the palace. She saw a door with the words, "Beauty's apartment," over it. Inside she found all of the things she loved and thought that maybe the Beast didn't plan to eat her after all.

On the first night, the Beast told Beauty she could have whatever she wanted and was the lady of the house. He asked her to marry him at dinner, and with a trembling voice, she said no. They continued having dinner together every night for three months. He requested her hand again and again, but she declined. He finally relented and asked her to at least promise to never leave him. She agreed, but wanted to visit her father, saying she would return within a week.

The following morning, she woke up in her bed at home. Her sisters put on a dramatic display about how much they'd missed her and pretended they were happy to have her home. At the end of the week, knowing of Beauty's agreement with the Beast, they convinced her to stay longer. On the tenth night, Beauty dreamt the Beast was dying. She awoke and realized how much she missed him. She returned immediately with the intention of marrying him.

She waited for the Beast to appear at dinner that night, but he didn't show up. She frantically searched the house and discovered him dying in the garden. She then realized that she actually loved the Beast and told him so. Her love magically freed him from the spell placed on him and he was transformed back into a prince. They were married and lived happily ever after.*

---

* Full story in Leprince de Beaumont's *Beauty and the Beast.*

Introduction

How do we learn to see ourselves in an entirely new way? Empowered, loving, loved, healthy, beautiful, gifted, blessed, peaceful, enough? And believe everything is perfect as it is? Let go of being victims? How do we shift out of the old stories and into the greater truth and goodness of life? Into trust, faith, and belief in the possibility of a life lived happily with all our needs are met?

In the fairy tale "Beauty and the Beast," Beauty is a victim, but once she's with the Beast, he won't let her play that role anymore. He repeatedly pushes her gently to accept abundance and freedom. He wants her to make her own choices, to love her powerful inner masculine and to be unafraid of it. He teaches her how to relate to her inner wild primal power. Beauty thinks he's a beast and must see through the façade—the curse an old witch put on him—to the loving prince, which is her inner masculine. She needs to love and accept him as a part of herself. As within, so without.

He's abundant and quite powerful. He loves her as she is and wants to relate to her, encouraging her to grow more fully into the truth of herself. He's a partner in her unfolding. She must open without fear, accept what comes, take on new roles, and let go of her old family patterns of acting like a child and victim. She'll leave her father's house of lack and limitation, and her critical sisters, to enter a new place of freedom, love, peace, and harmony. Beauty learns to speak up and to express what she wants fearlessly.

The Missing Feminine

"Beauty and the Beast" is a tale that concerns the loss of the feminine, the wounded masculine, and instinct. The mother is missing in the story, which is the initial indication that something is awry with the feminine. The empowered feminine and the divine mother are conspicuously absent.

The story shows us that the *feminine will not emerge until she feels safe*. When the masculine is a Beast, or a bumbling inept father, and the heroine feels powerless, she remains hidden. She won't open her heart to love him, or want to unite with him, until she feels it's safe to do so.

She won't feel safe if her power is projected onto someone or something else, and she believes that others have the power over her or to determine her wellbeing. If she thinks she's limited, controlled, or even protected by another, then she isn't free. If she depends on an external someone or something for her needs or desires being met, then she risks the possibility of feeling afraid to lose it.

Just as we saw with Psyche and Eros, Beauty must feel equal to the masculine for the sacred marriage to occur and right now the Beast scares the heck out of her. The sacred marriage archetype is significant personally and collectively. Fairy tales that persist across time are of archetypal significance, meaning they provide information about the deeper patterns unfolding in our time. We can see the marriage is important, since story after story culminates with the marriage of the hero and heroine. The feminine must resolve her fear of him to unite with the inner and outer masculine.

This isn't to say that only the feminine needs to be addressed, because the masculine is included here as well. This story gives us greater insights into the transformation of the masculine. Beauty's father, who represents her initial inner masculine, lets the young feminine take his place, to be devoured by a monster. As a part of her, her own masculine is willing to sacrifice her feminine self to save the old patriarchal masculine consciousness. The father is passive, incompetent, can't provide materially for his family, and fails to protect her, which are the reasons why she doesn't feel safe. But she also feels unsafe because she can't provide for herself, she doesn't protect herself from others, or her inner masculine. She doesn't stand up for herself, or her inner feminine.

In patriarchal cultures, the daughter is often sacrificed for material gain. We can see evidence of this imbalance all over the world in the challenges we are experiencing in ourselves and our environment. The masculine and feminine in a story are like the yin and yang of a whole. When one changes, the other automatically responds to maintain balance.

For example, if there is too much of an emphasis on work—masculine action—then the feminine suffers. That may appear as something like depression, or an illness like chronic fatigue, which forces us to slow down. When we honor what appears, then we follow the attempt by our system to create balance and work less. A culture that places the value on the masculine over the feminine, comes up with "solutions" to help us continue working, because not doing is not a consideration. This also means we ignore the body and our psyche's inherent wisdom to restore health and balance.

Beauty is initially isolated and in the intellect. She is childish and dependent, wanting to stay with her father—a masculine who is interested in material gain. The shadow, unconscious feminine is her sisters, who are interested in the material, socializing, expensive things, and status, as well as being jealous and judgmental. There is an imbalance in the characters with an over-emphasis on the outer world. The city, where they reside, also implies the activity associated with a busy life and being out of touch with nature and instinct.

When something isn't valued, it's ignored, unseen, and not validated. The mother is missing from this story, which means the a healthy empowered feminine hasn't been valued, and therefore, has gone into the unconscious. If something is in the unconscious for long enough, it's forgotten, and we don't even realize it's gone. However, it finds ways to remain in the culture and our lives, although it is often not recognized as such. Therefore, fairy tale after fairy tale repeats the motif of the absent, or silent, mother.

The Mother

The mother and the Mother, as the divine feminine or goddess, are missing. The mother represents qualities associated with the feminine, such as feeling, body, emotion, receiving, the heart, being and having enough, abundance, earth, relating, intuition and non-rational ways of knowing, an ability to just be, contentment, instinct, nourishment, and nurturance. The feminine relates to the moon, nature, and the cyclical rhythm of life. The Mother represents an earthy powerful divine feminine.

The masculine ways of a warrior patriarchal consciousness have superseded the feminine and the feminine nature has been something to be conquered, like the rest of the world. This isn't necessarily conscious and isn't to point the finger of blame at men, because women have, and are, doing it also. Many of us—men and women—reject the feminine because it hasn't been valued. Women have been portrayed as inferior and men as superior. This is part of our collective movement toward greater health and has a divine purpose. There isn't any reason to judge this, it's the way it is, and now we are bringing it to consciousness so we can move on.

How does the rejection of the feminine manifest in the culture? Nothing feels safe, inside or outside. The warrior archetype pervades our cultural discourse and seeks control over the feminine, nature, the body, emotions, and others. When they are perceived as different or out of control, they are approached with the intention to bring them back under control. We can repress emotions and disconnect from the body with drugs or unconsciously ignore its impulses and wisdom. Wild animals are exploited, caged, controlled, or killed. Homeowners are upset when wild animals infringe on "their" territory and pesticides are sprayed without thought for the implications.

Many aspects associated with the feminine are approached cautiously and with fear. We proactively seek safety in many areas. We don't even wait to see if we are unsafe but reject and repress in the effort to protect ourselves from discomfort and that which is seen as a possible threat. Our minds expect the past to repeat itself and we attempt to prevent the reoccurrence of challenging things that happened in the past.

But we have misunderstood. We are conditioned to believe that we must eradicate discomfort or any emotions that prevent us from participating *productively* in the culture. Emotions are feared as something that may cause us to lose control, or take us over, and we will never be able to escape from them. Many are convinced that we need to control emotions and avoid physical discomfort, of any sort, which can often be eliminated with a pill. We believe sexuality is a primal driving force and that it is to be tamed. There are heart attacks, breakdowns of the immune system, and illnesses in general to be fought. The unconscious and emotions are perceived as potential threats to our wellbeing and must be approached cautiously or they may take control of us. Our fears of the inner world are subsequently projected onto the outer world.

Now we have security for our nation, airports, banks, stores, information, homes, cars, schools, and children. We are in a paranoid culture where the surveillance is reaching unprecedented proportions and personal boundaries are considered irrelevant. Where is it safe when chemicals, pollution, contaminated waters, and terrorists, are often invisible and yet all around us? The other, food, water, air and world are perceived as unsafe. The body, emotion, nature, and earth are feared. There is a fear of the past and the future. That which is within, is reflected in the world. When we become acquainted with what is inside of us and stop being so afraid of it, we can find true freedom.

Innately Healing Experiences

If we open to the possibility that our life experiences serve our growth, then we might not be so afraid of what we encounter, and any fear of its ability to control us may be diminished. When we open to emotional and physical discomforts within ourselves and ask, "What's this saying? Why is it here?" we might see that there's more to what's happening than we previously realized. If we are openly curious, and can withstand the uncertainty, we may learn from what presents itself. Everything that happens inside and outside is here to teach us.

The human body is designed to heal. When we get a cut, it bleeds, and platelets form a clot once the wound is cleansed. A scab forms to seal the wound while it heals. When the time is right and the cut has healed sufficiently, the scab falls off. The skin will eventually mend to reflect its innate perfection. And we didn't *do* anything. If we didn't understand the process, we might be quite disturbed when the bleeding started. We get a small cut and all this red liquid starts gushing out, which we can't control. But we have learned to trust that the body knows what to do when we get a cut. We don't need to *do* anything. It knows how to heal us and make us better. It knows how to return us to our original state of health and wholeness.

Is it possible that this is a natural process for us with regard to all of life? That an uncomfortable emotion might show up to heal us? It might be perceived as the blood from a cut that arrives merely to cleanse a wound. Wouldn't that change everything? A slight shift in perspective can help us see differently.

What if we keep picking the scab as the wound heals? We'd probably end up with a scar. But, if we allow the wound to bleed until it is cleansed, and allow ourselves to cry until we are finished, or be sad for as long as we need to be instead of resisting, then we may be healed. We leave the scab alone until it is ready to fall off and we can trust that what shows up in our lives is helping us achieve better health. If we don't fall into a state of victim consciousness, or wallow in the emotions, they will pass.

We are moving toward an awareness of our innate health and wholeness. This is similar to a healing cut that is a movement toward health. In depth psychology, we open to what appears. We look at dreams, emotions, illness, and life to discover, "what is this guest showing us?" The outer world can be perceived in the same manner with all that happens as intending to assist us in the achievement of wholeness and health.

In the City

The family in the story lives in the city with a focus on the father's material success, the sisters' socializing and extraverted interests, and Beauty's introverted intellectual activity. Living in the city often indicates a lack of soul. Jung was "deeply concerned over the loss of connection with nature. He considered natural life to be the 'nourishing soil of the soul.'"[7] There is little space for nature and the rhythms of the natural life in this family's city living.

Instincts are the body's innate responses to conditions that don't require thought. The body operates on its own. Hunger arises when the body needs food. We feel sleepy and yawn when the body is tired. We have personal instincts and collective instincts, which have been handed down through the generations and are species specific. There are instincts for life and growth that are inherent.

Hunger is an example of how our society approaches food from the head and not instinct. This disconnection from instinct manifests in a variety of ways. For example, we often don't eat when we are compelled by an inner impulse, but by a clock. Most of us eat three times a day. What we eat is influenced by others based on the latest science, disregarding what we feel as individuals, or what our bodies need. If we need to lose weight, we are told to eat less calories or exercise more. Many of us don't wait for our hunger pangs, or know when we are full, or what our bodies need for better health. This lack of bodily awareness can be seen in the record numbers of people who are overweight, have eating disorders, food allergies, or are undernourished.

There is an innate knowing in the body. There can be feelings in the body about something being right or wrong before an actual event takes place. This instinct to know is often overlooked when these feelings aren't considered. A woman, for example, may get involved with someone who isn't a positive influence in her life despite her feelings that it isn't a good idea. She may stay too long in the relationship, deny to herself what's happening, and not act on her behalf.

Jung wrote of the "'primitive within myself.' This natural mind, formed over millions of years of evolutionary history, operates by its own set of logical assumptions. Jung illustrated the tremendous survival value of this differentiated instinct, now largely lost in civilized people."[8] The instincts are injured in Beauty's family, since they have spent so much time in the city.

Instincts can also be injured when we are taught to ignore what we sense in childhood. Children often know what feels *right*. They may sense when someone shouldn't be trusted, but we can override their feelings, and teach them to not listen. They learn what and when to eat from us. We teach them not to fall asleep when it's inconvenient and to sleep when it is convenient. We are culturally conditioned toward mind over body, to prefer intellect to innate knowing.

Beauty's father is a successful merchant. Many people begin reflecting on their achievements somewhere around the middle years of life. If not, an experience or situation, such as retirement or a significant financial loss, may be the catalyst for examination and change. At other times, it can be the psyche that compels us to move in a new direction. This story begins with the family ensconced in their wealthy lifestyle and its associated activities, but that changes.

The two older daughters are absorbed in the material world and are "very proud because their father was so rich. They gave themselves ridiculous airs, and would not visit the daughters of other merchants, nor keep company with any but people of high degree."[9]

The two sisters carry the feminine shadow aspects of the heroine, Beauty. The shadow is comprised of the rejected, repressed, and projected parts of us—good and bad. Doubling, since there are two of them, means they are critical to Beauty's development. They represent the parts of her that are selfish, materialistic, don't value herself, are judgmental and critical. They look to others and the world, to see how they compare to those around them, in order to determine their worth and rank. They seek validation outside themselves. They must perceive themselves as superior, and others as inferior, to feel good.

Some of their traits are going to be critical to Beauty's growth. She's always thinking of others and puts them before herself. She does things just so others don't feel bad. She ignores her needs to take care of her family's and postpones her development to stay where she is. The sisters, on the other hand, are out for themselves and Beauty will need to learn how to do that in order to discover her own path apart from her family.

The other issue with the sisters looking outside themselves to determine their value and judging others must be transformed. Beauty will have to turn within to determine her worth, then her actions won't be based on winning approval from others. She will be able to put her needs first and let others take care of themselves. This isn't meant to be selfish, but she must stop sacrificing herself.

Beauty is the youngest daughter, and not like her older sisters, so their qualities are rejected. She isn't interested in balls and parties, but spends her time reading. Beauty is introverted and the other two daughters are extraverted. They represent the part of the heroine that is self-absorbed and distracted by the physical world in a superficial way. She prefers the intellect and rejects the outer. She isn't interested in marriage and turns down suitors, saying she is too young, and wants to stay with her father. But we are left wondering if she will ever want to leave him. She seems content with life as it is. Beauty doesn't have any desire to grow up and move away from home.

Her instinctual knowing of how to respond in her own best interest is hampered. She isn't aware of the cycles of life and that it's time to become an adult and leave home. Beauty ignores her own needs, allows her sisters to treat her poorly, and avoids the outer world. Her inner knowing will heal as a part of her journey.

In the Country

Her father/masculine is a shadow as well, wounded in a variety of ways. He and some of the members of the family value the material, intellect, masculine, outer world, and the pursuit of pleasure, over feminine ways of being. When he loses his money, the family moves to their country farm and has to work to survive. His vocation changes from merchant to farmer.

As a farmer, he has to work with the rhythms of nature to succeed. The family has to be more tuned in to seasonal cycles and heal their wounded instinct. This man of "sense" values education and learning above feeling and instinct. Jung wrote about the "loss of connection with nature"[10] that,

> *Civilized man...is in danger of losing all contact with the world of instinct – a danger that is still further increased by his living an urban existence in what seems to be a purely manmade environment. The loss of instinct is largely responsible for the pathological condition of contemporary culture.*[11]

A move from the city to the country is an effort on the part of the psyche to heal. The loss of wealth, which may have initially been perceived as a catastrophe, is actually a movement toward greater wellbeing that will reconnect the family to the earth, nature, and instinct.

Beauty is initially sad about the loss of their fortune, but then realizes that she must be happy without money, which is a shift in consciousness.

She recognizes that she can adjust to the present situation and feel better. Happiness can't depend on life circumstances, or it will always be contingent on what is considered good and desired. Even though Beauty says this, there's still the part of her, as represented by the sisters, that doesn't agree.

Beauty accepts their new life and begins to enjoy her chores. Her sisters don't do anything to help. They are critical, mean, and make fun of her for being content. Their sole interest is in returning to the past and the old life in the city. The sisters' happiness is contingent on their circumstances in the outer world. If they merely accepted where they were, like Beauty, then they might find some peace.

Beauty learns how to nourish herself in the country. She cooks and cleans, gets stronger and healthier. The move from the city is positive, as she is transformed by a connection to the earth, nature, her chores, and a simpler lifestyle. She is shifting out of the head and into the body, or a more feminine way of being. This developing awareness isn't predicated on cooking and cleaning, but on the body, other ways of knowing, and instinct.

Instinct is perceived as more body-centered and intellect as more egoic, or centered in the head. A reason we have developed a fear of instinct as wild and out of control is due to its association with the body and animals. Beauty is coming into greater awareness of instinct and her body. She isn't as disconnected anymore.

As we follow along with the story, we can examine our own relationship to instinct. Do you listen to your inner knowing? Do you feel clear and certain about where you are? Do you take care of yourself in ways that are nourishing? What is your connection with nature, your body, and knowing? Do you honor that innate sense of what's right for you?

Hopes Reignited and Dashed

The family has been living in the country for about a year when the merchant father receives a letter that says one of his ships has come into port. This excites the two sisters and kindles their hopes of returning to the city when their father's fortune is restored. As he makes plans to leave, the two sisters request new dresses, but Beauty doesn't want anything. Finally, so her sisters don't feel bad, she asks for a rose, which is the one thing she misses from the city.

The rose symbolizes a love that transcends death,[12] indicating the importance of love, the heart, and transformation in the story. This suggests that love is stronger than death. Beauty is inadvertently saying she misses a love that is powerful.

According to feminist author Barbara Walker, "Worshippers of Aphrodite used to call their ceremonies the Mysteries of the Rose ... the rose was a female sexual symbol expressing the mystery of Mary's physical gateway."[13] This connection between the rose and Aphrodite is significant, since "Beauty and the Beast" is a sequel to "The marriage of Cupid and Psyches." Aphrodite isn't seen in this story, as she was in "Cupid and Psyches," but now appears symbolically and as a critical symbol. Beauty's longing is for the missing rose, mother, goddess, love, heart, the feminine, and ultimately the embodied Self.

The rose is also connected in the above quote to Mary, the mother as the physical gateway for the spiritual man. This is the Self embodied, or the Christ archetype. Mary is reminiscent of Aphrodite as mother of the god of love, Psyche's husband Eros. The meaning of this symbol suggests its significance to the story. What may seem on the surface as a random detail, upon examination, proves to be quite important. This often happens when we symbolically interpret stories. The symbols perfectly reveal a deeper tapestry of meaning.

The father goes to the docks and things don't turn out the way he expects. He doesn't find the hoped-for riches, which creates a space for greater consciousness. Loss is an opportunity for something new to emerge, but he's not interested in that at the moment, since *he* gets lost on a storm on his journey home. He and his horse—a symbol of power, instinct, and freedom—get confused and lose their way on a stormy night in a forest, which means they descend into the darkness of the unconscious.

The loss of his potential fortune activates him, which catapults him into the unconscious, as he becomes confused, doesn't know where to turn, or what to do. The father's wounded instinct means he can't perceive the right direction in the dark or during a storm. He loses his way, his power, and his sense of freedom, because of this challenge.

When we perceive our wellbeing as connected to, or dependent on, money, then the loss can be upsetting, because it shakes the very foundation we stand on. This is why he is knocked off his horse and loses his way. This is another place where power is projected and must be retrieved.

It's interesting because the father enjoys their new life in the country, but it seems that the thought of returning to the city, or more money, made him favor a return to the old life. There are times when the old doors close and there isn't any going back. This is one of those times.

The winds are so strong as he rides through the forest that they repeatedly knock him off his horse, suggesting he can't maintain his power, is unable to discern a new direction, and doesn't feel free when challenged. If he had access to a healthy feminine, he may have sensed a new direction through intuitive, instinctual, body-centered ways of knowing. Or, if he trusted the innate wisdom of life. The father is knocked off course because he doesn't understand yet that power and freedom don't come from money, but from within. His ability to know what to do, or where to go, doesn't come from the intellect, but from other ways of knowing.

The father encounters the rains associated with the storm. Water symbolizes emotion and the moisture nature requires to grow and sustain life. We may think of emotion as being negative, uncomfortable, or an indication that something is wrong. Sometimes that is the case, but it can also be healing. Tears nourish us and cleanse the heart so that after a good cry we feel refreshed, calm, and at peace. This is what it feels like outside once a storm has passed as well. The father is so afraid and concerned about his wellbeing, it's doubtful he's enjoying the cleansing power of his tears.

He's petrified by the sound of the wolves lurking in the dark forest. He hears them but can't see them. If his instinct was healthy, he wouldn't be afraid. The wolves symbolize the fearful thoughts, which devour him, knock him off course, and he's lost in them. This is how he gets activated. He experiences this loss and all kinds of crazy thoughts stalk him until he loses his way. The father's fear of nature, instinct, the wild, loss of control, and the untamed, is being brought to consciousness.

Shelter from the Storm

He sees a light in the dark woods and follows it to a palace, lit from top to bottom. This light in the dark is an indication of awareness in the unconscious and signifies something new coming into consciousness. This shelter in the storm is a place in the unconscious for the merchant and his horse to find refuge.

The merchant goes into the palace and sees a fire in the fireplace. Fire represents the heart, hearth, passion, and transformation. A burning fire means something is kindled in the heart that provides warmth. This is an important place. The fire of desire, love, or passion, burns away anything that doesn't serve. This is another way to transform consciousness. When we do things we love, we are in a space of wellbeing that can be healing. This palace indicates a new place in the unconscious that is nurturing and nourishing.

The merchant encounters a new state of consciousness in the palace, as it's staffed with invisible helpers who meet all his needs, without even a verbal request. He experiences the ease and effortlessness that's possible in life. He doesn't have to struggle, work hard, or use his intellect to get his needs met, which is new. This is the dawning light of a new truth coming to consciousness after the confusion of the dark. He thought he'd lost all of his money and ability to generate abundance, but here he gets a glimpse of something entirely different. It is a new inner paradigm.

That's not to say *he* gets or recognizes it, but he experiences it. It's like going to visit someone who lives in a way that's unfamiliar to you. You don't necessarily walk in and say, "Oh, I can do this," but it's now a part of your conscious awareness. Whether you realize it or not, you now know what's possible for you. I like to think of it as a vision for the future. It's possible for our futures as much as Beauty's.

This location of warmth and nourishment is an inner palace where all his needs are met. He gets a taste of a new life. The outer material success the merchant had in the past made him believe his needs were met through the outer world. When things get difficult, and he experiences setbacks, he loses his footing, and can't stay on his horse. He feels powerless and hampered by the lack he perceives in his circumstances. This is saying, don't look out for solutions such as the ship, but look within. What inner resources are available? What needs to be transformed within?

He believed the foundation of his power was the transient physical world. When it gets stormy and changes come, circumstances change, he falters and feels like a victim. That happens when our sense of self depends on things being a certain way, but we live in a world of change, which can feel like a threat to our sense of security. That's why the foundation for self needs to be inside. The outer shifts and you don't want a foundation on something that isn't stable and dependable.

As the father prepares to leave the palace the next day, he sees roses and remembers Beauty's request. He cuts a branch and then hears a tremendous roar, which is the Beast. The father's action, on Beauty's behalf, awakens the Beast and brings him into consciousness. For most of the father's stay in the palace, he's afraid he'll get caught taking what he needs. Funny enough, he's afraid of taking food, and clothes that were obviously laid out for him, but he doesn't think twice about cutting the rose.

He believes what he's taking has little or no value, which echoes Beauty's feeling about the rose. Remember she didn't really want anything, she only asked for something because she didn't want the sisters to feel bad. She asked for a rose, which she believed had little value, although she did miss them. The sisters, as the shadow, ask for exactly what they want—expensive dresses. Well, the Beast feels differently than Beauty and her father about the roses.

The Beast represents the emergence of a new symbol from the unconscious that values beauty and the natural world. Jungian Erich Neumann elaborates on the unconscious image as follows:

> When the unconscious content is perceived, it confronts consciousness in the symbolic form of an image. ... For this reason, even the instincts, the psychic dominants, which of all unconscious contents are most important for the psychological totality, seem to be linked with the representation of images. The function of the image symbol in the psyche is always to produce a compelling effect on consciousness. Thus, for example, a psychic image whose purpose it is to attract the attention of consciousness, in order, let us say, to provoke flight, must be so striking that it cannot possibly fail to make an impression. The archetypal image symbol corresponds, then, in its impressiveness, significance, energetic charge, and numinosity to the original importance of instinct for man's existence.[14]

The Beast represents the emergence of a new instinctive symbol in consciousness, which is such a powerful image that it does scare the merchant. The Beast's roar is formidable, and his presence is intimidating, to say the least. The merchant crosses a boundary and the Beast instinctively reacts to this ingratitude with a fierce and robust anger.

Boundaries

The Beast cherishes roses above everything, which immediately links him to Beauty, since she asked for it. The Beast realizes the value of the roses, beauty, love, the goddess, and feminine, but Beauty doesn't. She has a sense of longing, as though something is missing, but isn't really aware of what that is. The Beast is the instinctive part of the heroine that's intolerant of the personal and transpersonal devaluing of the feminine that is unseen and ignored. *He represents an instinctual reaction to a boundary violation that is much too significant to be ignored.*

The Beast represents the return of the lost *inner knowing* of what is acceptable and what isn't. What's wanted and what's not. When there's a loss of instinct, boundaries are unclear and uncertain. An injury to instinct means we stay too long, when we should leave. We let things happen that shouldn't and don't react when we should.

As the instinctive nature heals, awareness increases as to what nourishes and what doesn't, what is acceptable and what isn't, when we need to speak up and when we should remain silent. Sometimes, when we are learning to speak up for ourselves, we may roar like a wild, untamed beast. It can feel like an uncontrollable urge when we initially respond to a violated boundary. This pent-up roar is a voice that has been silent for way too long. The appearance of the Beast is a good thing for the heroine. His anger lets her know that a boundary is being violated and it's not okay anymore.

It doesn't necessarily mean someone else is violating a boundary but can be an inner violation that's our own. If we look at all the characters as aspects of one person, or the heroine, then the anger is inner directed, from one part of her to another. In this case, the Beast is angry with the father and there's a conflict between these two inner masculine energies. The new one that values the feminine and the other that doesn't, which may appear in the world as two different people, or between us and another person in our lives. Each one plays one of the roles, Beast or father.

Working through this can be frustrating, especially when we are trying to rediscover our own value, and someone else is challenging us. When there's a feeling of not being valued, and the Beast appears, he demands attention. And he is loud. He wants a sacrifice and threatens to kill the father. His action suggests that this is the only way to get the father to stop devaluing the feminine.

The heroine is learning to stand up for herself as these two masculine figures reside in consciousness together. Sometimes she'll speak or stand up for herself, meaning the Beast energy is active, and sometimes she won't, suggesting she's fallen into the old father consciousness. She'll revert between these two roles until, hopefully, the day comes when she will no longer sacrifice herself, for anyone.

The key through this phase is to keep working on the inner dynamic, even as the outer may continue to display the conflict. We have to keep going in to give ourselves what we are seeking from the world. When we acknowledge, love, appreciate, and value ourselves, then we don't need those in the outer world to do it for us. We aren't dependent on them for our well-being.

The father's beliefs are predominant in our patriarchal culture. There is an overemphasis on surface beauty as perfection and having to meet certain requirements to be considered beautiful. Many don't see or value the beauty of nature and perceive it as a commodity to be exploited. Those who don't meet society's standards of perfection for outer beauty can be or feel devalued. Inherent beauty and the uniqueness of each of us aren't often recognized. As a result, we can go to extremes in an effort to be accepted and meet societal ideals. The father and Beauty don't recognize or appreciate that natural or inner beauty.

What if our society valued love, and a person's beauty was measured by sensing their inner essence? We wouldn't judge others immediately by their looks but would have to take the time to get to really know them and their quality as a person before we could understand the depth of their beauty.

Speaking the Truth

The merchant tries to calm the Beast after he cuts the rose, but since his instinct is off, he makes it worse when he refers to the Beast as "My Lord."

The Beast responds, "My name is not 'My Lord,'...but 'Beast.' I don't like compliments, not I. I like people who speak as they think; and so do not imagine I am moved by any of your flattering speeches."[15]

The Beast states that this transgression can't be smoothed over by false sentiments, clearly defining the conflict and calling out the father. The father repeatedly demonstrates his disregard for the feminine. He doesn't value the roses, nor acknowledge the Beast's generosity, which upsets the

Beast. The father is given everything he needs and then has the nerve to take the rose. The Beast doesn't feel like the father appreciates what was given. *He* doesn't feel valued or appreciated. When the father says, "My Lord," which is showing respect, it is a respect the father doesn't really feel but is now saying merely to placate the Beast, who won't be calmed by such attempts at flattery. There's a conflict between what the father says and does. There isn't congruence there.

The Beast wants to hear the truth and wants honesty. Many in Beauty's family are deceitful and don't say what they really feel, which needs to change. When we are in our power we can express our truth without fear of the other's reaction. The Beast's appearance means things that used to be acceptable, aren't any longer, and he's going to speak up. He represents a shift from the passive father to a more outspoken, active, masculine who now willingly stands up for the feminine. He demands attention and gets angry if things are wrong. He values Beauty and that is an indication that the heroine is beginning to value herself. This means Beauty will stand up, occasionally to start, for herself.

The Beast is an aspect of the heroine's psyche and a transitional figure. He is powerful and wants to kill the passive father in the psyche, because the father is entitled, ungrateful, and unwilling to speak up for, or protect, the feminine. The Beast sees him as a problem in the psyche.

Beauty is conflicted if both the father and Beast are active. The two of them can't remain in consciousness for long, and eventually, one will have to go. We know which one is in the best interest of the heroine, for the moment anyway.

We want to examine our own inner and outer masculine figures. Is he more like the father or Beast? Are you afraid of the masculine? With dreams of locking him out of the house? Or maybe dreams of being in bed with the father? And what about the outer male figures around you? What's their relationship to the feminine?

Beauty doesn't feel safe when her father fails to defend and protect her. He does the exact opposite when he sacrifices her for possessions, superficiality, and status. He and the world aren't safe for her, which is probably why she went into her head. As the Beast emerges, he begins to stand up, defend and protect the feminine, so she can stop feeling so unsafe. She hasn't been able to do this for herself. She isn't standing up for herself when the masculine in her consciousness is her passive weak father.

When the Beast says he will kill the father for taking the rose, the father explains that he took the rose for his daughter. Basically, it's her fault. The Beast says fine, he'll take the merchant's daughter instead then. He gives the father a trunk full of gold in exchange, since that's what the father values, and he heads home.

The Sacrifice

The father sacrifices Beauty—the thing he supposedly values most in the world, his kind and most beautiful daughter—for gold, which is a symbol for the masculine and something that has worldly value. The masculine values money over beauty and the daughter, the young feminine, is exchanged for material gain. The father didn't receive the money he expected from the ship, but from the Beast. The father took a journey looking for money and he got it.

On the one hand, the feminine is sacrificed for money, but gold is also a symbol for the Self, a transpersonal center of our being. It can represent the destination of the story and in the individuation process. This suggests the possibility of a deeper meaning to the cultural loss of the feminine. The loss may be seen as assisting in the expansion of awareness and search for the Self. Women are at the forefront of the current spiritual movement in terms of the number of participants. It may be the devaluation of women that compels them to pursue higher consciousness, since the outer doesn't value them, they look to the inner. Another way of seeing this is that many don't feel valued by the physical world and are searching the spiritual to find it.

When something is devalued, and in the unconscious, we have a sense that something is missing, which in this case is the feminine. We search and search the world, as we have been taught to do, looking to fill an emptiness that the world cannot fill. We are all on a journey to bring the feminine, soul, to consciousness.

This re-emergence of the feminine requires a transformation of the angry masculine, which we see in the developing relationship between Beauty and the Beast. There will be a change for us in the way we live. The old materially based ways can no longer be followed, since that was the reason for the loss of the feminine to begin with. We need to look inside to meet our needs and not base our wellbeing and sense of self on consumption and the outer world. We don't need to learn to manifest in ever greater quantities, but to create lives that truly nourish, sustain, and fulfill the soul. And, the soul loves beauty.

The Beast carries the light of consciousness and a new kind of abundance. This includes a redefinition of abundance from being materially-based to being soul-based, which honors all life. This involves trust, knowing life supports us so that we can release stress, struggle, strain, and effort. It's a new perspective in which our needs are met, before we even ask. What is required, then, is a whole new view of how life works. Manifesting means we control. Surrendering means we let go of control and allow, trust, and see more than we consciously desire come to us effortlessly. We see the world in a radically new way. This isn't a materialistic perspective, but a soul perspective.

The natural instinct descended into the unconscious because of our outer-focused lifestyle, which disconnects us from nature and the earth. We have been taught to believe what we need and desire are material objects, but that's not it. When we lose contact with the earth, we can miss the inherent truth of the abundance of life. When we look around us, we can see how plentiful the world is. The Beast values a natural object, the rose, which is a symbol of the embodied Self. He has tremendous abundance, but it doesn't matter to him, what he cares about is living the Christ archetype.

The key is to *receive* what's offered. The father didn't freely receive in the Beast's house, since he was afraid and felt guilty. He was worried he might get caught taking something and wasn't in tune with the natural abundance of life. He didn't receive gratefully, although he did thank the invisible fairies, but was afraid of being discovered having taken what he needed. This indicates that the father's worldview is based in fear and lack, whereas the Beast instinctively understands and willingly accepts the generosity of life that's possible by living with an eye toward beauty and soul.

The Beast and Instinct

The Beast is angry when the father takes what the Beast most cherishes. The father is passive and wounded; trading his daughter, his "most cherished" possession, for money. The Beast carries greater consciousness and represents the path of growth. It's clear the heroine's masculine needs to heal because neither the Beast, nor the merchant, are healthy, or balanced, ways to act. The Beast carries the instincts but is isolated and disconnected from life. No one is with him or wants to be around him because he is wild, ugly, angry, and primitive. Jung wrote, "What is needed is to call a halt to the fatal disassociation that exists between our so-called higher and lower being; we must unite the conscious aspect with the primitive."[16] And further:

> The...loss of roots...is a disaster not only for primitive tribes but for civilized man as well... The life of instinct – the most conservative element in man—always expresses itself in traditional usages. Age-old convictions and customs are always rooted in the instincts. If they get lost, the conscious mind becomes severed from the instincts and loses its roots, while the instincts, unable to express themselves, fall back into the unconscious and reinforce its energy, causing this in turn to overflow into the existing contents of consciousness. It is then that the rootless condition of consciousness becomes a real danger. This secret vis-a-tergo results in a hybris of the conscious mind which manifests in the form of exaggerated self-esteem or an inferiority complex. At all levels a loss of balance ensues...[17]

The Beast was created when the instinct went into the unconscious. The poor self-esteem of the father and the Beast suggest an inferiority complex in the masculine and Beauty. She frequently faces the rejection of her sisters and their devaluation of her. The sisters carry the rejected, but also extreme, superiority complex. The heroine will vacillate between superiority and inferiority as long as they remain unconscious. The Beast rages as a result of his feelings of vulnerability, victim consciousness, and inferiority.

When so-called masculine qualities are preferred over feminine, women can feel they aren't as appreciated as men and men may feel superior to women. This belief can be unconscious, subtle, and unseen, even though it's happening for many. Girls may take on male characteristics in order to compensate for being female. Women can face rejection that makes them feel inferior physically, emotionally, psychologically, financially, etc.

This isn't to blame men, or to say women are wrong for having masculine interests or attributes, but merely to reveal the conditions that exist for some of us in our culture in order to change them. This also isn't to say everyone falls into this category. If we happen to grow up with the good fortune of feeling loved and appreciated in and as ourselves, then we can be models of what's possible. For those who weren't so blessed, becoming aware of this dynamic can be helpful.

This sense of inferiority and superiority doesn't need to be fought by bringing the Beast out in the world and fighting our way from inferiority to superiority. When we attempt to demand that others' value us, it doesn't usually work. The inner work transforms the outer world. It is the only way to really be free of this dynamic. This isn't to say it won't come up in the world, because it probably will, and we might still feel irritated when it does, but the intensity of the energy behind it is usually less. The idea is to work through it so it doesn't remain a never-ending battle.

The feeling of being *enough*, and of being equal to others, has to come from inside. We can contemplate and feel the enoughness within and often remind ourselves that we are enough exactly as we are. If our sense of worth depends on conditions of the outer world, then we aren't free. *If we feel equal, regardless of what others say and do, then no one has power over us. Then, our wellbeing and value don't depend on the actions of others.*

Beauty's father goes home and tells his family what happened with the ship and the Beast. The sisters immediately blame the unfortunate turn of events on Beauty, since she asked for the rose. Beauty's response is to simply offer to go in her father's place. She will have to face her fears of the Beast, anger, isolation, power, death, the masculine, and the instincts while with the Beast. She's happy to sacrifice herself for her father and does so willingly. She's leaving her passive father's house and her family of origin in consciousness.

When instinct is injured, and a woman doesn't know when or how to act, she's sometimes forced by circumstances out of her current situation. She might not recognize the conditions that hamper her growth, or if she does, she doesn't know what to do about it and feels helpless to change anything.

Childhood conditioning can teach a us to ignore our instinctual body-centered awareness, intuition, and other non-rational ways of knowing. If these signals and knowing are repressed, by the time we reach adulthood there may be little indication of the information that's possible through these other channels. When the feelings and information do come, we might not even see or feel them. We may just dismiss it as a passing sensation without recognizing its information or even an answer to a prayer.

The father's house is comfortable for Beauty and she had no intention of leaving, so life intervenes. Her instinct has to be recovered in order to know what serves her and what doesn't, when to stay and when to go. She has to learn to stand up and speak up for herself and respond to her own knowing. This ultimately means reconnecting to her inner wisdom. This is why she must leave the passive father, who doesn't have access to instinct, as he clearly demonstrates.

Beauty Leaves Home

The father initially protests weakly, but then agrees to sacrifice Beauty to the Beast to protect himself. He accompanies her to the Beast's palace, which means a descent into the unconscious. The Beast appears as they eat dinner and the sight of this immense unknown part of Beauty terrifies her.

When we are used to a passive role in life, the power of repressed energy may frighten us. The depth of anger and rage can feel overwhelming when it surfaces. Passive and aggressive often go hand-in-hand. Aggression has more energy than the passive stance, but it is fear-based energy, which is still not healthy. This energy can help the feminine as she moves toward her power, in the sense that she has the inclination now to protect herself, as opposed to the passive masculine who didn't. Although, when the protection comes from anger, it's unbalanced. She goes from passively allowing to, "This isn't acceptable anymore!"

When a limit is reached, the anger is activated, which makes her more conscious of what she really feels. The anger motivates her to act against her own inner passive father consciousness. Since the anger is an out-of-balance movement, it can be exhausting, and can't be maintained as a permanent mode of operating. The anger can't be directed toward others either. Although, it may come out that way, the intention must be to resolve it, and not get stuck blaming others, or staying in a situation that's finished. There must be consciousness with it. Any time anger comes up, look inside. Look inside to see if you feel hurt or afraid. We don't want to get stuck in passivity or anger, since neither suits us. But, the anger can be an interim step in seeing where our boundaries are and becoming empowered.

Despite being afraid of the Beast's appearance, while she and her father dine, Beauty remains committed. She later tells her father to leave her in the "care and protection of Providence,"[18] which Jungian Edward Edinger writes, "is the classic statement of the ego attitude needed in the face of an individuation crisis. And with such an attitude, support from the archetypal psyche is usually forthcoming."[19]

Ugh, surrender can be such a challenge when faced with this kind of fear but surrender we must. This isn't passive, but in this situation where nothing can be done, we must accept what is. This opens the way for synchronicity, dreams, or some other form of help.

Beauty surrenders to the possibility of her own death, before entering the next phase of her journey. *Surrendering* to Providence means letting go of control. Life can't be fully embraced until death is accepted in the face of the unknown and the fear of it is acknowledged. Beauty must die to being a passive daddy's girl and victim. She also must let go of her father, family, old role, and the past. She can't continue to take care of her family and sacrifice herself for the old masculine-oriented way of life. To discover her own path, she must release the father. Leaving the family of origin, physically or psychically, is required on the path of individuation. This is a death to the old egoic self.

Beauty's move to the palace represents a shift in consciousness. She symbolically moves into a place in the unconscious, since the palace is in the forest. The only reason she can make this move is because she spent time in the country, which was her initial foray into the world of nature and instincts. This grounded her and began her reconnection to the earth, instinct, and her body. It humbled her, the parts of her that were caught up in the material world. Remember, she isn't just leaving her father behind, but also her materially-driven sisters and their superiority complex. She's trying on a new state of consciousness in which she coexists with the Beast, an unconscious masculine, in an effort to bring him to consciousness.

The new state of consciousness opens Beauty to other ways of knowing and she has a significant dream on her first night in the palace. The response to her surrendering to Providence is in the form of an archetypal lady in a dream. This beautiful feminine tells her she will be rewarded for her willingness to give up her life for her father, or *with* her father might be more accurate. She's told that the decision to let go of her past will have a positive outcome. Beauty shares the dream with her father in the morning to give him hope, but once he leaves, she's afraid and cries about her situation.

Edinger writes that during these periods of isolation,

> *The ego feels utterly deprived of comfort and support, both from within and from without. Trust, based on projections and unconscious assumptions, is abruptly terminated. This state is a transition period. It is the limbo of despair following the death of an old life orientation and preceding the birth of the new one.*[20]

This quote is significant because this is *exactly* what it feels like. When we feel vulnerable, during a transition, we can be tempted to call on someone from the past and what's familiar for help, but that isn't the answer. The tendency may be to avoid the fear that arises, but it's important to accept what's felt, regardless of how uncomfortable it is and know that this too will pass. It will change. We are fully supported through this transition, even if we don't see it. We can focus on being surrounded by a peaceful loving presence, within and without. Here the guiding, loving presence appears to Beauty as a lady in a dream.

Beauty surrenders herself to the Divine (or call it what you will), which is an inner presence that can't ever leave. It is always there and available. After connecting with this inner calm, Beauty decides to explore the palace, the new unknown aspects of the psyche, instead of crying, during the little time she has left (before Beast kills her, or so she thinks).

She discovers an apartment with her name over the door, which suggests the Beast may not kill her after all. Why else would he go to the trouble of setting up a space for her with all of her favorite things? She has a place where she belongs in this new consciousness.

Dinners with the Beast

That night at dinner, the Beast asks Beauty if he can join her. Her response is that he can if he would like to, but he can see that she's afraid. He tells her it's up to her and then, asks if she thinks he's ugly. She says she can't lie and follows up saying, he seems like he has a good nature. I guess she forgot about his threat to kill her father for cutting a rose. There's still a duality here.

She has to become comfortable with this powerful, angry part of herself. It's her unconscious masculine that's frustrated with the father for not feeling valued. This means she wasn't standing up for herself with her sisters, or her father, until the moment the Beast appeared as a symbolic image out of the unconscious.

Now she has to learn how to speak up, even though she's afraid to face this angry masculine. It's not easy, or familiar, for her to tell the truth and speak up for herself, but this is a start.

The Beast says he's a stupid monster, but with a good heart. This contrasts with her intelligence, since she's the smart one in the family. He appears scary on the outside and certainly has anger issues, but Beauty has to penetrate his tough exterior to reach the inner truth. In his house, she can have whatever she wants, since she's the mistress. She just needs to ask and all of her wishes will be fulfilled. The Beast says she's powerful, but she doesn't see herself that way. She has to take back the power she projects onto him.

This is what's possible for us. We can have what we want. Imagine the kind of world where we receive what we desire. The Beast is saying that we have the power inside of us to be able to make things happen. Although, he's an inner energy and not an outer one, which means we need to go in first, not out.

Beauty thought she'd lost her freedom and was going to die. Instead, she finds out that she's the mistress of an immense palace and can have *anything* she wants. How can that be? She went from victim to victor in one moment. When someone has been in a passive role for their whole life, it isn't always as simple as that. She has to grow into it, and accept it, in order to fully realize this new sense of self and new worldview.

He tells her that if she doesn't want him around, all she needs to do is say so. He gives her the power to decide her own fate; it's in her hands. Beauty can either learn to relate to this powerful instinctual part of herself or not. She has to learn that she's free to do as she pleases, to say what she feels, and to not be afraid.

At the end of dinner, the Beast asks Beauty to be his wife. She nearly faints from the fearful thought of telling him no. Beauty isn't ready to acknowledge and integrate this powerful Beast as a part of herself or unite with him. She tells him the truth about her feelings, even though she's petrified. She must speak, regardless of how he might respond, in order to move more fully into her power. The Beast told her father that he only wanted to hear the truth. And he meant it.

This may only be a fairy tale, which can make it easy to dismiss and not recognize the depth of fear when speaking up for ourselves and saying our truth out loud, for maybe the first time. When we've been silent, only spoken out of fear, or said just what we believe others wanted to hear, speaking may feel like facing death. It depends on the depth of conditioning.

A difficult childhood compounds the fear, as well as a history for women, and men at times also, of not being free to speak openly. Challenging the status quo isn't always encouraged so finding our voice may constellate fear. The answer is to just take baby steps, if necessary, toward the life that's wanted. Feel the fear and keep going, acknowledging and feeling whatever arises along the way.

When Beauty tells the Beast she won't marry him, he's crushed and rejected. He's so saddened by her response that his hiss scares her all over again. He feels his emotions deeply and expresses them. Opening to the feelings of rejection that have happened across a lifetime can reveal immense sadness. The depth of his sadness at her rejection softens her heart toward him.

She can't say yes to his proposal because she thinks he's ugly and he scares her, which means she's judging him based on outer appearances and his fearful actions. Beauty isn't looking past the superficial for the deeper inner truth. Here we see shades of her sisters in her. The two sisters are critical to individuation, which means Beauty is going to have to learn to value the inner over the outer.

The Beast has dinner with Beauty and asks her to marry him every night. She continues to say no, since she still can't see past the surface ugliness, although she enjoys his company more and more with each passing day. She grows less afraid of him, but is unwilling to integrate this energy, or to acknowledge and accept that this is a part of her. She declines his request every day for three months.

Three is the number associated with transformation, which means something is going to happen.

Beauty's Request

Beauty looks forward to dinner with the Beast and enjoys his company. Finally, after three months of him asking her to marry him, she courageously tells him she never will. She likes him as a friend, but that's the extent of her feelings. He tells her he loves her, and accepts what she feels, but asks her to promise she won't ever leave him.

That's an issue for her because she's seen her distressed father in a magic mirror the Beast gave her, and she longs to visit him. She wants to let her father know she's still alive and actually doing well, because he thinks she's dead. The Beast surprises her when he agrees, if she will just return within a week. If she doesn't, he warns, he will die of grief. Remember, he has that thing about congruence and doing what you say you're going to do.

Has she learned the value of her word? We must look at ourselves to determine if there's alignment between what we say, or know, and what we do. If you know what you want, are you taking action on your behalf, and following through? If you promise yourself something, are you speaking up, taking steps to create your dreams, honoring and listening to your feminine? If not, then this may be the time to begin exploring your inner knowing.

The Beast carries Beauty's power, freedom, abundance, and instinct. He wants her to take these qualities back, stop projecting them onto him, and accept them as her own. She still believes he controls her, that she has to ask to go home, but he told her that what she expressed would be honored at the very beginning. In their time together, she has learned to relax and trust him, but she still acts as though she isn't free. She thinks he holds her captive, but he *asks* her if she will stay with him and never leave. He doesn't want her to feel like his prisoner but wants it to be her choice to be with him.

He tells her she can go home to her father and that it's her decision. She can choose to return to him or not. He asks for her word that she will come back, not because she isn't free to do as she wishes, but because he loves her, values her, and wants to be with her. If Beauty doesn't return at the time that she promised, the energies of the Beast will go back into the unconscious, and he'll die. She'll return to the passive masculine consciousness—her father's—and stay in the past. It will be a regression, instead of a movement into the fullness of her own power.

Beauty wakes up the next morning in her bed at home. She discovers the Beast has sent her a trunk of beautiful dresses to wear. When she decides to keep only the simplest one, and give the rest to her sisters, the trunk disappears. *She has to receive the fullness of good, even in her family of origin and not shrink from in the sense of needing to play small to protect them. Beauty must embody her worth and stand in her power when she's with her family, and not regress to get their approval.* The Beast knows this. He magically appears to her father and tells him the dresses are only for Beauty. The trunk returns and Beauty keeps the clothes, much to the consternation of her sisters. The Beast continues to force, or remind, her to accept her worth. He's encouraging her to not ignore her worth with her family.

Beauty has to integrate the sister's consciousness, since they are the ones who *want* the dresses and appreciate them. The Beast forces her to receive this abundance in the midst of her family. Be the person you have become, even with those from your past. There can be a fear of making others feel bad if we are "too much," or not playing the inferior, humble role. Don't be too proud, or think too much of yourself, or talk about yourself too much. These are some of the rules, many of us grew up with. Stepping out of these limitations and allowing our light to shine, especially with those who it irritates, will free us. I'm not suggesting going around bragging just to annoy others, but to be authentic and speak up for ourselves when necessary. It gives others permission to do the same.

This trip back to her father's house could be perceived as a regression, but in the scheme of things it needs to happen. Beauty has to go back because she isn't yet ready to step fully into her power. She hasn't made the decision herself to be with the Beast, since she still has some allegiance to the old passive masculine and judgmental sisters. Beauty doesn't feel like she's enough, or should outshine her sisters, which is why she tries to give the dresses away. But she has to accept her abundance. Her sisters are influencing her behavior and must be transformed.

Beauty reverts to the old role and goes back home because she still doesn't feel safe and secure in her new role yet. She regresses in a sense into passivity, because something needs to be cleared. There's more childhood inner work to be done, old beliefs to clear. She still doesn't realize she is free and powerful. What from her past is holding her back? That is exactly what she returns to her father's house to discover.

Are you standing, and speaking, up for yourself? Have you been taking action toward that the life you dream of and the person you want to be? Do you feel powerful in and out of your family? Can you be authentically you wherever you are? Are you open to receiving the good being offered to you? Do you feel safe to receive?

Beauty has to understand that security doesn't come from the past, her family, acceptance by others, playing small, money, the outer world, or in what's familiar. She must give up the old roles of not being enough, not asking for and accepting what she wants, as well as powerlessness or victim consciousness, which she's inherited from her family. These patterns of behavior include the servant and playing an inferior role, so others can feel okay about themselves. When she was with the Beast, there wasn't anyone to challenge her as she wore the beautiful dresses and was the lady of the palace. When she returns home, these new roles are challenged by her sisters, and she falters. She retreats and plays her part in the old patterns.

The Jealous Sisters

Her sisters are very jealous of Beauty's circumstances, her dresses, and her relationship with the Beast. He knew Beauty had to keep the dresses and wear them in front of her sisters, risking their displeasure, in order to stand in her power. She has to feel these rejected feelings to transform them. Avoiding them keeps them in the dark. The sisters are envious of Beauty's abundance and her relationship with someone she enjoys. They know he values her and it irritates them. They can see that once again she's happy and content with the life she's living. There's an inner conflict. The sisters' husbands are shallow and self-centered, probably like their father. The sisters are the part of Beauty that doesn't think she can have what others have, which keeps her locked in a situation because of her belief.

The sisters, as aspects of the heroine, mean Beauty still feels she isn't enough. If Beauty is envious of others, she doesn't see or realize the abundance that's being offered to her. She's also basing her sense of self on the outer world circumstances, which we saw in her family when they lost their wealth. Not only does she feel she isn't enough, but what she *has* isn't enough either. She still doesn't fully accept that she can have what she really wants and that her value comes from inside.

The sisters plot to keep Beauty with them for longer than a week, hoping the Beast will get angry and kill her. At the end of the week, the sisters carry on until Beauty agrees to stay. She believes they suddenly really love and care for her and falls for their dramatic displays of affection. She's been longing for this forever and now she thinks she's finally getting their love. She doesn't see that they are manipulating her. Her instinct is off and she isn't picking up on their manipulation of her.

The sisters represent an inner part of her that is lying to her about what is important, what matters, and is keeping her in the passive father's house instead of going forward into the life of fulfillment she really wants. She doesn't trust and feel safe enough yet, so she wants the comfort of the past to lull her back to sleep. The sisters represent the longing for what was. They don't want responsibility, power, or greater consciousness; this part of her still resists the Beast as her masculine. She must make the decision to step fully into this powerful role, as the Beast keeps telling her, the choice is hers.

Beauty can have what she wants. As a victim, she believes she can't and has to tone down what she wants to be accepted. Because she thinks that she isn't enough, she believes she has to change herself to be loved. She's been conditioned by the idea that she has to remain passive, as a servant, dependent on the father, and cater to her critical sisters.

A Dream of Beast

On the tenth night, which symbolizes the number one and new beginnings, Beauty wakes from a dream of the Beast dying. He reproaches her, in the dream, for her ingratitude, which was his original charge against the father, meaning she has regressed. *She's not grateful and doesn't see what she's being offered.* Nor has she learned congruence and to honor her word. We can see that she's freer and more authentic at the Beast's than she is in her father's house.

We again need to look inward to discern where we are. Have you regressed? Are you standing in your power, honoring yourself, and following through on what you know is right for you? Or are you seeking the approval of those who have always been unwilling to give it? This is the time to let go of all that no longer supports who and what you are becoming. This includes releasing old limiting roles you have played that don't serve you anymore.

The Beast never asked Beauty or her father for anything and gave freely to them. He gave Beauty his love, he valued and appreciated her, and saw her as so much more than she saw herself. *He carried the vision of who she could be and encouraged her to strive for that.* His only request was for honesty, integrity, and companionship from Beauty. He didn't ask her to do anything she didn't want to do and she broke her promise.

When she awakes from the dream, Beauty realizes her mistake. She now knows that in fact she does care very deeply for him, and wants to be his wife, even though she still doesn't love him.

This dream is necessary to her development. The possibility of losing her new masculine awakens her to act on her own behalf. Her instinct kicks in! Yes! She sees that being in her father's house isn't acceptable and doesn't serve who she really is. She sees that this life isn't hers any more. She has served the needs of others and really wasn't acting in her own best interest, until now.

What did Beauty ask for in the story? She asked for the rose, and then later, to go to see her father. She asked for the rose to appease her sisters and asked to go see her father because she saw in her mirror that he was distressed. She was still taking care of her family. The dream makes her realize she's given her power away and may lose her freedom.

Now, the aggressor energy of the Beast has to die, or be transformed. Once Beauty is in her father's house, she sees how things are there with new eyes, and knows after the dream what has to be done to step more fully into her new role. This perceived regression was merely to reveal the ways she was still willing to diminish herself to accommodate others. This means she ignored who she was, and what she needed, to take care of her family.

The two sisters, who are so significant to her individuation, are the reason why Beauty returned to her father's house. She had to fully release the servant energy to step into her power. She had to reclaim that instinctual knowing she had lost touch with, which tells her what she wants and must do for herself.

In truth, Beauty really feels angry (as the Beast) for her family's ingratitude at her sacrifice of herself for them, which weaves the Beast and Beauty together. The Beast is an expression of her frustration at not being valued and appreciated by them, which is ultimately a reflection of her own inability to appreciate herself. She diminished herself for their benefit. *In order to fully receive the good that is being offered to her by this new life, and take action on her own behalf, she must release the desire to please and take care of others.*

Beauty Returns

Beauty needs to feel it is safe to let go of her family of origin, those patterns, beliefs, and her past. It's time to let it die, and the aggressor will be transformed along with the belief that she needs to defend and protect herself. Since her inept, passive father did not protect or keep her safe, and her sisters were unkind, she lived in a situation in which she felt vulnerable. This may constellate the aggressor as a protective masculine energy. The Beast responds when needs are ignored, boundaries are invaded, the feminine is unvalued, and when feeling unsafe.

When Beauty realizes she's safe in the palace, and that her safety doesn't depend on others or outer circumstances, she can relax, be herself, and open her heart. There isn't anything to fear and therefore defensiveness, protection, or aggression aren't required. *No one needs to save Beauty, nor does she need to save or take care of anyone else. She doesn't need her family to be safe. Her safety and security now come from her trust in herself as powerful and capable. She knows her needs are met inside and not from the outside.* This is the end of warrior/aggressor archetype, since it's no longer necessary.

Inner peace leads to outer peace. Beauty is now free to be herself, follow her heart, and do what she loves. She returns to the palace and waits for the Beast to appear at dinner, but he doesn't come. She remembers the dream of him in the garden, where the roses are, and rushes out to find him dying on the ground. She throws herself on him and hears his faintly beating heart. The Beast opens his eyes and tells her he starved himself, since she didn't honor her promise.

Beauty is horrified and tells him she wants to marry him. The grief she feels at the possibility of losing him reveals to her that she can't live without him. She sees now that she loves him and kisses him.

> As soon as her lips touched his cheek, the palace sparkled with light; fireworks and music filled the air. But nothing else could claim her attention but her dear Beast, for whom she trembled with fear. How great was her surprise to find the Beast had disappeared, and in his place she saw at her feet one of the most handsome princes the eye ever beheld, who returned her thanks for having put an end to the charm under which he had so long remained.[21]

She finally feels safe enough to open her heart. Now she *knows* that she feels love and accepts this rejected part of herself, which frees the prince from being a Beast. She has seen past the superficial to what's deeper.

The Beast, Beauty, the sisters, and the inhabitants of the palace that were enchanted, are all transformed.

The prince explains that a wicked fairy put a spell on him, but when there's a call to greater awareness, the culprit is often called wicked, or a monster, when in fact it's critical to achieving higher consciousness. The prince may have been ungrateful for all he had, and the fairy wanted him to realize his blessings by turning him into a stupid ugly monster. The prince learned to love without expecting anything in return, which changes him.

Beauty is transformed through her relationship with the Beast. She reconnects with her feelings and instinct, speaks her truth, and stands in her power. She eventually realizes that virtue and love are more important than intelligence or surface beauty, which she had valued before she knew the Beast. These insights were required for her to become a powerful princess, able to stand up, and be herself.

The union of Beauty and the Beast is the integration and healing of instinct, power, and freedom that are required to free Beauty from her old limiting story. The unconditionally loving open heart and power are associated with the realization of the Self. When Beauty acknowledges her love for the Beast and agrees to marry him, everyone appears in the palace. This is an indication that wholeness is realized. And as the story goes, they live happily ever after.

Three

Rapunzel: The Way to Wholeness

*O*nce upon a time, there was a couple who had wanted a child for quite some time and were expecting. The witch next door had a garden, which the couple could see from their back window. Everyone was afraid of the witch because she was so powerful. One day the mother saw some rapunzel lettuce in the garden and developed a craving for it. Her longing grew stronger with each passing day until her husband noticed she was looking pale. He asked her what was wrong and she said she would die if she didn't get some of the lettuce. He initially resisted, knowing the consequences of getting caught, but then consented, climbed over the wall, and stole some lettuce. She ate it hungrily, but the next day, she wanted more.

And her desire was even stronger. Once again, he reluctantly climbed the wall, but this time the witch caught *him. He pleaded that his pregnant wife would die if she didn't get the lettuce. The angry witch said he could take what they needed, but she would take their child when it was born. The father agreed. The moment the mother delivered the child, the witch arrived, named the child Rapunzel, and took her.*

Rapunzel lived in the house with the witch until she was 12 years old, which is when she was moved to a tower in a forest. The only way into the tower was for the witch to call to Rapunzel and she would let down her long braid for the witch to climb.

A prince watched all of this one day and tried it for himself once the witch left. Rapunzel was initially startled, but the prince calmed her and then asked her to marry him. They agreed that he would bring pieces of silk to her every night and she could weave them into a ladder to escape. One day, when the witch came to visit, and Rapunzel wasn't thinking, she absentmindedly asked the witch why she was so much heavier than the prince.

The witch was very angry, she cut Rapunzel's braid and banished her to the desert. When the prince arrived, he climbed the braid and found the witch. She told him he'd never see Rapunzel again. He leapt from the window and landed on a thorny bush, which scratched his eyes. He wandered blindly through the forest for years lamenting the loss of his love.

One day he reached the desert and heard a familiar voice. It was Rapunzel with her twins, a boy and a girl. Her joyful tears fell into his eyes and his sight was restored. They lived happily ever after.*

Introduction

Rapunzel lives happily in her little tower, until the masculine appears. He activates something in her for a greater life, one that is more than she's

---

* Full story in Manheim's *Grimms' Tales for Young and Old.*

ever dreamed. She's no longer content with living in isolation and wants to emerge into the world. His arrival signifies that it's time to begin a journey to bring out her gifts and share them with others. Before the actual move into the world though, the inner union will have to take place.

Jung realized there was a need for a central living myth, since our culture seems to have lost our sense of meaning in life and reason for being. In "Rapunzel," the heroine on the path of individuation must *discover this deeper meaning of life to transcend the beliefs she inherited* from her parents and the culture. She must take an inner journey to discover the truth and connect with her Self to find the meaning inherent in her existence. According to Jung,

> *The myth of the necessary incarnation of God...can be understood as man's creative confrontation with the opposites and their synthesis in the self, the wholeness of his personality... That is the goal...which fits man meaningfully into the scheme of creation and at the same time confers meaning upon it.*[22]

We meet the opposites as we progress on the path of individuation in order to maintain balance and find that transcendent center Jung refers to as "Self." When we are finally united, having consciously unified the opposites, we have transcended duality, the egoic mind, and live from the Self. Jung suggests that the "purpose of life is the creation of consciousness,"[23] which is created when we are aware of and fully present to that which arises in each moment. Rapunzel integrates the parts of herself that have been relegated to the unconscious as she becomes more conscious.

The Mother and Father

Rapunzel's parents have been trying to have a baby for a long time. They didn't know how to create and sustain life, but finally their wishes are fulfilled.

The mother and father don't have a *connection to their own wholeness, or a sense of the deeper meaning of life,* which would give purpose and direction to their lives. They look to the outer world for pleasure, fulfillment, and gratification. The mother represents the negative mother complex, since she's out of touch with the cycles of life. She isn't content, despite the fact that she's finally pregnant with a long-awaited child, but still she wants something more. She thinks a baby will resolve her unhappiness, and that once she has it, all will be well. What she doesn't realize is that her dissatisfaction is rooted in herself and can't be fixed by anything other than an inner transformation. Initially, the mother is barren and wants a baby. However, when this desire is fulfilled, she then wants lettuce, which she eats, and then wants more. This leaves us with the feeling that she isn't ever going to be satisfied. She seeks her nourishment from the world but doesn't realize that what she's really looking for is within. The outer isn't the true source of fulfillment or happiness. In one way, she's looking outside herself.

In another way of perceiving this, she looks to the unconscious—the witch's bounty, which comes from the garden to nourish, yet she remains unsatisfied. It's never enough, inner or outer. She takes the gifts from the unconscious, but still can't free herself from her sense of deficiency and inadequacy, she just consumes everything in sight.

You would think the mother might take care of herself, since she's pregnant, but she doesn't. She ignores the needs of her infant and herself. Disconnected from the new life growing in her womb, she only thinks of her desire for the lettuce growing in her neighbor's garden. This causes her to waste away, to the extent that her husband believes she will die if she doesn't get what she wants. He feeds his wife's dissatisfaction, which causes it to grow, and goes along with the idea that the solution to her hunger is in the outer world.

The father believes his wife will die without the lettuce from the garden, which in a sense, is true. When Adam and Eve ate the fruit from the tree of knowledge of good and evil, they became identified with the body, which meant they believed they would eventually die, since the body dies. In fact, when the mother in this story does die, she won't be conscious of the immortality of the soul and wholeness which exists, and she longs to taste. The walled garden, protected by the witch, represents the Garden of Eden, which once existed in unity and wholeness. There wasn't any knowledge of good and evil—judgement or duality—in the garden. *All* needs were met and fulfilled there. The mother longs for that state of consciousness.

The witch guards and tends the Garden now. She keeps intruders out to protect what's vulnerable to those with an insatiable appetite.

It's a sense of inadequacy, incompleteness, and an out-of-control need to consume, that prevents and keeps us out of the garden of wholeness, as we search endlessly in the outer world for what can only be found inside.

The husband's fear of losing his wife causes him to violate the boundary of the garden wall and take the witch's lettuce. He steals from the part of the feminine that can create, sustain, and protect life. Although, the witch lives in isolation, obviously because she has to, since the couple disregards her boundaries. The witch knows the inner world and its bounty, because it's her domain. She can grow things and bring them to fruition. The father and mother violate the witch's boundary and have to pay the price for their transgression. The father doesn't respect the witch, nor does he value her gifts when he steals from the abundance of a woman who has access to life in order to feed the insatiable feminine.

The husband could say no to his wife's appetite at any point and stand up to her, but he doesn't. He might realize, if he was healthy, that she's out of control and the outcome may be undesirable. This is probably a long-playing pattern that's being repeated. If he had learned from the past, he might have known that the outcome would be the loss of the young feminine.

The Witch

The witch represents the shadow—that which is hidden, or in the unconscious. In this case the witch and garden are concealed by her walls. According to psychologist Robin Robertson, "The shadow appears when the ego has accepted too limited a view of itself."[24] The shadow shows up in dreams when it's time to look at what's been repressed and is an important symbol in the process of individuation.[25] This integration is significant to the development of greater awareness and self-knowledge. In accepting the shadow, the disowned aspects of us, we no longer project them onto others. This is essential to the movement toward realizing wholeness.

The first stage of the work with the shadow can appear as depression, which is seen in the mother. It causes us to slow down; it pulls us under, into the unconscious, in order to see and feel what has been ignored. The mother sits immobilized, staring out the window, and longing for the lettuce. Instead of looking within and feeling her sense of inadequacy and emptiness, she wants to consume something, anything to avoid the discomfort. *If the feeling is felt, instead of projecting it onto the world with the belief that the fulfillment comes from outside, she would learn something about herself.* The depression would take on new meaning, as a sign from the psyche to look within, to deeply peer into the darkness of longing to discern what this is really about. What is truly wanted here? What will nourish the soul? She longs for what the witch has and is.

The etymology of the term "witch" relates to wisdom and wit, which come from the same roots, and is consistent across many languages. Walker suggests *witch* is derived from the Anglo-Saxon *Wicca/Wicce*, which comes from *witga/witega*, a seer or diviner, from *witan*, meaning to see or know.[26] The witch sees and knows. Jungian Clarissa Pinkola Estes writes of the wise *witch* that relates to the word *wild*, which:

Has come to be understood as pejorative, but long ago it was an appellation given to both old and young women healers, the word witch deriving from the word wit, meaning wise...the witch, the wild nature, and whatever other criaturas and aspects the culture finds awful in the psyches of women are the very blessed things which women need most to retrieve and bring to the surface.[27]

The things "the culture finds most awful in the psyches of women" are what we need to retrieve. Wisdom, healing, feeling, meaning, being, nurturing, nourishing, creating, are all feminine ways of the soul. The wise woman is content and doesn't long for something outside herself, like the mother in the story. This feminine is associated with female, but doesn't belong only to women, since men have this in them as well.

Walls

The witch's walls protect her and her garden from the world, since the world is perceived as a threat, and we can see why. She creates beautiful nourishing things, but is afraid to share them, because she isn't valued. This is why she lives behind her walls and lives in the unconscious. She's afraid of losing herself, being hurt, and having her boundaries invaded, again. As a child, she may have experienced physical, emotional, psychological, verbal, or sexual abuse. Her boundaries were invaded in one way or another, causing the walls to form as a protective measure, since she didn't feel safe.

We can explore our own lives to see if we are at all defensive and protective about ourselves, our creations, or what we desire. Are you and others honoring who you are and do you have healthy boundaries? What are your boundaries protecting? Are you hiding anything from yourself and others? Are you comfortable with the cycles of creation? Do you know how to nourish yourself? Are you sharing your gifts? Do you seek fulfillment from the outer world instead of the inner? The characters and their experiences can be related to us.

The mother longs for the aspect of herself that the witch represents. They are both isolated from life. The witch carries the wildness of instinct that knows how to heal, nourish, nurture, and feel, is close to the earth, and is in tune with the rhythm and cycles of nature. She is wise, content with life as it is, and knows how to sustain life as it grows. The mother's longing is for something deeper. She wants the witch's gifts and wants to know how to nurture her inner life, although she isn't aware of these deeper desires.

The first time the boundary is invaded, the witch overlooks the transgression, but the second time, it enrages her. She's the gardener and protects her bounty from those who wish to exploit her, and who have an insatiable hunger. The witch isn't afraid to express her anger when her boundaries are violated. She's not willing to just let the father sneak into the garden to steal from her but will not hesitate to speak up.

It would be difficult for anyone to get close to the witch because of her energetic walls and anger. She hasn't integrated a healthy masculine energy yet. The new inner masculine honors and respects boundaries, and as such, defensiveness and protection aren't necessary. He helps the feminine stand up for herself—not aggressively, but in a positive way. He assists her in carrying out her good choices. She then has the strength to walk away from things that don't honor her. A healthy inner masculine makes her fearless and when he's present, she's in her power. She doesn't need to be saved, rescued, protected, validated, or taken care of. If she gives her power away, then she allows others to hurt her, influence how she feels, determine who she is, and decide who she will be. *If she is in her power, she knows herself as the soul and approaches life with open curiosity instead of fear.*

The same goes for a man. If he has a strong healthy masculine nature, then he's clear and isn't defensive or protective. This isn't about repressing anger, because that emotion has been transformed. He's able to be open and receptive, because he's comfortable with all of his feelings. He has good boundaries, honors his own feminine knowing and values it.

The openly curious stance to life means that all that occurs is received without judgment or fear. Just as with depression, we inquire as to the *reason* for whatever shows up. This approach can be utilized for all of life. What does this mean? What appears within or without is explored to reach a deeper understanding. All that comes to us in our lives is a reflection of our consciousness. We can peer into whatever challenges us and discover what keeps us from being fully open to love, which is our true nature. Love is the energy that moves the world and permeates all of creation. Ultimately, there's nothing to defend ourselves against or protect ourselves from.

Sacrificing the Baby

The witch agrees to the husband's request for lettuce because of his love for his wife, but his fear of losing his own life causes him to sacrifice the baby. His boundaries and his sense of what's right and wrong are off. The witch knows the parents can't nurture and care for the infant, since they can't take care of themselves. To protect the innocent feminine, the witch takes Rapunzel from her parents and hides her behind the walls to keep her safe. This means that the new feminine energy is in the unconscious, which is the psyche's self-preservation mechanism for what's special and vulnerable. Rapunzel represents the soul that's untouched by the world.

If it's not safe to have a part of ourselves, or ourselves in general, out in the open, then we unconsciously repress or hide it. It can be a talent, or even a parent's preference for a child of the opposite sex, that makes certain qualities, or gifts, retreat behind walls so to speak. The witch then stands guard at the door to the unconscious and won't let anyone get close to what she protects. She uses anger and defensiveness to protect, because the masculine can't.

Rapunzel leaves her parents, if not literally, then symbolically. In many stories of the hero's journey, the hero often doesn't grow up with his parents. The parents usually do something which causes them to lose the child, as we see in this story. Here, it's the soul that moves into the unconscious.

A child needs to feel safe and have its needs met. What is seen, mirrored, validated, and acknowledged in a child is what the parents value. This is how children learn what to be and become. In order to feel loved, they often exhibit the qualities which they believe are most desirable to others, while repressing those which are ignored, rejected, or devalued.

Rapunzel's parents aren't the healthy nurturing parents she needs, which causes who she really is to disappear from view, like the witch. As the soul, Rapunzel remains hidden from the parents. Why? Because they don't recognize their own souls or its needs. They aren't aware of their deeper desires and don't know how to satisfy their soul's longing.

The witch and Rapunzel hide together for twelve years in the witch's home, protected by her walls. Rapunzel spends time with the witch to integrate the witch's qualities. Rapunzel looks at the parts of herself the witch carries, and she integrates them. She acquaints herself with intuition, with the rhythms of life and the cycles of nature, and with the garden, where she learns how things grow.

We can look at how developed the witch's gifts and knowing are in ourselves. She keeps things that are young and vulnerable out of sight as they grow. She knows about the inner life and nourishing the soul. Our own souls have often been relegated to the unconscious because the culture didn't value, see, or acknowledge them. It prefers the material over the soul, which requires things like poetry, art, gardening, beauty, love, story, music, and nature. The soul doesn't operate on clock time, but with the rhythms and cycles we've been talking about here. It thrives on meaning and discovery. It's enchanted with life and lives slowly and meaningfully. The soul requires attention and tending.

The rhythm and cycles of nature are at play in all of life. The witch sits and walks in nature, spends time in the stillness and silence, relaxes, and then an idea comes. She knows what to do with that seed of an idea. It is planted, nourished, and nurtured it as it grows. She's aware of how to take inspired action and doesn't force things before they are ready. The seed isn't dug up out of impatience or the petals of a flower pulled open to make a flower bloom faster. She trusts the unfolding process and allows it to be as it needs to be. When it's time for things to die, she lets them die. She isn't afraid of death, because she knows it precedes new life. The witch is at peace and content in winter. She's as happy during the fallow times as she is in the creation phase of life.

Are you in harmony with the cycles of creation, destruction, and decay? What's the status of the soul in your life? It's the inner witch that protects the soulful part of us.

The witch plays a dual function. She's the angry protector, as well as the one who knows and understands things at a deeper level. In this story, she's secluded because of her fear of others, which means the heroine can't stay with her. We know this because of her anger and isolation.

At the age of thirteen, Rapunzel's integration reaches the point that she no longer needs to live with the witch. The Self, as the organizing principle of the psyche, draws Rapunzel into a new situation for her to grow into greater awareness. The witch knows that it's time to move Rapunzel to a tower in the depths of the dark woods. Rapunzel is strong enough now to go more deeply into the unconscious.

Moving into the Tower

The move to the tower is an upward movement that's a reaction to her downward connection to the physical, earth, soul, being, and the feminine, at the expense of the intellect, spirit, doing, and the masculine. Rapunzel has been isolated from the masculine whom the witch feared. We can perceive this as the next step in discovering the gifts of the inner realms. In this phase, she experiences spirit. In the tower, she is disconnected from the earthly physical and goes deeper into the unconscious to connect with spirit and to discover a new masculine energy. Rapunzel goes to the other extreme in order to eventually find her center.

The tower "was originally conceived as a vehicle for connecting spirit and matter,"[28] which is exactly what needs to happen for the heroine. The witch taught Rapunzel how to connect to the earth, nature, soul, body, her wild nature, and to her intuition. Now she needs to shift her focus to something beyond matter. She can't remain a child and stay with the witch forever.

How did the witch teach Rapunzel to connect to the earth? Through the garden, time spent in nature, exploring the inner world as intuition, knowing, the body, feeling, and her primal nature. Rapunzel was able to feel the flow of the rhythms of growth, like a seed planted in a garden. She also learned to see what was hidden and know that which was normally ignored.

Our own creations are patterned on a natural flow. We sit quietly, receive, listen to dreams, witness imaginal wanderings, and enjoy times of doing nothing but just being. When the soul is experienced as a fully embodied presence that engages with life as it unfolds, it's nourished by all that's done. Activities such as baking, cooking, gardening, sweeping, watching the leaves fall, listening to the birds chirping, or seeing a caterpillar transform into a butterfly, result in a sense of delight over the simplest things. Instead of ravenously consuming what's seen, like Rapunzel's mother, it's experienced in a way that's satisfying.

While in the tower, Rapunzel goes deeper inside to connect with stillness and silence. She's being present to the inner peace and allowing it to permeate her body. Rapunzel experiences the Source that's inside of her, which is the wholeness that already exists. This is how a new foundation is created that's permanent and always present.

It's interesting that the image of Rapunzel sitting high up in the tower beside a window, mirrors that of her mother at the beginning of the story. It's important for Rapunzel to find something inside herself to fill her emptiness and not to look outside for happiness as her mother did. This is a time of greater isolation for Rapunzel and the first step in separating from the witch. She's exploring the inner world more deeply, but now in greater isolation.

The Gatekeeper

The witch is the gatekeeper to Rapunzel and her gifts. She's the only one who has access to the young innocent feminine—the soul. We can be fully present to her anger and frustration at being ignored, and her desire to hide. The soul and its gifts are inside, and she protects them. While the soul is developing inside, and becoming a stronger presence, the outside may appear as though nothing is happening. Everything is taking place behind the walls, or deep in the forest, and hidden from the sight of the world.

This is an inner transformation. There is a shift from dependence on the world of form for fulfillment to receiving from within a sense of fullness and peace in which nothing is ever missing.

Rapunzel's move to the tower coincides with her transition to becoming a young woman. The witch feels the need to protect Rapunzel even more and moves her to a place that is virtually impossible to get in or out of. Conditions have been created in which Rapunzel can't leave, even if she wants to. During this phase, her life becomes more about what's within than what can be accomplished in the world.

It appears as though Rapunzel is content with her life exactly as it is. She sits alone in her tower singing to amuse herself and is happy with the witch's daily visits. True fulfillment occurs when we allow our gifts the freedom of expression and aren't preoccupied with outer desires, as we saw with Rapunzel's mother. The song is sung in isolation when the masculine is wounded, and the garden remains hidden behind the walls of fear.

What phase of this transformation are you in? Are you sharing your gifts? Is any part of you or your life isolated? How are you honoring your soul? Have you understood what it is and embodied it? What's your relationship to nature and the rhythms of growth? Is the witch still active for you?

The Prince

The beauty of Rapunzel's song draws the prince—a new masculine energy—out of the unconscious. We can read this as *following our hearts* and *doing something* with our gifts. This isn't necessarily in the world yet, but it's a time to explore our abilities and bring our deepest essence to fruition through some type of creative expression. What's your inner song? What makes your heart sing? We need to spend time seeking to understand what we are capable of and what we desire.

Rapunzel goes deeper into the unconscious in order to discover this new masculine aspect of herself. The prince is an energy that's needed for balance. He has a horse, which means he has the energy that's required to navigate through the world and can help her to be free. The prince needs her energy, sight, knowing, gifts, and fresh innocence to be effective in the world. He serves as a bridge between the worlds for Rapunzel.

This is a time to conduct an inner search for power and freedom. We can really feel these qualities deep within ourselves and explore how powerful and free we actually feel. If we don't feel these qualities, then we need to look at why. This is an inner discovery and not an outer search. If power or freedom are rooted in outer conditions being a certain way, then they aren't based on truth and are impermanent.

As an outer character, Rapunzel may see the prince as her salvation, and he may perceive himself as her savior. But she can't look outside of herself, for anything or anyone to save her, or she's giving her power away to them. This means she isn't ready to go out into the world. As an inner aspect of the heroine, he's the energy of power and freedom that she must embody. The witch has carried the power up until now and Rapunzel must reclaim that for herself.

The prince represents a new phase in her healing process. He helps her to see her situation more clearly and to realize that she isn't free. She must discover what freedom is and how it will look in her life. One way is for Rapunzel to find it is to weave a rope and escape from the tower with the prince, which is a logical response to get them out of isolation and into the world. The other way is to search for freedom inside.

The arrival of the prince in a fairy tale is often misinterpreted as rescuing the heroine, which is exactly what it looks like here. When we read this literally, and see the turn the story has taken, it's an understandable assumption. The masculine energy is needed for balance, but not to rescue her. On an inner level, these two energies have to come together, since both are required to operate in the world.

Empowerment

True empowerment occurs when the inner masculine and feminine energies work in harmony. Inner power and freedom must be discovered and grounded in the body first. Then, Rapunzel—as the intuitive feminine—supplies the plan for their escape, and the prince—as the intellect—helps complete the task. This is an opportunity for them to learn to work together to reach a goal. The prince goes out into the world to acquire the silk they need, and Rapunzel uses her skill to weave the rope.

The prince's desire to free Rapunzel is similar to the father's desire to free the mother, which suggests that isn't the path to true freedom for the heroine. If we see him as either in relationship with her, or as her inner masculine, the idea that the masculine is the way to freedom is an erroneous idea. It's what most of us have been conditioned to believe as well. His appearance is the impetus for her to *want* to escape. He's the desire to move forward and seek freedom, because, as stated previously, she was thoroughly content just sitting in the tower. Rapunzel thinks the masculine is the path to freedom, but it isn't. She can't free herself through outer action in the world, nor can she escape from her current situation by running to a new one. We've been taught that freedom comes via the masculine, war, fighting, struggle, the intellect, action, doing this and that, or taking certain steps.

True freedom isn't in the hands of the masculine, and never was. If freedom comes at the point of a sword, by a law, or a situation, it won't last, since it's based on circumstances that can change. If we seek permanent freedom, the only way to find it is to look inside.

The couple plans to *escape* from the witch, but this isn't true empowerment. They aren't in their power if they are running away from something out of fear. Rapunzel must go even deeper. The father was afraid to lose his wife and managed to stay with her, but at the expense of the innocent young feminine. The prince and Rapunzel have to do things differently to change the outcome. The prince will have to face his fear of losing Rapunzel, since her father ignored his fear and continuously fed her mother's insatiable appetite.

Is your masculine still serving the old feminine by attempting to feed and satiate her unending hunger? This looks like the need for more and never being satisfied with what is as it is. This is about being enough, having enough, and doing enough. Rapunzel wasn't looking out for fulfillment when she was alone in the tower, but she was in a place of complacency. She wasn't even aware of the fact that she wasn't free. The impulse of life toward wholeness creates a situation that awakens the desire for freedom. Rapunzel was fine with her situation, until the prince arrived. Her growth was stunted by the arrangement; she needed to emerge and evolve into something more.

The Witch and Prince

The prince comes to visit every day and brings bits of cloth for Rapunzel to weave. Then, one day, Rapunzel makes a terrible mistake during the witch's visit. She accidentally tells the witch about the prince when she innocently asks the witch why she's so much heavier than he is. The witch is furious to hear of Rapunzel's betrayal. She's broken some unspoken rule with the witch and dared to step beyond the confines of her old role.

The deeper truth is that Rapunzel's so-called *error* is the Self's way of continuing her growth in consciousness. She inadvertently tells the witch that the masculine has stepped across the boundary, but this time it isn't her father. The first time the prince enters the tower, he was deceitful, and

Rapunzel was frightened, but she calmed down as he explained himself. From that moment on, he was a welcome visitor and that's where he differs from the father. He's not stealing anything to feed the insatiable feminine appetite, which would keep them both in bondage. The prince values Rapunzel and wants to be free with her.

The witch isn't interested in whether the prince is a healthy or an unhealthy masculine. She's afraid of him and reacts unconsciously to the memory of being harmed in the past. This is an egoic reaction. She pushes others away because she doesn't want to get hurt again. It is an old pattern that's ready to be resolved.

This may appear to be justified defensiveness. If we are telling ourselves old stories about how we need protection, then we may not be really seeing what's actually in front of us. These narratives may be a projection of the past onto the present, and into the future, making our experiences inauthentic. The present situation is being perceived through a lens that isn't clear. These old stories may contain judgment, blame, fear, and unmet expectations. It sometimes can make us feel really vulnerable to open to the masculine again and to trust him.

The witch just pushes him away without questioning his authenticity and doesn't want him around. As such, she represents resistance to allowing the masculine in. This means Rapunzel still has some fear about him and isn't yet ready to be in the world.

If we have any anger or fear that causes us to push someone, or a situation, away, then it means something is unresolved. The response is to take a deeper dive into the emotion, or experience, while being fully present to what's being activated. Even if it appears to be a perfectly reasonable way to respond to the circumstance, we want to explore what beliefs are surfacing as a result of the experience we are in.

The witch is angry about the masculine's presence. This old attitude has outlived its usefulness and is now a problem. The witch's feelings toward the father's intrusion were acceptable, but the prince isn't the father, and this energy must now be transformed. The father was stealing from the witch in order to feed the insatiable feminine hunger, but now, the prince's intentions are to partner with Rapunzel to free her. These two masculine energies have different motivations.

The witch's anger is evidence that Rapunzel doesn't feel safe, so instead of pushing the masculine away and hiding, she must address the fear itself. Maybe Rapunzel thought she was fine as she planned to leave the tower, and the witch, but as the time drew nearer, she (as the witch in her consciousness) got scared and reacted by pushing him away.

The witch can represent an internal voice that criticizes our desire to break away from old patterns in consciousness. It's possibly replicating a familial condition that's ready to be transcended. The internal witch may sound like someone from the past. This attempt to change the narrative may be met with shame, fear, guilt, and uncertainty about what to do. If the outer world doesn't appear to be changing in the way you desire, keep looking at dreams and what's being triggered by outer situations to determine what is occurring in the unconscious that's keeping you where you are.

Rapunzel doesn't feel it's safe to leave her isolation, because she isn't ready to live her truth in the world. This means there is more fear to be transformed through witnessing and going deeper inside to find out who she really is. If she doesn't feel safe, then she isn't free. That has to be healed *before* she goes out into the world. It's not time to share her gifts yet, since this is what she feels.

When we are in this situation, we want to keep working at our gifts and doing what we can to get stronger, but also continue deepening into our sense of self. That freedom we believe will come from this or that action, is inside. We are the freedom we are searching for in the world.

Rapunzel is conditioned to hide, to be in the tower, follow the witch's rules, and so now, as she prepares to break those rules, she may get triggered emotionally. She's already defied the witch by allowing the prince in, but now, as she contemplates escaping and gets closer to that possibility, she panics. This conflict between the desire to remain hidden, and the longing for freedom, must be felt.

Fear of the Other

The angry witch reacts to Rapunzel's transgression by cutting her braid, which represents Rapunzel losing an old form of connecting with the world (through the prince and witch). The witch's intention is to permanently sever the link with the masculine, so he will never see her again. While Rapunzel had her long hair, she remained in the tower as the other two came and went. Without the braid, this is no longer possible. Something new needs to happen.

The witch is afraid of the prince because she projects her power onto others, and as such, is used to being the victim where they are concerned. In the past, her boundaries, needs, and desires were ignored, which is how she learned helplessness and not to stand up for herself. When the witch responds with anger, she becomes the aggressor with the intention to destroy what frightens her. What she's really afraid of is her *own* power, which the masculine—the prince—carries for her. She plays the role of powerlessness to his powerfulness. The only way for her to protect herself is to respond with anger, which at least means she's not playing the helpless role. This situation—an invasion of boundaries—is often a re-enactment of childhood, or what's happened in the past. The mind expects the past to repeat and tries to protect itself accordingly.

While the witch is projecting her power onto the masculine, he's projecting his power onto the feminine. Rapunzel's father gave his power away and was the victim, while Rapunzel's mother, and the witch, were perceived as having the power. In many stories, the father is often passive and ineffective, while the destructive tendencies are displayed in the angry feminine as the witch or evil stepmother. Rapunzel ignites the witch's anger, like her father did, which means she's a victim of the anger of others, like him. She carries the insatiable mother, angry witch, and the helpless father, within her. Her power is being projected out onto the world, and others, since the anger stems from an inability to facilitate change. It doesn't matter how hard she tries, things just seem to stay the same.

In life, this dynamic can play out with anyone who catches the projection of a parent or activates that consciousness. This is often a partner, but it can also be anyone who is perceived as an authority figure. When a strong emotion appears regarding another's behavior, we can explore it to see if there is a connection to a situation from the past, possibly with a caregiver. Does this person's behavior remind you of someone? Are they carrying your power? If anyone is making you feel angry, helpless, or powerless, then the response is to reclaim your power from them.

Anger and Action

Rapunzel's father couldn't protect her from her consuming mother, which is why Rapunzel had to go live with the witch. He didn't respect boundaries and that made the young feminine vulnerable. The heroine's masculine energy is utilized to speak up for herself and set healthy boundaries. If he's wounded, as the father and prince are, then this needs to be transformed for Rapunzel to go into the world and be empowered.

Now, the witch doesn't want to turn over the "care" of the feminine to the prince, because she believes this masculine is also disempowered and unable to protect Rapunzel. She's right, since he and Rapunzel planned to "run away" from her. The prince didn't stand up to the witch, any more than Rapunzel's father, and therefore, he isn't any different from him in that respect. Rapunzel must learn to maintain her own boundaries and discover her true power within. Her power can't come from fear, but it must be based on love and come from the heart.

Anger serves to draw our attention to unknown boundaries that come from past wounds. When anger arises and we peer into it, we may realize a boundary is being invaded. It's entirely possible that a day comes and something that always was okay is no longer tolerable. The presence of anger is how we begin to recognize boundaries we might have previously ignored. If they were ignored as a child, then we often don't even know where they are. Life will teach us by triggering our anger to reveal the boundary. Once we see it, and notice that it's being invaded, then we can explore our options and determine how to respond. The important thing to remember is that the outer reflects the inner. As we explore the situation thoroughly, we want to see if we are ignoring the boundary ourselves and not assertively maintaining it.

One of the fascinating things about this is that we can feel angry when we do something we were told not to do as a child. If a parent had a rule that we disobey as an adult, we can feel anger toward ourselves for breaking it as we ignore the rule and move past that internal boundary. The anger may have protected us in childhood, to keep us from upsetting a parent, but here, the anger points to a limitation that's not serving us anymore and must be dismantled. Again, by being present to the anger and witnessing it in ourselves, we don't have to follow old restrictions and can free ourselves from outdated beliefs. In this way, we learn to dissolve unnecessary parental restrictions in our consciousness.

Rapunzel was the victim of her caregivers. She did need to be saved from her passive father and consuming mother, and now, from the angry witch. This old pattern means she has the belief that she needs to be rescued from the other, which in this case, it's by the prince. Rapunzel isn't yet aware of her inner power, or of her ability to save herself, but is projecting her power onto the witch and the prince. She believes her freedom depends on them. In this view, the prince and the other characters are external to herself.

Internally, she still sees action as the way to freedom. It's not the time for her to go out into the world yet, since she's still afraid, and believes the masculine is the way out of her current predicament.

If the witch was empowered, then the prince would have shown up and, if appropriate, she might have just told him to leave and he would have departed. No trauma and no drama. If she didn't fall into the old erroneous expectation that she's the victim any time the masculine appears (since she believes he has the power), then she could have also responded to his arrival with open curiosity. The witch may have wondered, "What's this new masculine here to teach me now?"

Cutting the Braid

The truth must emerge, sooner or later, and Rapunzel is the one who reveals her secret to the witch. The witch is so angry that she cuts off Rapunzel's braid, which was how the prince and the witch were able to reach her. This is a significant shift, a door has closed, and that means things won't ever be able to go back to the way they were, ever.

A change in hairstyle indicates a change in the persona, which is the face we show to the world. By cutting Rapunzel's hair, it's the witch who puts an end, once again, to an old phase. Rapunzel must leave the tower and her old pattern of being a victim. Sometimes, it's more comfortable to return to what's known than to enter the unknown.

We saw Rapunzel begin to act on her intuition in the tower, as she and the prince planned, and were executing, their desire to escape. It was during this time that Rapunzel became acquainted with a masculine she didn't know before. She also established contact with a spiritual aspect of herself that provides new solutions to new situations. While she was in the house with the witch, she had become familiar with the soul and feminine, and in the tower, it's the spirit and masculine. The link between the above and below were being explored deep in the forest. The braid was a bridge between the worlds for her.

A braid is three parts woven together to make one, which suggests the possibility of the braid as a symbol of the Trinity. The Trinity is perceived as the connection between the above and below, within and without, which now has been severed by the witch. The old idea of the Trinity as an outer separate Father, Mother/Holy Spirit, and Child is being released. The bridge can't be an outer one, but it must be discovered within. The desire for connection and belonging is often believed to be fulfilled in the world, but now the connection must be found within.

All of us are on a spiritual journey. Many of us have been conditioned to orient ourselves around the material instead of the spiritual, even if we were brought up in a religion. For those of us who grew up in a culture that's predominately Christian, those doctrines permeate our consciousness and affect us regardless of our own personal religious practices. The old concept of the outer Trinity as the link between heaven and earth, above and below, spirit and matter, is removed here to create the space for something else. It's no longer an option for Rapunzel to believe her power resides in the prince, witch, or outer Christian heavenly Father, Mother/Holy Spirit, or Child.

Rapunzel has directly experienced the Father/internal spiritual aspect of herself during her isolation in the tower and has some awareness of it as an inner presence. She connected with the Mother/soul while with the witch. And now, just like the Son/Child Jesus, she is being sent to the desert to be tested. Rapunzel still has remnants of fear and inadequacy remaining, which will be challenged in the desert and transformed.

If Rapunzel believes that an outer power—as a person, thing, or deity— is required to fulfill her needs or desires, or to give her freedom, or is necessary to her wellbeing and sense of connection, then she's giving her power away and needs to reclaim it. She will have to pull back all of her projections from any outer sources and look inside to find that unshakable foundation. Rapunzel will have to do this in a place with no links to the outer world. Then she will be able to stand in the fullness of her own power and *know* that she doesn't depend on anyone, for anything.

In the Desert

The witch severs the braid and sends Rapunzel to the desert. The braid isn't *just* a lock of hair, but it's a huge part of her identity and she has to let it go. The heroine loses the prince and the witch with a snip of the scissors. She must be feeling bereft during this new phase—miserable according to the story—as her isolation is taken to an even deeper level. This is a challenging time that calls for introspection in a place without *any* distractions. Rapunzel loses everything in the outer world. All that is familiar is stripped away and she's forced to look inside. Sometimes life has a way of creating the space and time for us to contemplate and discover a higher truth. If we can see that this is what's happening, then we can take advantage of these opportunities to develop greater awareness.

It's often in hindsight that we discover the reasons why we needed to go deeper before moving on. These times of reflection are sometimes externally imposed, which may make us feel as though we don't have any choice in the matter. As time passes though, we might feel grateful as we begin to see, while we're still in it, exactly what we're supposed to learn. This will help us to accept where we are. Even though it might not feel like it in the moment, this isolation is required to create something new.

In this level of isolation, we might feel seriously challenged to discover all we need within. If the feelings of disconnection in all areas of life are triggered, try to remind yourself, repeatedly if necessary, that it's all inside. When there isn't anything or anyone to project onto, we may keenly feel unloved, unvalued, that we don't matter, inadequate or not enough. And if you are really in it, the phone won't ring, there won't be any emails, no responses will come to your work, you'll feel disconnected from family and friends, and have to continually remember that it's all inside. The connection, love, peace, fulfillment, enoughness, and freedom, are all a part of the wholeness that you already are but may have overlooked. Keep searching inside, no doubt you have the time to do it while alone, be patient and trust that it will come.

Our heroine will grieve for all of her loses. It's not just the prince and witch that are absent, but she's faced with the fact that she never had parents, nor did she live a normal life. Rapunzel must come to terms with her past, feel her sadness about the life she lived, and discover the deeper meaning of it all. There may be feelings of rejection and the realization of how lonely she really felt all those years in isolation. This can be literal or not so literal. It may mean feeling as though she never fit in anywhere, didn't know where home was, or who was her tribe. She might recognize her deeper longings that went unheeded, emotions that were overlooked, or gifts that were rejected and went into the unconscious.

Rapunzel must face her fears, emptiness, and a deep loneliness in order to establish a firm foundation in a transcendent center and embody her innate wholeness. She can't run away and hide anymore but is being forced to face what remains when everything that's mattered to her is gone. Whatever was projected onto others must be found inside. She may have thought that the witch, and then the prince, were required for her to feel whole. Rapunzel may have believed the witch held her prisoner, and the prince—or God in heaven, or some other thing outside of her—would set her free, but now she sees that's not going to happen. The two people she depended on are now gone, which means she's going to have to figure this out for herself.

While in the desert, she must look inside to discover her greater truth. When Rapunzel accepts the importance of her current situation, she will realize the deeper meaning of her experience. It's time for her to forgive the witch and her parents for the ways in which they seemed to have hurt her. As she peers deeper into her so-called past, she will realize that each experience was necessary to bring her to this moment. Each person—who seemed to hurt her—actually served her growth and her coming into greater consciousness. Her soul will be felt as a presence, which has never been touched by anything anyone ever did, or any experience she's ever had. It's healed, whole, and complete. This understanding resolves any issues around worth, contentment, safety, or clarity with regard to her path, which empowers her. Her time in the desert is a gift. She's establishing an inner awareness in place of any outer dependencies she erroneously looked to for fulfillment and the illusion of wholeness.

Rapunzel is deep in isolation as she explores and questions much of what she has learned from others. It is during this process that she will discover what is true for her now. She must stand in her power and remains undaunted, as she faces her deepest fears, which are recognized as merely thoughts. The fearful thoughts come and go but something remains, untouched and unmoved by them, which is the transcendent center. *If she feels like a victim, she sees it and let's it go.*

Our heroine faces the truth of the longing that her mother couldn't face. She resolves the misplaced desire for worldly things and sees that what she's really been searching for is her own experience of embodied wholeness. This is the emergence of the Child in the Trinity as she *surrenders the need to defend and protect herself,* since she's finally safe. The realization comes that there isn't anything to be afraid of, since the outer mirrors the inner, and they are one. If it's safe inside, then it's safe outside. She stands unaffected by her fears as they are transformed, and they lose their power over her.

The Lost Prince

While Rapunzel is in the desert, the prince returns to the tower. But when he reaches the top of the braid, he finds the witch is there instead. He decides to leap from the window and kill himself with the desire to flee from the pain of his loss. He initially leaps from the tower to end his life, but instead, lands on a bramble bush that scratches his eyes and renders him blind. The story doesn't tell us about her time in the desert, but about him wandering in the forest, lost, blind, and alone.

The prince's connection to the intuitive feminine was severed by the witch and he believes he will never see Rapunzel again. He's truly lost and feels like life isn't worth living without her—the feminine—now that he's experienced what life was like with her. The prince doesn't have access to nurturance and nourishment, nor can he create and sustain life in her absence. There isn't any generativity without her, and her loss feels unbearable. His desire may have been to destroy himself, but fate won't allow it, and he loses his sight instead.

He doesn't have any sense of direction, which is a natural part of the process during the chaos and uncertainty of a new creation. During this birthing phase, we often don't know where to go or what to do. We may feel like we are meandering aimlessly without direction and the signs can be confusing. It may be possible to determine where we are in the transformative process as we turn our attention within. Most of the time though, there isn't any action in the outer world as all of the energy is focused inside.

The prince loses his sight because the old way of seeing doesn't work anymore. The old way of using the intellect to determine what to do next will no longer suffice, and the outdated view of the feminine also has to change. Rapunzel carries the intuitive sight and now she's gone. He's lost without the benefit of intuition and mourns for all the losses he never grieved. Weeping is known to clear the eyesight. The witch appears to have taken away his happiness, just when he thought his dreams would be fulfilled.

The blind masculine—when unable to see where to go and what to do—can go into fight-or-flight mode. He may either confront or attack, charge forward and ignore his fear, like the witch did. This masculine may want to run away from any emotions or the situation, as the prince and Rapunzel originally planned to do. Running is often an avoidance of the unknown, and the discomfort of not knowing what's going to happen.

What's really being run from is oneself. There can be a fear of truly knowing ourselves, because it's unfamiliar. We are being called to accept the truth of the unknown, which is that it's the true nature of all life. Nothing is ever really known for sure. We don't really know ourselves, nor do we know what's going to happen in the next moment, and we don't even truly know the people we love apart from our projections.

Longing

Hope and disappointment are a major theme in this story. There's hope that things will get better and then disappointment when they don't. When we are repeatedly disappointed by life, there may be a reliance on hope to maintain motivation. This idea is based on the belief that what's wanted is off in the future somewhere. It will come later, after some magical event, like a marriage, retirement, wealth, or birth of a child. There's optimism and an anticipation for the time when things will improve. This future is one in which we follow the proverbial carrot at the end of the stick, but it always remains just beyond our reach, because it isn't here now. If our wellbeing depends on particular circumstances being a certain way, then we aren't free. Rapunzel's time in the desert will resolve this belief as well.

This longing echoes Rapunzel's mother's desire for a future in which she's finally satisfied, but that time never arrives. She longed for the child and then the lettuce. There isn't any peace or joy in the now with life as it is. The true fulfillment of wholeness is here in this moment. Everything that's needed is already here. This present is full and not empty. It's enough and not lacking in any way, despite the ego's belief to the contrary.

It is not always obvious if the feeling is one of contentment, or a repression of emotion that comes from having given up on life. One is an acceptance and satisfaction with life as it is and the other isn't bothering to try to create the life that's desired because the life that's wanted is no longer thought of as possible. In the latter, the pain of loss and disappointment is avoided altogether. Because the desired outcome didn't manifest in the past, there can be a feeling of unworthiness, or of not deserving what's wanted. If that which is sought isn't here right now, then something must be wrong, and it's probably never going to happen.

Trust is needed. We can cultivate a belief in the goodness of life, a feeling of deservedness, and know that everything is fine as it is, which will carry us through. We are enough and can be empowered to pursue the life we desire. When we are open and *expect* that what's happening is in our best interest, then we aren't afraid of it. There isn't any need to hide, to be saved, defend and protect, or run away. *We don't look for someone to save us and we don't look for someone to save.* When we go into fear and helplessness, then we constellate the savior to help us. This is the current common conception of Jesus. We need to release the idea that there's anything we need outside ourselves to save us —Jesus, prince, the government, family, or otherwise. Rapunzel left the tower and returned to earth in the desert. Jesus was tempted by the devil in the desert, which was him facing his egoic-based fears. Jesus, when confronted, had to remain stable, grounded, and in his power.

The ego tempts us through outdated beliefs in the necessity of the material for fulfillment and happiness. Every time we look outside of ourselves for satisfaction, we are encouraged to turn back in. Our sense of self is derived from the inner world and not the outer. Our worth, value, and peace are always there. When we root in that steady, still, ever-present awareness, anything can happen in the world and we remain undaunted. When we free ourselves from a dependence on the world being a particular way in order to be happy, then we are truly free.

Rapunzel's Rebirth

Rapunzel mourns her losses in the desert. She experiences the depth of her sorrow from having lived most of her life in isolation and without freedom. It's a time to grieve for the loss of her parents and their inability to be there for her or to see her. As such, she has spent her life hiding and afraid, unable to be herself in the world. She feels the sadness of what appears to be an unlived life. Whatever she feels, anything she believes and thinks, she witnesses it like a visitor who is leaving. Rapunzel feels whatever comes up that has been repressed, unseen, and unfelt by her, and allows it to flow. Her feelings come and go, thoughts come and go, and yet she remains present and grounded in the awareness that's her true nature.

Rapunzel is being reborn into wholeness.

After her mourning, among the tattered remains of her life, Rapunzel discovers the deeper meanings of events. If she hadn't gone to the desert, but had escaped with the prince, it's fairly certain that she wouldn't have been happy. She would have re-created her old situation in a new location because she hadn't shifted to a new consciousness or changed her expectations and ideas about who she is. Her husband may have stepped into the role of her father or the mother/witch, and she would have perceived him as critical to her wholeness and possibly her freedom as well. Rapunzel didn't know how to be in an equal relationship with anyone, since her entire existence was about what the witch wanted instead of considering her own desires. The witch had complete control over Rapunzel and her life, until the prince arrived. She might have entered a relationship with the prince and tried to please him to keep him from rejecting her, as she did with the witch, and not lived her own truth.

Rapunzel had to have this experience in order to successfully leave her isolation and live within a community. If she had resisted this time alone and the lessons it brought, she might not have been prepared to accept the good that was coming. Rapunzel has been in isolation almost her entire life, and living with others—learning to trust, feel safe, and loved—would have been a challenge had she not accepted her truth, wholeness, value, and power first. Had she not come to realize in the depths of her being that she's joyful and free, her happiness would have been contingent on circumstances, like her mother.

Our heroine is sent to the desert to discover her truth. She realizes the ego isn't anything more than the story about who she thought she was. It had moments in which it was a good story and those in which it was believed to be a bad story. Either way, it was a story. The Self is beyond the story. It sees the story but knows that it's untouched by whatever happens. This is where true freedom is found. This is the unshakable center in which we stand, undaunted by anything that happens.

The desert is a place of deeper isolation without distraction. During this time, the requirements of the material world are set aside so Rapunzel may discover herself. She learns to hold her center, to nurture, and nourish herself. Getting sent into the desert was meant to be punishment, but is a blessing in disguise, since she discovers and realizes her true self there, and that changes her life. This is a period of transformation that opens Rapunzel to the love inside herself. Love is the power that sets her free. It's the only power there is and it's setting us free as well as we surrender to the flow and wisdom of life.

Now, Rapunzel realizes her happiness is always within her and doesn't depend on the world around her. Most of the material things we surround ourselves with and many of the activities of the world, provide us with very little true reward. Whatever we get from them, it's often temporary.

Facing Fear

When Rapunzel faces her own fears of isolation and loneliness, she discovers something new within herself. She comes to realize she isn't alone, and nothing is missing. The transcendent center is her support, sustenance, and nourishment. As such, she now stands on the foundation of her own truth with the strength and ability to build a healthy life. She spends time in the stillness and silence in order to bring forth her new gifts.

While in the desert, Rapunzel also gives birth to twins, who symbolize new masculine and feminine energies. She carries the infants to term and manages on her own. She's discovered something new in herself and has brought it from the unconscious into her full awareness. The desire for freedom was awakened by the prince, or spirit. Now, she has discovered the truth of herself. This is the perfect moment for the prince to return. His appearance is inevitable because in wholeness nothing is missing. He's the personification of the energy needed for the next step, which is to bring her realization back to the community.

Rapunzel cries when the prince appears, and her tears heal his vision. He can now *see* her, and as such, see where they need to go. His sight returns because she—as the feminine—carries the intuitive sight. Intuition guides us in the right direction, and the healed masculine energy respects and follows it because he's learned through his aimless wandering that following the intellect doesn't work. That didn't get him anywhere. In terms of cycles, there's a rhythm to the inner and outer work. When the inner is being tended, the outer may appear to be confusing, uncertain, and no observable progress is seen. Rapunzel learned who she is in the desert. She's seen her true self, so now, the prince can see her as well.

Reunion

Now there are four of them, Rapunzel, the prince, and their two children, which is the number associated with wholeness and stability. This is also a new representation of the Holy Trinity, which is no longer the Father, Son, and Holy Spirit, but Father, Mother, and Child as the Son and Daughter. This is the true fullness of completion.

The reunion of the masculine and feminine is cause for great happiness, not only for them but also for the collective. Their reunion indicates that Rapunzel is living her truth in a healthy balanced manner. She knows her worth and is ready to accept the abundance of the prince's kingdom. She also knows she's free. The desert experience was exactly what she needed to prepare for what is to come, in order to know that she is love, joy, and wholeness. The result of this realization is the true nature of an abundant life.

All of the characters in the story thought their happiness depended on something outside themselves. The mother wanted the lettuce and the father was afraid of losing his wife. The witch and prince were afraid of losing Rapunzel and Rapunzel was afraid of losing the prince. Each sought something outside themselves that could not be possessed.

We are taught to look to the world to feel whole and complete, but the characters in the story demonstrate that this isn't the path to real contentment. Lasting fulfillment comes when we realize our true nature. When we become aware of the transcendent center within us, we find the deeper meaning of life and our own reason for being. As we move out of our old egoic stories, and experience life without a story while centered in the true self, our consciousness evolves, and we are transformed. We live in wholeness; we embody love and joy and know a freedom that can never be taken away, since it is our natural self.

Rapunzel, the prince, and their two children return to the prince's kingdom and live happily ever after.

CHAPTER

Four

Ashputtle (Cinderella): Death of the Good Mother

*O*nce upon a time a wealthy man's wife was dying. On her deathbed, she told her daughter to be a good girl and that she would watch over her from heaven. The father remarried an unkind woman with two mean daughters. The woman took Ashputtle's clothes, the girls moved into her room, and she was relegated to the kitchen to do all the work, while they just sat around. The girls taunted her and called her names. They referred to her as "Ashputtle" because she was always dirty from work and sleeping by the hearth.

The father was going to a fair and asked the three girls what they wanted. The stepsisters requested dresses, diamonds, and pearls. Ashputtle asked for the branch of a tree that brushed his hat on his way home. She planted the sprig he brought her on her mother's grave and watered it daily with her tears. When she sat under the tree weeping, a little white bird was perched in the tree. Whenever she made a wish, the bird gave her what she wanted.

There was to be a three-day celebration at the king's castle to find a bride for the prince. All the girls in the kingdom were invited. The stepsisters were excited about the three balls, but when Ashputtle asked if she could go, her stepmother said no. She couldn't because she was dirty and didn't have anything to wear. Ashputtle begged until her stepmother relented. Her stepmother dumped a bowl of lentils into the ashes and told Ashputtle that if she separated them in two hours, she could attend the balls. Ashputtle secretly called the birds and they completed the task for her.

She took the bowl of lentils to her stepmother, but still she wasn't allowed to go to the celebration, and so she cried even harder. Ashputtle begged her stepmother once again, and once again, she gave in. Although, this time she said Ashputtle could attend if she picked two bowls of lentils from the ashes in an hour. Ashputtle called in the birds and they completed the task for her. She took the bowls to her stepmother, who said she still couldn't go because she had nothing to wear and didn't know how to dance. She would be an embarrassment to them all.

When the family left for the castle, Ashputtle went out to the hazel branch that had grown into a tree and asked for a gold and silver dress. A moment later a dress fell from the tree with slippers. She put on the dress and went to the castle where no one recognized her. The guests all thought she must have been from far away. The prince danced all night only with her, and then offered to walk her home when she was ready to leave, because he wanted to know who she was.

She ran away from the prince and once she reached home, she slipped into the dovecote. When her father arrived, the prince told him she was inside of it. The father broke open the dovecote, but it was empty as she'd already slipped out unnoticed. When they went into the house, Ashputtle was lying in the ashes by the hearth in her dirty rags.

The following day, once everyone had left, she went to the tree and asked again for a gold and silver dress. The bird dropped down a dress that was even more beautiful than the one from the day before. The king's son was waiting for her when she arrived and danced only with her all night. When Ashputtle was ready to go home, the prince offered to walk her home, but again she slipped away. He followed her to a pear tree in the garden. When her father arrived, the prince told him that she was in the tree. The father chopped it down, but Ashputtle wasn't there. He went inside and found Ashputtle lying in the ashes as usual in her dirty dress.

On the third day, Ashputtle went to the tree after everyone left and asked for a gold and silver dress. A dress, more beautiful than the others fell from the tree with gold slippers. She was the most beautiful young woman at the ball and the prince only danced with her. When she was ready to go home, the prince offered to take her, but she left before he realized it. Although, he expected it this time and had the stairs covered with pitch. Ashputtle lost her slipper as she ran down the stairs and the prince picked it up.

The prince went to Ashputtle's house the next morning and told her father that his bride's foot would fit in the slipper. The first sister tried on the shoe, but her foot was too big, so her mother told her to cut off her toe and shove her foot in it. The prince and first sister rode off, but a little bird alerted the prince to the blood that was dripping from the shoe. He returned and the same thing happened with the second sister. He took her back to the house.

The prince asked the father if there were any other daughters in the house. He answered no, only a kitchen drudge. The prince insisted they call her. Ashputtle washed her face and hands in the kitchen. She entered the room where the prince was, and tried on the slipper, which fit perfectly. The prince recognized her, so they climb onto his horse and the birds announced that this was his true bride.[*]

---

[*] Full story in Manheim's *Grimms' Tales for Young and Old*

Introduction

This story is more familiarly known as "Cinderella," but we will refer to her as Ashputtle in this interpretation. Our heroine becomes a victim and servant when her mother dies. She works and works, but regardless of how much she works, the critical stepmother won't give her permission to do what she wants. She can't enjoy life, play, or have fun because there's too much work to do. The inner stepmother is constantly judging, and wanting her to do more to be enough, in order to finally achieve her freedom. The stepmother just won't relent. She persists, along with the entire rest of the family, telling Ashputtle that she isn't, nor will she ever be, enough. Ashputtle will have to face, and transform, the consciousness of each member of the family within herself. The good news is, she won't do it alone. Ashputtle will be assisted every single step of the way.

Ashputtle's story is very alchemical in nature, since it has many motifs associated with the alchemical art. Alchemy reflects the old mystery religions, which were practiced during a time when the feminine, and feminine qualities, were valued. Alchemy is one of the compensatory links from the old religion to the present, and symbolically conveys the transformation of consciousness.

Alchemy, myths, and fairy tales, like the mystery tradition, emphasized the cyclical nature of unfolding, as opposed to a linear path. The alchemists believed in *kairos*, a Greek word meaning "at the right time," suggesting things happen at an appropriate moment and can't be rushed. In nature, a flower opens at the perfect moment. We have learned to believe more in an artificially constructed concept of time than in nature. In an alchemical perspective, life is allowed to unfold, and we don't force it to meet our will.

Truths such as, "as above, so below" and "as within, so without" are repeated throughout alchemical writings. The idea of a relationship between the inner and the outer rests on the assumption that what's within us is mirrored in the world around us. The "above" refers to the unseen, formless reality, and the "below" is the physical world. They are interconnected and influence each other. There are correspondences throughout all of nature, of which we are a part. We are affected by and influence all that is around and within us.

Jung's discovery was that the alchemical process and the movement of the psyche toward wholeness were the same. The alchemical transformation of base metals into gold was merely an outer process reflecting the alchemist's real interest, which was an inner transformation of consciousness. The alchemical writings and art were not literal, but symbolic—like dreams, myths, and fairy tales—which is why alchemical meanings are debated. The alchemists said they were transforming metals because searching for God within oneself could mean death for those who were discovered at that time. They were left alone with their vessels, since it was believed that what they were doing was impossible. Their alchemical art hid a secret.

Fairy tales can be perceived in a similar manner, as alchemical treatises in that they symbolically describe the process of transforming consciousness. They address the redemption of the feminine, as did alchemy. The feminine that needed redeemed was the soul that was lost, or trapped in matter, and required rescuing. These stories are also compensatory, addressing what's neglected by the current culture.

What is rejected and rests among the ashes in our story? Ashputtle, the young feminine, has been cast aside, is unvalued, unseen, and must be redeemed. She tends the fire like the ancient Roman Vestal Virgins, or priestesses, tended the sacred fires.[29] *Ashputtle's work, which she does while the others are distracted with the frivolity of the culture, may be perceived as a sacred task.*

Fire was important to the alchemists who said, "Take fire, or the quicklime of the sages, which is the vital fire of all trees, and therein doth God himself burn by divine love."[30] All is love and it is this divine love that compels everything to grow toward the light of truth. There is an energy that causes us to move toward greater consciousness. We seek to know and understand and live according to a higher ideal. If you follow your dreams, it becomes evident that there is something guiding us to an unknown destination. Dreams contain a wisdom beyond our own waking consciousness.

The fire of the sages can be seen in consciousness a conflict or a desire, which purifies. In the mysteries, the fertilizing power, or light, of the moon is in trees and is released, or awakened, through rubbing.[31] This speaks to the heat of friction as a transformative agent. That reflected light within trees is a burning love of the god/goddess that must be released. The friction, or rubbing, such as desire, can reveal the love and light of the divine that sleeps inside of us.

We can transform ourselves and release the love within, and our inner light, through a conscious engagement with the friction, rubbing, conflicts, or desires we experience in our lives. When we learn to sit with the discomfort that can arise when a typical response to a situation is thwarted, we transform the emotion in order for more light, peace, and love to emerge.

The fire can also be a passionate engagement with some creative activity. When we do what we love, we are immersed in the silence and stillness, which opens a healing channel for divine love to flow through us. That's why it feels so good to do things we really enjoy, like baking bread, tending a garden, making furniture, cutting the grass, or anything else that brings us into the moment and quiets the mind.

The solar masculine and fire is the opposite of the lunar feminine and water. The moon is a symbol associated with the feminine and the goddess. Venus, the goddess of love, was born from the foam of the sea. The ocean is intimately connected with the moon. As the moon waxes and wanes monthly, the tides ebb and flow. The moon also symbolizes the unconscious or watery emotion. Watery emotions, such as grief and sadness, are transformed as they are witnessed. We can sit with the waxing and waning of the emotions and develop a steady presence as they shift. The moon's phases are reflected in the tides as well as human emotions. Women also have lunar cycles such as menstruation and phases as they age from virgin, to mother, and then crone. Information and revelations of the unconscious have their own natural rhythm as well.

The alchemists began their work with lead, a base metal, the *prima materia* (primary material) that was transformed repeatedly to reach the final product of gold. In psychology, gold is the Divine Child, Christ, or the Self, which is what we are seeking. The *prima materia* in our story is Ashputtle's shadow, which is her victim and servant states of consciousness. Ashputtle sees herself through the eyes of her conditioning. She believes she is what others reflect, and have reflected, to her about who she is, and her value or lack thereof, which is the consciousness that's being transformed. She isn't who or what she's been told.

The alchemists believed that there was an original substance from which the world was created. In the alchemical process (and Biblically), the beginning is also perceived as the end. "In order for something to be transformed, it must first be reduced or returned to its original, undifferentiated state substance...primary matter."[32] Edinger associates this with Jesus' saying, "Unless you turn and become like children you will never enter the kingdom of heaven." (*Matthew* 18:3)[33]

The "child" is a state of consciousness you experience before all the conditioning about who you are, and what the world is, was set in place. When you return to that awareness, you become like a child and are born again into the kingdom of heaven. A child doesn't have the dualistic, jaded, judgmental, "I already know everything" mind of an adult. They don't have an adult's habituated approach to life. Life's initiatory tasks burn away the illusion of separation, multiplicity, and erroneous beliefs that conceal primary matter. This journey will reveal to consciousness an awareness of its own divinity.

Being Good

The story opens with the death of the archetypal good mother. Ashputtle's mother passes her legacy to her daughter when she tells her to be "good" on her deathbed. This type of comment from her mother, especially at this particular time, can be detrimental. The desire to please her mother means she'll often try to be good for her mother's sake. She may believe that if she's good enough her good mother will return. She may think good will come from being good, but as we have seen in the story, that's clearly not the case. When the outcome is contrary to what's expected, it leads to confusion for her. Despite this, Ashputtle continues being a good girl long after her mother dies.

Ashputtle's father remarries after the death of her mother. The stepmother and mother are two faces of one mother, which is also confusing for Ashputtle, because her mother was good but now is unkind. Ashputtle tries and tries to be good enough to meet the demands of the stepmother, in order to receive a loving response, but it doesn't come, since the good mother is dead. But, despite this, Ashputtle goes on trying.

What does it mean to be good? What do you do to be good, or to be perceived as such? Do you go in the opposite direction and rebel against what you are told? Or do you ignore yourself and cater to others? Often times something is sacrificed in either case. If you don't care about what others think about you, and go on your merry way following your heart, then you are on the right path.

The idea of being good can lead directly to victim consciousness: "I am good, I do everything right, I help others, I do what I am told, why don't I have what I want or need?" That's Ashputtle. That person over there does this and that wrong, they aren't good, they don't follow the rules, why do they get what they want and need? This is the stepmother and stepsisters. These beliefs come from the confusion the mother created in Ashputtle when she told her to "be good." Just be quiet, do what you are told, take care of the needs of others selflessly, be a servant, and continue to be kind even if others are mean to you. At least that's her interpretation of what she was told.

The belief in the necessity to "be good" hampers our freedom. If we are told that dancing is bad as a child, then to dance as an adult may constellate an inner voice that tells us that we're bad if we dance or it's not safe. That voice can regulate behavior and curb our ability to follow our hearts and do what we love.

Do you feel free to do what you want? It's not enough to just say you believe it. The question really is "Are you *doing* what you love?" Were you encouraged to follow your heart even if others didn't approve? If you were told to be good and that meant playing it small, ignoring yourself, your desires and needs, putting others first, being quiet, listening instead of speaking, etc., then what happens if you don't follow these rules?

The Stepmother and Sisters

Ashputtle weeps over the death of her mother, especially since she's been replaced with the terrible stepmother. The new mother has two daughters with white faces and black hearts. White and black are opposites, which means the daughters contain the opposites and duality. They represent black and white thinking—pure white faces on the outside and black hearts on the inside.

As described in an earlier chapter, doubling in a dream or story places the emphasis on the item that's doubled as an important factor for growth. This means issues of duality, or opposites, are of significance, in addition to any qualities the sisters carry. Here, the sisters are the "bad girls" and Ashputtle is the "good girl," which means these opposites will have to be brought to consciousness and integrated. All characters are aspects of the heroine.

The stepmother and daughters project the inadequate and rejected parts of themselves onto Ashputtle. The father doesn't defend or protect her at all, and so Ashputtle carries the family's shadow. She's the black sheep, and a victim of their unkind behavior. She takes care of all their needs and serves them.

Ashputtle's initiatory journey begins with the death of her mother. This marks the start of a descent into the underworld for her when the good mother is replaced with the negative mother. The stepmother is the critical, mean, rejecting, judging, inner or outer feminine. Nothing is ever good enough for her. She's the way she is because of the culture and her upbringing. She's never been good enough, which is so uncomfortable to accept that she projects it onto the easiest target—Ashputtle.

The stepmother doesn't know her own inner goodness and so when she sees it in Ashputtle, she rejects this young feminine. There is the inherent inner goodness and then there is the "be good," which we have been told. Being good means we do what others think is good and don't do what we've been told is bad and selfish. We introject the voices of the negative mother and sisters, who remind us that we aren't ever enough.

This negative inner mother, like the witch, is an inner voice that serves as a protective mechanism. It is developed in childhood to keep a child from experiencing the rejection of the mother, or other important figures. This inner character assesses everything in order to keep the child out of harm's way and to avoid incurring the mother's displeasure. This is the voice that encourages her to do things perfectly to make her mother happy, but alas nothing seems to work. Though that doesn't stop Ashputtle from continuing to try, and try, and try. She wants to win her stepmother's love and approval, or bring back the good mother. She doesn't realize neither are going to happen, which can lead to feelings of helplessness, fear, confusion, uncertainty, shame, and feelings of not being enough.

As an adult, this inner critic continues the commentary, which causes victim consciousness to arise. This consciousness causes an adult to continue to perceive himself as a victim, even when he isn't. Ashputtle is good, does what she's supposed to do, but that voice just won't stop with the criticism that it's not enough. And you know what? That's what life will reflect. This is what the alchemists realized, "as within, so without." She strives for ever greater levels of perfection outwardly, hoping to change the inner voice, and finally be enough.

The idea of "not enough" may not only apply to us but can also pervade our lives. Where else isn't there enough? Has it been projected onto other areas such as our creative endeavors, money, partner, time, love, energy, support, friends, family, material goods, neighbors, work, community, government, country, other countries, or the world? We can explore all of the areas of our lives to see where else this idea of inadequacy might be active.

Alchemical Implications

The *nigredo* is an initial blackening stage in the alchemical process. The sisters have black hearts, which means the heart needs to be transformed. The heart closes due to difficult conditions in early life and stays closed as those situations are repeated throughout life. These early situations, like Ashputtle's, create feelings of being unsafe, which causes the heart to retreat. The sisters, as the split-off aspects of Ashputtle, need to be brought to consciousness for her to release the love in her heart. We can see that there aren't many outlets for Ashputtle to open her heart, to give or receive love, once her mother is gone.

The sisters' faces are white. The second phase in the alchemical process is whitening, or *albedo*, which has to do with ash. Jung wrote about the importance of the ash by quoting the alchemical text *Rosarium philosophorum*, which says, "Despise not the ash, for it is the diadem of the heart, and the ash of things that endure."[34] Isn't this fascinating? The diadem, the crown of the heart is ash, which we thought had no value. Certainly, we see that *Ash*puttle isn't valued by her family, while her name also implies that she is someone who endures and does, in fact, have value.

This whitening can also refer to the wisdom received from life experiences. When we encounter a challenge and look at it, turn it over, sit with it, come to an understanding as to why it happened, and allow the wisdom inherent in the situation emerge, then we experience the whitening. This is the purification process in action, and it is purifying the heart, which will result in an unconditional love for all.

The second whitening phase refers to what remains once the purification of our consciousness is complete. This purification stage is one in which all that isn't essential is burned away. The ash remains at the end, which represents an experience of the Self, but not yet as an embodiment, which is the final stage of reddening.

The idea of the white face and black heart also echoes our "Psyche and Eros" story in which the people were worshipping surface beauty and missing the deeper beauty within. Our culture is like this in that there's a preoccupation with the superficial. The mean sisters then are an agent of whitening for Ashputtle. They assist in the burning away of any false ideas, any beliefs that keep her from seeing the love that's in all, and her erroneous perceptions about how the world works.

Projection

Fairy tales compensated for the loss of the divine feminine in Western Christianity and this story opens with the death of the mother. In a greater sense, it's "the" Mother, the goddess, love, and abundance that has largely disappeared from consciousness and is being brought back into awareness. The mother in fairy tales is usually dead, silent, or wounded and is often replaced with an evil stepmother, witch, or old woman. The divine feminine returns as we heal, transform, and reclaim our feminine.

When the divine feminine disappeared, women were devalued. We have to bring our culturally created fear-based beliefs, like not being enough, to consciousness. Of course, it's easy to say, but can be a challenge to live. *Ashputtle will have to know herself (and her worth), so fully that she can stand her ground and be empowered in the face of those who believe she's inadequate.* Remember the comment above about becoming like a child? Children come out of the womb believing they are loveable. It is their state of consciousness and then we are taught that we aren't enough by those around us.

The sister's black hearts suggest their hearts aren't open, nor can they love. This is obviously the case, since their behavior is wretched. Why are these girls like this? Well, let's take a look at their mother. Before Ashputtle came along, someone had to carry their mother's sense of inadequacy and the most likely choice would be them.

The stepmother projected her disowned qualities onto her daughters, and then, they project it onto Ashputtle. The sisters aren't much different from their mother. We receive the wounds of our family of origin; they are passed on to us for us to heal and to help us grow. All three of these figures in the story are critical and unkind. Their black hearts are inside, but what appears on the surface are white faces that show purity and goodness. Isn't that interesting? Ashputtle is beautiful, presented as pure and good, and inside she has something else going on, which is seen in the sisters. The sisters in a sense are Ashputtle's rejected critical nature, as is the stepmother. It goes both ways.

It's easy to project the shadow—the disowned aspects, onto these two sisters, and forget that it's another facet of the heroine. She has to reclaim this rejected quality and approach it with compassion. The story centers around Ashputtle as the main character, therefore, we would perceive the others as her disowned and projected qualities.

How does a critical nature serve us? It seeks to find what is wrong in order to correct it, which in this case, as has been previously stated, was to win the approval of the mother. It's to bring the good mother back, despite that impossibility. There are parts of us that exist beyond logic. If enough of the things that are wrong are found and resolved, then the mother would return, and things would improve. The inner critic is projected. If someone is critical of others, they are also critical of themselves, even though we can't see it. It's an attempt to feel, even for a moment, that they are enough. When we have compassion for this aspect of ourselves, we can transform it. *When we see that we are enough as we are, we can stop looking for what's wrong and needs to be healed, fixed, or perfected.*

If we view all of the characters in the story as conscious and unconscious aspects of the heroine, then she has repressed the sisters' part of herself. She can't consciously accept the stepsisters' behaviors as her own because her mother told her to be "good." She's so invested in being perceived as good that she can't accept anything that challenges this self-image. The disowned shadow aspects are split off and projected.

Ashputtle suffers from the actions of the sisters and stepmother. As we bring consciousness to those things that cause us to suffer, we transform them. Our experiences reflect our inner world. Therefore, that which appears in our lives tells us about our beliefs, expectations, and limitations.

Suffering Servant

What is the suffering about for Ashputtle? What are the stepmother and sisters saying and doing to her? They exclude her and won't let her sit with them for tea. Imagine, she works hard all morning and prepares the tea for her stepmother and sisters, while they socialize. She'd like a little spot of afternoon tea too but is told no, which feels like an abandonment that causes her to feel unworthy and isolated. This means Ashputtle is splitting off certain aspects of herself that feel unacceptable. She doesn't believe she deserves a break and to join the others, which is reflected in her having to work as they have their tea.

Ashputtle toils while the rest of the family relaxes and enjoys themselves. This is the crux of her story: she's treated as a servant, while the others are free to do as they please. She feels she must always work and take care of others to get her needs met, which never happens, and to win their approval, which never comes. We must transform the part of ourselves that believes we have to take care of others and ignores our own needs in the process.

When we *connect to our inner sense of freedom*, we can relax, be ourselves, and do what we want and love. When we feel safe, we can let go of control, trust that we are supported, and our needs will be met. In the beginning, the sisters and stepmother can do what *they* want and Ashputtle can't. They are the ones who appear to prevent her from being free, but they are inner aspects of her. She may serve others but resents them for it.

Ashputtle utilizes criticism to push away her feelings of unworthiness and resentment, which is why her sisters and stepmother are critical. She wears rags and is relegated to the kitchen to work, while the others wear fine dresses. *She has nothing and the others have what they want and need,* which puts her into victim consciousness. They make fun of her rags, which activates feelings of shame, inadequacy, and helplessness, since she can't do anything to change this. She can't express her anger toward them, because she's the good girl. There isn't anyone who intervenes or protects her with the father absent. Although, even when he's there, he either passively allows this behavior to continue or joins in. The actions of the stepmother and sisters can constellate a lot of emotion for Ashputtle. They create extra work for her just to be mean.

The sisters taunt Ashputtle, by putting peas and lentils into the ashes for her to separate. Initially, when the sisters do this, she picks the peas and lentils from the ashes herself. There are three items she separates, which are peas, lentils, and ashes. This is like a separation of mother, sisters, and Ashputtle. What is true and untrue? This sorting is a discernment process in which she utilizes her experiences to understand herself. Are they merely showing her what she believes about herself and the world? What needs to be separated to be seen? The way to tell if this situation is important to her growth is to see whether she gets activated by the event, which no doubt she does... who wouldn't? The emotion could be repressed though, which means she might have to depend on her dreams to let her know.

The ashes are what remains when a fire burns. The heat of the fire—emotional intensity—is what burns away what doesn't serve Ashputtle. The experiences with the stepmothers and sisters activate her in order to resolve the inner beliefs that are out of harmony with her true self. The separation is between what is true and what is untrue. They are whittling away at the beliefs she has about herself and the world that are inaccurate. This is a process that is increasing consciousness for our heroine.

If Ashputtle feels like a victim, angry, helpless, or any of the other highly charged emotions, then what she experiences is a result of her inner situation. When emotions are activated, it's an opportunity to examine what's happening. If her sisters or stepmother do something and she doesn't feel any discomfort, and isn't repressing anything, then it isn't a reflection of her beliefs. The repression can be tricky and dreams can help to reveal when repression is happening.

Separation

Ashputtle cooks, cleans, does the wash, and tends the fire, which means she is transforming her experiences, as these are all alchemical purification processes. She also carries the water, which means she has access to the spring, which is the source of life. She works with the duality of fire and water, which can be passion, desire, or anger, and grief. She cooks and washes those things that activate her. The fire may also consist of tending the inner fire of a creative passion, which is also healing, as was mentioned above. Tending the waters means to participate in activities that nourish the soul. These actions all transform consciousness. As we follow our hearts and do what we love, our consciousness changes. We free ourselves from restrictions as divine energy flows through us, and we are absorbed in something we love.

Ashputtle's activities ground and balance her, which complements the dualistic critical thinking of the sisters and stepmother, who are in the head. The cooking and cleaning puts Ashputtle into the body and the present moment. When the heart is closed, the head takes over. Normally, the mind sorts and separates the good from that which isn't useful, but here we have something different happening.

Ashputtle sits with her activating experiences and burns through them, until only the ash remains. We might initially think, as she separates the lentils from the ash, that she's extricating that which is edible and nourishing from that which isn't—since the ash is normally thrown away and the peas and lentils kept for a meal. It's as though she's dividing that which is beneficial from that which is useless. However, if we look deeper, from the alchemical perspective, we see that she's utilizing her experiences to transform herself. The peas and lentils can be changed by the fire and become ash, which means they were impermanent. Therefore, she's separating the impermanent peas and lentils from the permanent ash, which cannot be reduced any further.

She's seeking the greater truth of herself. The actions of her sisters and stepmother are the means by which she will discover her meaning and truth, what's permanent and impermanent within herself. The sisters' and stepmother's behaviors activate Ashputtle emotionally and the emotion transforms her when she engages with it consciously. These experiences are a gift as they reveal her beliefs to her and begin to create the space for her to see something deeper within herself. This is the beauty of sorting. That which is in the unconscious is pushed to the surface to be seen and burns to ash in the persistent heat of attention.

Separation (*separatio*) is another alchemical process. This is an early stage in alchemy in which the opposites are separated. The ancient alchemical document "The Emerald Tablet," recommends the separation of fire from earth, or spirit from matter. This is achieved by discerning the deeper truth, or meaning, of what happens. The matter is the body and spirit is the fire that clarifies creation. The fire burns through whatever isn't truth in the psyche by way of experience and emotion. Remember the previous comments about the fire emerging from the tree through rubbing? Spirit is being revealed through the friction of experience. Everything serves a purpose. Ashputtle is learning to see through her experiences to their deeper truths and to the light they contain. We reach that truth by peering into activating experiences patiently, until they reveal their hidden meaning.

The Outer and Inner

Instead of projecting onto others what she doesn't want to see in herself, Ashputtle has to see that the outer world is mirroring her inner condition, and then take back those projections. This conditioning hampers her awareness of who she really is, and it must be seen through in order to embody the Self. The process of separation is a realization that what's being met in the world is one's own beliefs. *Instead of pushing what is encountered away, rejecting it, being afraid, blaming, or resisting, it is approached with open curiosity to see what life is revealing that needs to be brought to awareness.* These opposites will be seen through to take the heroine beyond the dualistic black and white thinking associated with the sisters.

This dualistic thinking is judgment about what's encountered. We change that entirely. We stop pointing the finger of blame at others and *accept that everything that appears to us has something to do with our inner world.* Everything. We aren't victims of anything, even if we don't understand it. There isn't any need to be an aggressor either, because it all reflects us or has appeared for our growth. We can take responsibility for our lives when we understand that we aren't powerless, and everything has value. The ash isn't thrown away and the phoenix rises from the ashes. Whatever we transform brings us closer to the truth of our being. This is also called suffering. Whatever causes suffering can be transcended by seeing through it. When we finally see everything has value, there isn't any judgement because it all is in service of love and ultimately results in good. Even though at times it might not initially feel that way.

The sisters create more work for Ashputtle, but as aspects of the heroine, she creates more work for herself. Does she look for things to do to avoid her feelings? Do her fears of inadequacy cause her to do more work than she needs to? Is she being a perfectionist? Does she believe she has to do everything alone and can't ask for help because, well, who will help her anyway? There isn't anyone on her side and she feels isolated, which will continue to be her experience until she changes it inside. Her tasks are the path of her awakening.

She tends the hearth, which symbolizes the heart, and as we have seen with the sisters, that must be transformed. Any fear that causes the heart to close will have to be burned away. Ashputtle learns to tend the heart and heal it through love, and weeping, as in tears of grief.

Ashputtle rests on the hearth as well, since she doesn't have a bed. She's hidden in the kitchen and rests the heart of the house. The house is a symbol of the heroine and all that takes place there is within her. The good, kind, loving soul lives from the heart.

The Hazel Branch

The father first appears in the story when he's leaving for the fair. He asks the girls what they want him to bring back. The sisters want material things but Ashputtle, curiously, asks for a branch from the first tree that brushes her father's head on his way home.

Ashputtle's belief that she must be good to receive her mother's love means she denies her own wishes. She doesn't ask for anything of value, because she doesn't believe she deserves it. Since Ashputtle's desires are in the unconscious, she doesn't even know what they are. The tree branch is something that appears to have no value, as opposed to her sister's requests, which are things the culture says have value. She has to learn to ask for what she wants and needs. She must understand that she can provide for herself and receive what she desires. Her sisters are the part of her that is willing to ask for what they want. Then the other part of her denies this desire and only asks for a tree branch. This request for the branch though, small as it is, is a step in the right direction in her beginning to receive good.

The branch is something that is alive, natural, and can grow. It's a tree that can be planted, which will eventually produce, and continue to produce infinitely. She may not have consciously realized the value of what she asked for initially, but possibly on a subconscious level she chose what would most benefit her.

The father's hat is knocked off his head by a hazel branch, which indicates a shift from the head into the body and emotion. The hazel tree is used by water witches, or dowsers, to find water. They utilize a forked twig to locate underground streams, usually for a well. Ashputtle already knows how to tend the fire and here we have a link to the opposite, water. This is a way to find the nourishing hidden waters of life.

Ashputtle plants the hazel branch on her mother's grave and her tears cause it to grow. The roots are in "the Mother," which is the Great Mother, or the good mother. This earthy mother is loving, generous, and abundant. She's what is dead and missing from the story. This is the world which Ashputtle has been exiled from, since she lives in the stepmother's house now.

A tree symbolically connects the earth and heaven, its roots grow deep in the unseen, the dark earth, while its branches reach toward the light of heaven. A bird, which lives in the tree, also symbolizes the connection of heaven to earth. It's believed to be a creature that's able to deliver messages between the gods and humans. The bird is an embodiment of the mother spirit watching over Ashputtle.

As Ashputtle cries and allows her grief to flow, she will open her heart, become aware of what she wants, and begin to ask for it. At the same time, her roots and connection to the unseen will flourish as well. She's learning to depend more on the unseen inner world for her stability and comfort, than the seen physical world of form.

Transforming the Victim

Ashputtle usually feels like a victim and doesn't feel free. In general, she believes she can't have what she wants and doesn't normally bother to ask, since she probably wouldn't get it anyway. She isn't a victim in all aspects of her life, but other than receiving the branch, she doesn't see evidence that things are changing yet. The garden, where the hazel tree is planted, is a transitional space where things can grow. When we feel like victims in one area of our lives, it can feel as though it's global and permeates our entire life, when there are actually differences. We transform this consciousness of being a victim by challenging our habitual ways of thinking. We can look at the situations where things *are* working out, recognize things *are* changing even if it's only in small ways, and not break down into thinking everything is dire. This is a way to work with our thoughts when victim consciousness gets activated.

Victim consciousness is pervasive in our society in both men and women. We may carry this archetype without even realizing it, in most instances, and need to be really honest in order to free ourselves from it. When the victim archetype is activated, we often feel either a sense of helplessness and sadness, or frustration and anger, which then activates the warrior or aggressor archetypes. The sisters and stepmother carry the aggressor energy and Ashputtle the victim.

When we feel like we don't have the power to change a situation, the fear triggers feelings of being a victim. Instead of going into the head and going global with the idea, we can descend into the feeling and the body to explore the sensation. We can learn how to accept what's been triggered, and just *feel* the feelings of helplessness, frustration, shame, or whatever is constellated.

When victim consciousness is present, it can influence how we perceive life and how we relate to others. We may feel defensive, hesitant, and reluctant to interact. We can anticipate, possibly unconsciously, that we aren't safe, and then approach novel situations cautiously. If we've been hurt by someone before, we might protect ourselves from the possibility of being hurt by them again. We are guarded and on the lookout for signs that we need protection. We can even construct encounters with others, where we weren't victims, into stories in which we are. These stories may be entirely untrue. When we really look at what we are telling ourselves, we might discover that it's not what *actually* happened. This is where the old victim consciousness can begin to unravel.

If Ashputtle tells herself she *never* gets what she wants, that isn't true. If she's honest with herself, then she will see that the tide is turning. Initially, she didn't have anything, but the energy begins to shift when she asks for the tree branch, which she receives from her father. The grief she expresses at her mother's grave is opening her heart and will allow her to receive, if even in small ways. *She's learning how to trust again, which will happen before it shows up around her.* When she's not judging, she accepts and trusts that what is occurring is for her greater good. It's not just her grieving that changes things, but also the transformation of herself through her consciously engaging with her experiences. We know this is happening because the tree in the garden is growing.

Ashputtle has to learn to trust again, to value herself, stand up for what she wants, and believe she deserves good. She has to develop a healthy inner masculine to be in the world and to take action toward what she wants and needs. The weak passive absent father in her consciousness will have to be transformed. This new masculine won't be a defensive warrior who protects her from others, because, as we can see, there isn't anything to protect her from, since the outside mirrors her inner world. If she encounters something she doesn't like, she can look inside to change it within.

There are times when situations stop serving us, we outgrow them, and have to move on. When we are clear, we have the ability to discern such things, and can let go when we need to. If there's any uncertainty, then our dreams can provide assistance. There are two sides to the belief in what we deserve. Do we deserve something better and need to move on? Or, do we believe that no matter what situation we are in, it's never enough, and we always want something better?

The Invitation Arrives

The king represents the introduction of a healthy mature masculine father energy, but alas there's no mention of a queen, which means the mother is missing from this household as well. He organizes three days of celebration in order for the prince to find a new bride. It's interesting that the celebration is then referred to as a wedding in one version of the story. This is the beginning of the psyche's movement toward the union, or integration, of the masculine and feminine. These things happen in threes, and so it's three days of celebration, or three balls. Three is a number associated with transformation and rebirth.

Has a new masculine arrived? Look for evidence in your life. Is there a transformation underway for you or a union taking place in which you are uniting the feminine and masculine energies? What are your dreams saying? The dreams may show a male and female coming together but can also appear as things such as fire and water, squares and circles, or the sun and moon. What old ways are you being invited to step out and what new ways do you need to step into now? Are you listening to your intuition and taking action on what you are getting?

When the king's invitation arrives, the stepsisters excitedly begin to prepare for the celebration, with Ashputtle's assistance of course. She helps like a good girl, but weeps and begs her stepmother to go. This is the first time we hear of her crying about her situation, and these are the tears of a victim. She feels helpless to change this and feels like the stepmother has all the power. In this moment, she believes her freedom is in her stepmother's hands, since her stepmother is the one who has to grant permission, but now, at least Ashputtle knows what she wants and asks for it. *She persists in her desire to go and doesn't give up,* which means we are seeing a new tenacity in her. She isn't accepting her stepmother's rejection or resistance this time.

As a part of Ashputtle's own consciousness, the stepmother represents an inner conflict between the part of her that wants something and another part of her that believes she can't have it. What's keeping her from what she wants? It's Ashputtle herself, or the inner voice of the stepmother that says she can't do what she wants and always comes up with what appear to be valid reasons why not.

Ashputtle's Pattern

Her stepmother eventually relents and tells Ashputtle that she can go if she separates the lentils from the ashes in two hours. So, there's a glitch. Some condition must be met, to get what she wants. But, instead of falling into victim consciousness about it, Ashputtle recites a magical prayer asking for help, and this brings the birds to her aid, which is evidence of a change in her. She doesn't feel like she must complete this task alone, and in fact can't. The birds are a new aspect of consciousness that connects heaven and earth. This is an exercise that teaches Ashputtle how to join with the unseen, in terms of requesting assistance, to complete a task. She isn't in this alone anymore, but she can ask for help and receives it.

The stepmother is initiating Ashputtle, but not her own daughters. The daughters will follow in their mother's footsteps and remain in alignment with cultural beliefs, which means they aren't going to change. This can help us to see the wisdom in our challenges, which occur in order to facilitate our growth into greater consciousness.

The heroine is going through another round of separating the lentils from ashes, which was elaborated on previously as a separation of what's true from what's untrue, and the temporary from the permanent. What is it that remains unchanged throughout all experience?

Despite Ashputtle's successful completion of this task, her stepmother still refuses to let her go. She tells Ashputtle that she isn't enough, doesn't have the right clothes, is too dirty, can't dance, and everyone will laugh at her. She will be humiliated if she is *seen* because she's inadequate. Ashputtle has been ignored, rejected, and hidden in the kitchen for years. Now she wants to emerge and step out into the world, but she's afraid. The stepmother says, "You can't because you aren't enough." Remember this is a part of Ashputtle. She weeps out of sheer frustration. What does she need to do? Here is the demonstration of the good girl belief. Regardless of how often she meets the demands of the stepmother, it's just never enough to satisfy her.

The stepmother relents at Ashputtle's tears again and gives her another test. This time it's *two* bowls of lentils she must pick from the ash. If she meets *this* condition, *then* she'll be enough and can go.

Ashputtle again prays for assistance, and the birds appear to complete the task for her. She meets her stepmother's demands, but once again, the stepmother refuses to let her go, citing her inadequacies, and this time adding that they would be ashamed of her. Ashputtle's inner stepmother critical voice isn't giving up. Ashputtle is coming up against her own sense of inadequacy and we are watching the opposites play out: "I am enough, I am not enough, I am enough…" Then there's the "I can go, I can't go…" This can be exceedingly frustrating. "I can do this, I can't do this it's too hard," and sometimes we give up.

This is the manner of Ashputtle's conditioning. When she asks for what she wants, the answer she gets is no. So, she cries, and goes into victim mode, until the stepmother relents. The stepmother sets a new condition to be met in order to change the no to a yes. Ashputtle does it, the stepmother still says no, but now because Ashputtle is inherently not enough. She goes into victim mode again, the stepmother sets a more difficult task, which of course gets done, but it's still not enough.

When this pattern is inside, then it might play out as we're trying to emerge with, for example, a new online business doing what we love. The business is set up, but the sales just trickle in. Then we figure that we just need to advertise, but still that only yields a slight increase in business. The next idea of how to be seen more, succeed, and generate more interest is followed, but that also falls flat. Then another, and another, and another, but it never seems to be enough to get that business off the ground. What's felt? Frustration that it never seems to be enough to succeed. This is the outer world scenario of the stepmother and Ashputtle.

This pattern repeats over and over, and Ashputtle learns that no matter how much she tries, it's useless, because nothing changes, since she's inherently not good enough to get what she wants or needs. This becomes an inner belief about the way the world works. It's conditioned helplessness and victim consciousness. Others needs are met, and she can even be an agent of fulfillment for others, but her own needs remain ignored and unfulfilled.

This must be looked at deeply, since outer success can be a cover for true fulfillment. We can be very successful in the world, believe we are doing what we want, have convinced ourselves that our needs are being met, when our soul's *real* needs aren't being addressed. What do you *really* need in your life? Do you feel like you have the time, space, freedom, or finances to do it? Are you helping others achieve their goals and not living your dreams?

Voices of the stepsisters and stepmother must be brought to consciousness. To really transform a habit of consciousness, or way of being, we need to learn how to see it, feel it, and really bring it into our awareness. In order to change those voices, first they must be heard. Then the feelings associated with these inner voices must be felt, because normally, like the stepmother, the uncomfortable feelings are avoided and projected onto others. When the discomfort of inadequacy, or helplessness, is felt, it loses its power. The projection of not enough onto other people and things must be retracted. The projections of others' inadequacies onto us must be seen as well. The more these feelings are brought to consciousness, the less they influence and control us. When the belief changes, just as it did with victim consciousness, we are freer to act on our own impulses. In many instances, the erroneous ideas about our value or worthiness aren't true and are just a habit. Look inside and outside for evidence that you are enough. Peer deeply into yourself and feel this truth resonate within your cells.

The Prince Sees Ashputtle

The family leaves for the ball on the first day of the celebration and here we witness another change in Ashputtle. She doesn't cry, fall into victim consciousness, or feel sorry for herself, but instead, she takes action. Her stepmother's directive, about her not going to the ball, doesn't matter now. Ashputtle walks out to the tree and asks for a gold and silver dress with silver shoes. She knows, because of the past responses, that her request will be fulfilled by the tree and birds. Her faith in the good that's available to her grows stronger with each passing day.

The union of the silver and gold of the dress and shoes are an indication that the masculine and feminine are being united now. Gold is the alchemical opus, the Self, but symbolically gold is also associated with masculine, fire, or spirit. The silver is perceived as feminine and associated with the soul, moon, and water. They are opposites. Ashputtle asks the unseen realms for what she wants, receives it, and then moves forward.

On a practical level, a possible scenario for this union is as follows. We experience a challenge in life and get activated, since we don't know how to resolve it. If we sit quietly, until the difficult emotions pass and we feel calm, then a solution often comes. If the answer doesn't come immediately, usually we feel better and can let it go for the moment. The action that arises from a place of peace will come with a solid inner knowing and clarity. Once Ashputtle *knows* what to do, she does it.

We are witnessing her transformation from a victim to empowerment as Ashputtle links with a higher source of wisdom to achieve her dreams.

In her beautiful new dress, Ashputtle goes to the castle, which represents a new state of consciousness. It's such a significant change for her that those who know her don't even recognize her. They can't *see* her in this new role. This can be a bit of a challenge when those around us don't recognize that we have changed, and still perceive us as we used to be, but undaunted, like Ashputtle, we must persist.

At the ball, she dances only with the prince, and he, with her alone. Again, speaking of discernment, she knows her true masculine, focuses on the one, and doesn't get distracted by variety. Ashputtle and her new masculine keep their eye trained with devotion on the one thing that is desired. He's dedicated to her. This is important when moving out into the world from seclusion. She must not disperse her energies in too many directions but keep her attention on one activity at a time. Her emergence is a delicate process. Any step she takes in the direction of her dreams is action and intention toward what she wants.

When we connect with intuition, we may receive a constant stream of new ideas. This is one way of perceiving this commitment to only one other, like the Ashputtle and prince. We can start an idea file or journal of ideas, but remain focused on completing what we have started, even if we can only take small steps regularly, that's enough. Just remain dedicated to the dream and emerging as who you really are.

Ashputtle now recognizes what she wants and needs and responds appropriately. She's listening to herself and honoring her needs by taking action toward their manifestation. When she feels tired, she tells the prince that she wants to leave and prepares to go. He wants to escort her home, but she's not ready for that yet. Again, she knows and acts on her limitation in the moment. She's afraid to be fully known, or seen, and so runs away from the masculine when he wants to know more about her. She feels vulnerable and unsafe after the way her family has treated her. She's also not strong enough yet to reveal her new identity to her family and that's okay.

The prince follows Ashputtle home but loses sight of her as she slips into the dovecote, which is the home of the birds that have helped her. Doves and pigeons are associated with the feminine, mourning, water, and the soul. The dove is a symbol associated with peace and the Holy Spirit, which is the feminine aspect of the Christian Trinity. In some traditions, it is believed that the soul takes the form of a dove at death. We could perceive the Father as the king, the Mother in the symbol of doves, and the Child as Ashputtle and the prince combined. The Child represents the successful union of spirit and soul.

The castle is the king's house and the dovecote is the Mother's home. Here we can see the movement back and forth between the above and below, the inner and the outer. The castle and spirit represent the above, while the dovecote and the soul are the below, which means the embodiment. The birds, like the tree, unite the two. The prince is associated with spirit and above, while the princess represents the soul and below. Neither the above, nor the below, has a value judgment associated with them. The Father's house is spirit, the Mother's house is soul, and the two unite in the body.

First, we had the separation, in order to see what was what, and now we are working on the union. In alchemy, these unions are called *coniunctios*, which is the union of opposites that creates greater harmony. The outer conflicts create an inner peace as the stillness of spirit is being embodied. The first ball at the castle is the first *coniunctio*.

The prince is undaunted as Ashputtle escapes into the dovecote, because he knows what he wants and goes after it. He isn't passive like her father. The prince tells her father that the girl from the ball went into the dovecote, and the father breaks into it, but Ashputtle isn't there. In this *coniunctio*, the soul realizes it's not the body. The soul that was previously distracted by emotions, thoughts, ego, and the body, and thought *that* was who it was, now understands that it's something other than what was believed. This occurs as a direct encounter with the spirit inside, which is the stillness and silence within.

Sometimes, the soul may experience an earth-shattering surprise when it realizes it's not the ego/body, but it's the still silent void of spirit. This is a foundational shift when looking inside, like the father and prince peering into the dovecote, and seeing that there isn't any-*thing* there.

The prince and father don't find Ashputtle—the soul—in the dovecote. She escaped unnoticed, went back to the hearth, and put on her dirty clothes before being discovered. It's interesting that the father is the first one to get an inkling that the prince may be looking for Ashputtle. This indicates the old masculine is shifting his view of her, which can only happen when she changes her beliefs about herself. This dance with the masculine mirrors her shift toward the heart and greater love.

A back and forth motion between the opposites—the different aspects of Ashputtle's being— is the manner in which they are united. Head and heart, back and forth, spirit and soul, inner and outer, enough and not enough, back and forth. As she encounters new experiences in her life, she's trying to remain grounded in the truth and not get swayed by emotion or old beliefs. That's the soul identifying with spirit—the still inner silence— as who she is, as she walks through life. She's learning to courageously stand firm in unfamiliar situations and allow the emotions to arise, while staying rooted in her calm center, and witnessing the emotions as they pass. She isn't the emotions or thoughts that come and go, but she is the peaceful spirit within.

Ashputtle is dismantling her old beliefs about herself and building a new self upon the firm foundation of the unchangeable stillness of being. The dreams will reflect the back and forth, up and down, destruction and creation, black and white, as the opposites are united. This prepares our heroine for the next stage in the evolution of her consciousness.

Being Seen and Hiding

On the second day, Ashputtle doesn't even bother to ask her stepmother if she can go to the ball. She just waits for everyone to leave, goes to the garden, and asks the birds for what she wants. There's no point in wasting her time with her stepmother. Why? Because she now knows from experience that her stepmother is not in charge of her good, nor does she need the mother's permission to do what she wants. This is a big step in taking her power back and towards freedom. She can do what she wants to do. We can do what we want to do and our good does not depend on outer sources. This means the parent, corporation, boss, partner, spouse, government, or anyone, can't keep what we want and need from us. Ashputtle is receiving what she desires, just not through the old channels she used to believe were how her requests would be fulfilled.

The birds respond to Ashputtle by throwing down a new dress from the tree, and it's even more dazzling than it was the day before. She expects that good will come to her, because of her past experience with the birds, but this time it's even better. Imagine that. That she can ask for something, and not only is it not denied, but life is gifting her with more than she asks for. She's realizing that she deserves good and is opening more and more each day to receive greater abundance.

The prince is the first person in the story to see and value Ashputtle. He dances only with her at the second ball and everyone notices the beautiful young woman. When she gets weary and tells the prince she wants to leave, he follows her home again, but this time she sneaks away by climbing a pear tree in the garden.

Pear trees are associated with regeneration, the feminine, and as stated previously, unite the above and below, heaven and earth. The roots grow deep into the dark unseen realm and the branches stretch up into the sky. The tree represents creation, balance, and harmony. Pears indicate a fruition of the work she's been doing. Ashputtle is learning that she can meet her own needs now, with a little help from her friends, of course.

For the second time, the prince goes to the father, who again wonders if it's Ashputtle the prince is seeking. He chops down the pear tree with an axe, which is associated with cutting, and therefore discernment. Here we have an outer discernment taking place where before it was an inner one (with the tasks of separating the peas, lentils, and ashes, or the impermanent from the permanent in Ashputtle). This discernment is through the masculine axe now—the old and new masculine together—as they (as parts of her) attempt to understand the feminine. What is and isn't the truth of who she is?

The first masculine act of discernment occurred when they chopped down the dovecote, which is the manmade home of the birds. This is when the soul becomes aware of spirit. At this point, the stepmother is beginning to lose her power over Ashputtle, as Ashputtle realizes that something else is answering her requests. Her prayers are being heard by something that she can't see.

In this second masculine act of chopping down the pear tree, the separation of the above and below is in something that's a natural object. The masculine seeks to know what is the power that fulfills her wishes and what is her. This power is still projected out and needs to be realized as the action of divinity within herself.

Remember, initially it was her stepmother with the power, then the birds, and finally the tree. The power to answer requests and take care of her needs must be seen as within her and not some distant separate Father, which is giving her what she asks for, or not. Our world, our reality, is being created through the filter of us and we, through growing consciousness, are embodying more and more of spirit. In the second coniunctio we have the spirit and soul uniting with the body, as embodied spirit.

The tree was alchemically significant, as it contains the essence of the feminine. Therefore, cutting down the tree is searching for the feminine in matter or nature. The desire here is to assist the soul in her emergence from hiding. Where is she? The soul? The divine feminine? This is an inner search for the truth of her being.

Ashputtle moves further and further into her power. She vacillates between the opposites, as she learns to reside in her center—moving out and in, above and below. The world around her has less and less control over her. The trees and birds are above and below, the castle and Ashputtle's home are in and out. She is learning to stay out of the egoic sense of self and reside in the stability and clarity of self as Self, regardless of where she is and what she does. She isn't letting others define her, or basing her actions on their desires, but is learning to stay rooted in her Self—the transcendent aspect of her being.

Our dreams will reflect this back and forth experience and reveal where we are in the process. You will be going up and down stairs, high in a skyscraper, or riding on a plane that is ascending or descending. Then dreams of being on the ground, walking or moving through mazes, inside and outside, people will fall from above, and rise, say in a hot air balloon. There will be dreams of chaos and the changes will become clear as new behaviors are exhibited by you and others.

Ashputtle enjoys "being enough" at the ball, but then reverts to her old "not enough" self at home. The old self and old roles are more comfortable because they are familiar. The new roles may be uncomfortable because they are unfamiliar. As she repeatedly unites with the prince, she discerns what is her truth and what isn't. Ashputtle is attempting, through her experiences, to embody and live from her Self. That's what the discernment is about: discovering the ash, or what is permanent when all else is burned away by the alchemical fire. It is the union of the inner and outer, the above and below, as the old alchemical axiom suggests.

Then we reach day three, which is the magical number associated with rebirth. Ashputtle's dress is more beautiful than ever and now has golden slippers. Gold is the alchemical destination—the Self. Once again, the prince and Ashputtle only dance with each other. That is the dedication and focus they both need, in order to reach the destination.

Again, the same scenario repeats when Ashputtle is ready to go home, although now the prince is on to her and has a plan. Her left slipper comes off on the stairs, which the prince has had covered in pitch. Here again we see the downward movement as Ashputtle descends the stairs but loses her shoe as she moves back to the physical. The prince learns from the past and does something different this time. He hasn't been able to figure out who she is, and tries a new way to discern her true identity. Since she's missing the shoe, she can't emerge on her own now without the energy of the masculine. The girl who fits the shoe is the princess.

The Prince Finds Ashputtle

It's an interesting phrase: "whomever the shoe fits, will become the bride." It suggests that something more than looks will be required to fulfill the role of princess. Who can stand in these shoes? The prince knows he won't be able to discover who his future bride is merely by appearance. He needs to be clever to find the right woman to marry.

When he reaches Ashputtle's home, and the first stepsister privately tries on the shoe, her mother tells her to cut off her toe to fit into it. Then, the prince and sister leave together. They go out of the house and into the world. But this isn't the true and authentic feminine. This version of Ashputtle doesn't fit the role she was intended to fill, something has been cut away, and she's not in her wholeness. The cutting of the foot is a fear of "too muchness." The stepmother instructs her daughter to just cut off the part of herself that's too much, since she won't have to stand on her own anyway. Of course, that's not an empowered stance. These shoes, and the stepmother's beliefs, are too confining for this stepsister.

When rooted in the Self, there isn't any need to be special. Nor are there thoughts of too much or not enough. From this center, we realize that we are each a unique being and as such we are all enough as we are, despite the messages we might receive from the culture. As the opposite of "not enough," being enough in the world can feel like too much, especially if we're used to playing the role of not enough. There can be a fear of overwhelming others when we allow our gifts, our Self, and our full beauty to be seen. What if others think we are "too big for our britches"? Remember the stepmother said Ashputtle would be an embarrassment, so that belief may still be lurking in the dark corners of her unconscious. When we are used to being small, unseen, unheard, and ignored, then being seen and heard can challenge us and make us feel unsafe.

We can imagine this as Ashputtle, when it's time for her to leave the safety of what's familiar, sending her stepsister out instead of going herself. A false version of her goes with the prince, as the fullness of her true self remains hidden. The stepmother's voice is still telling her to tone it down, play smaller to be accepted, cut away something that's critical to her standing in her power. None of which is going to work. That's clear from the fact that this cutting away is a wound that causes her to bleed and renders her unable to stand up for herself. If she went out into the world like this, she would have to depend on others to fill her needs and take care of her.

Blood is alchemically about moving back into life. The blood of life. This is the third stage of the alchemical process and movement from the white, *albedo*, to the red, *rubedo*. The *albedo* is intellectual understanding, but *rubedo* is when we actually live the union in the world.

What does this look like? As an example, this book is read, and the ideas are understood; that's the whitening. But, when the book is read and the reader acts, looks at her own life, sees the parallels, and does what's suggested, it's the reddening and embodiment. I've seen this with spirituality before when seekers will read spiritual books and think they understand the concepts, then believe they are "spiritual." When it's suggested that the ideas must be *lived*, however, I've been met with blank stares of disbelief. Often, I'll see a response like, "Oh, but that's really hard." That's why it's the reddening and critical to transformation.

The sister's stockings are white, and the blood turns them red, which is another indication that the union of the masculine and feminine is happening. White is the *albedo*, spirit, wisdom and intellect, while the red, the *rubedo*, is the soul in the world. The birds, Ashputtle's allies in her awakening to her Self, are the discerning aspect here that reveals the sister's real identities. The birds say Ashputtle isn't emerging as her true self, something is still being hidden. This is about embodying what's been learned. It's about getting out of the head and into the body, and about being able to live our authentic selves in the world without having to diminish who we really are in order to be accepted.

Truth Revealed

When the prince and stepsister leave, the birds tell the prince that he isn't with the true princess, because she's bleeding on the shoe. Ashputtle doesn't feel safe to fully reveal herself yet. We must not rush this process, like the butterfly emerging from the chrysalis. The first three times Ashputtle goes to the ball—out into the world—she returns home of her own volition. This time, as the stepsister, the prince brings her back home. She went out for a brief time and ends up at home again. Patience is required to embody the Self in the world, since the emergence can take multiple attempts. It's like she's testing the waters as the sisters.

This whole scene then repeats with the second sister. Again, we see the doubling aspect, which suggests the importance of this action to the heroine's development. Ashputtle still feels as if she must diminish herself to be in the world, so she cuts away, at the insistence of the inner stepmother, another part of herself. This can also be perceived as a necessary cutting away of that which doesn't reflect her full truth.

After they leave the house the second time, again the prince turns his horse around when the birds reveal the second stepsister's true identity. The horse symbolizes power in the world. He brings the "false bride" home. The masculine can't unite with anyone other than the "true bride." She must be his equal, able to stand on her own, in order to feel it's safe enough to live her soul's truth. The masculine and feminine must be equal within, with no preference of one over the other. Ashputtle won't be in her full power until she allows her Self to be free. She must reclaim all of the discarded aspects of the feminine and be willing to live them in the world.

The prince returns to the house with the second stepsister and asks if there are any other daughters in the house. The father says no, only the servant. He actually refers to Ashputtle as, "the little kitchen drudge my dead wife left me." This old masculine aspect of the heroine still doesn't value her, but now he's being replaced by the prince—the new masculine—who is seeing with ever greater clarity and appreciates what the old masculine discards. The stepmother adds that she's too dirty to be seen. They are both—father and stepmother in the psyche—protesting at this point, saying she isn't *enough* to be the prince's bride. This is the inner conflicted dialogue that Ashputtle hears as she tries to leave her past behind. The beauty is that there's the new internal masculine voice of the prince. He has the horse, which means he has power, and is undaunted by the old parental voices. They don't have any power over the prince and can't influence him either. He ignores them and insists that he try the shoe on Ashputtle.

When he slips the shoe on her foot, he realizes that he has finally found his "True Bride!" He *sees* her and he *knows* her! She acknowledges her own value and understands her parent's limiting story about who she is really isn't true. Ashputtle knows that she's worthy of love and appreciation. She is love. Ashputtle sees her Self and awakens to her wholeness. The consciousness that is her truth is fully realized by her.

As they leave the old house, and state of consciousness, behind, Ashputtle and the prince ride together on one horse. The two doves fly to her and land, one on each of her shoulders. She now resides in the center as the center. The above and below, within and without, masculine and feminine united. She's enlightened and the consciousness of wholeness is embodied.

The doves also peck out the stepsisters' eyes, which means they are symbolically rendered incapable of seeing the world through eyes of judgment or duality. Their sight is transformed from an outer vision to an inner one, so that they may discern the deeper truth of situations. Ashputtle won't judge anything as good or bad, but she will see everything through the unitary eye of love, goodness, and truth.

There isn't anything in life for Ashputtle to either resist, or control, anymore. All that wasn't true for her has been cleared out of her consciousness, so she can live from her transcendent center, which is the truth of who she really is—the Self in wholeness. Ashputtle resides in a new state of consciousness now and takes on an entirely new role. She's able to stand in her power as the princess, and rule from a place of love, with heart, and in non-judgment. This is the True Bride united with the Prince, which is why they lived happily ever after.

CHAPTER

Five

The Handless Maiden: The Gift of Sacrifice

There once was a poor miller walking through the forest. He met an old man he'd never seen before who said he would trade him riches for what was behind his mill. The miller knew the only thing behind the mill was an old apple tree, so he agreed to the deal. The stranger said he would return in three years and take what was his.

The miller went home and found his wife waiting for him. She asked what he had done, since all of the drawers and chests were full of riches. He told her about his bargain with the old man and she was aghast. She said their daughter was sweeping behind the barn and that he had made a pact with the devil.

Three years later, on the appointed day, the daughter washed up, drew a circle around herself, and waited for the devil to come. He was angry when he arrived because she had cleaned herself and so he was powerless over her. The devil arrived again the next morning but couldn't get near her because she had cried on her hands and they were clean. He angrily ordered the miller to chop off her hands. The miller was horrified by the request, but the devil threatened to kill him instead.

The miller apologized to his daughter for what he was about to do. She held out her hands and he chopped them off. She cried on the stumps so hard that she washed them clean and the devil wasn't able get her on the third day either, which meant she was free. The miller said he would care for her, since she was the reason he received all the wealth, but she refused. Her parents tied her arms behind her the next day and she left home.

She was hungry from walking all day and ate a pear that was hanging from a tree in the king's orchard. The king counted his pears the next morning and asked the gardener about the missing pear. The gardener said that an angel had helped a spirit cross the moat and that the spirit had eaten the pear. The king replied that he would watch with the gardener that night.

The king, his priest, and the gardener waited in the dark and watched as the girl ate another pear. The priest asked her if she was of this world or the spirit world and she responded that she had been forsaken by all but God. The king took the beautiful girl as his wife and had silver hands made for her.

A year later the king went off to war and left his mother to care for the queen. The mother sent word to the king when the queen gave birth to a boy. But the messenger fell asleep at the creek and the devil changed the message to say that the baby was not of this world. The king replied to his mother to take care of them, but again, the devil changed the message when the messenger fell asleep, ordering the mother to kill the queen and child.

The old mother couldn't bring herself to have them killed, so she bound the baby to the queen's back and told her to leave and never return. The queen went to the forest, prayed for assistance, and an angel appeared and led her to a cottage. The sign over the door read, "All are welcome." They were greeted at the door by an angel who cared for the queen and her child for seven years, during which time her hands grew back.

When the king returned from the war, he asked his mother where the queen and his son were. She told him they had been killed, but when she saw his anguish, she admitted to merely sending them away. The king vowed not to eat or drink for as long as it took to find them.

The king searched for seven years before he discovered the cottage in the forest. He went inside, declined the angel's offer of food and drink, and laid down on a bench to rest. He covered his face with his handkerchief.

The angel went into the next room and informed the queen and her son that her husband had come. When they entered the room and saw the king, the boy couldn't believe the wild man was his father, since the queen had told him his father was in heaven. The king didn't believe she was the queen either, since she had hands, but the angel retrieved the silver hands from the other room and the king knew then that it was truly his wife and son.

He took them back to the castle and they lived happily ever after.

Introduction

This is a rich fairy tale, since it provides details regarding the transformation of both the masculine and feminine. The masculine plays a significant role in this story, which allows us to follow his development in greater detail. His transformation is critically tied to the heroine's and they depend on each other to evolve.

The Handless Maiden's father sacrifices her, and her hands specifically, to the devil for financial gain. Hands are required to live, to create, receive,

---

* Full story in Manheim's *Grimms' Tales for Young and Old*

and give. She will need to learn how to work with the unseen realms to have her needs met, since they can't be met in the typical way. The manner in which we have been taught to care for ourselves, or get our needs met, isn't available to the heroine, and so she's forced to learn a new way of being in the world. Her situation requires her to depend on the Universe for the essentials she needs to live.

The Handless Maiden will heal her fear of not being safe, which has led to poverty consciousness in her family of origin. She will learn to surrender, to let go of control, and to trust life, in order to be able to receive true abundance and know her needs will always be met.

A Poor Family

The father is a woodchopper and mills wood for a living. Since he can't provide adequately for his family, they are poor. It is his desire for wealth that makes him susceptible to deception. He doesn't see the value of what he has—in the apple tree and young feminine—and so loses it in an exchange for what doesn't have any real value in terms of life.

As he walks along one day, an old man approaches him and wants to give the miller riches for what is behind the mill. The father assumes he's talking about the old apple tree. It seems like the miller would know the value of an apple tree, since trees are the source of his livelihood, but his actions don't reflect that awareness. This tells us something is amiss in consciousness. You would think the miller might realize it's unusual for the old man to want to trade, or buy, the apple tree for all that money, but he doesn't. His instinct is off. He doesn't see that he needs to be cautious in this situation, nor does he sense the wrongness of the transaction.

All he must give is an old tree, which doesn't have that much value to him anyway, to receive all these riches? *What's the hidden cost of this bargain? What is he sacrificing that he initially believed didn't have value?* These are very important questions. Have we agreed to something that seems like a bargain, that's in our favor, while ignoring the real cost? Like possibly taking a job for the money, meanwhile the cost is to our well-being? Or deciding to stay in a situation that doesn't honor the deeper needs of our soul, because it's easier, cheaper, someone else wants to, or we feel like we don't have any other choice?

The Apple Tree

The apple tree represents generativity, life, abundance, awareness, as well as food for nourishment and life. It symbolizes knowledge, wisdom, coming to consciousness in the Garden of Eden, and also the feminine, the mother, and that which unites heaven and earth.

As long as they have the apple tree, the family has an abundant food source, but obviously the father doesn't see it that way. The tree demonstrates the cycles of life, which are feminine. The tree is like the moon that waxes and wanes. In spring the tree buds, blooms, and the fruits come into fullness in summer. Then the tree releases all that it holds in the fall and becomes barren in the winter. The cyclical nature of the tree reflects the cyclical nature of life. The father doesn't know how to move through the phases of life and isn't tapped into the abundance that is natural and available.

When we have access to the Tree, we are connected to the source of life and abundance. We are then open to the constant stream of the gifts being offered to us. The gifts that are received are timely and are a response to the needs of the culture. This is a state of consciousness that doesn't depend on externals but is solely rooted within. Then our well-being isn't contingent upon what's happening in the culture.

This family doesn't recognize the gift that they have available to them in the tree. They are, and probably have been for a long time, stuck in the barrenness of winter, since they are so poor. Barrenness is created by an old patriarchal mindset that sacrifices the feminine for the masculine. There is too much activity, mind, lack consciousness, controlling, and doing, at the expense of being, feeling, instinct, creating, contentment, sharing, receiving, and knowing.

The tree represents wholeness and abundance. It is generative in that it contains the fruit, which provides seeds for more trees. The tree stands in wholeness, rooted in the earth, and it contains all it needs to create that which it was made to produce. The devil breaks down that sense of wholeness and thrives in an environment of not enough. Since we have the devil and the apple tree, which are significant symbols in Christianity, it would be remiss to not address this from that angle.

We can look at the biblical creation story symbolically, like a fairy tale. The story says that Adam was alone and lonely in the Garden, and so, as he slept, God took his rib and made Eve. They lived in the Garden where all of their needs were met. Then one day, a serpent (devil) came along and tempted Eve by making her believe that something was missing, which could be gained by a bite of the fruit. They ate the fruit of the tree of knowledge of good and evil, which means duality, and awakened to separation. The serpent awakened in them an awareness of the sense of inadequacy and inequality that was unconscious. This is when they began to hide parts of themselves and were booted from the Garden to toil in order to get their needs met.

This story is usually explained as Adam and Eve were in the Garden, where all was going perfectly well, and then the serpent showed up. But, in my Bible, it says that Adam was lonely *before* Eve was created. If everything was so very hunky dory in the Garden, and all of Adam's needs were met, then there wouldn't have been the need for God to create Eve. Lonely means something is missing.

I don't want to digress too much into this story, but the point here is that things were out of whack *before* the snake appeared. We might say the snake went to Eve because she was open to listening and was *willing* to break the rules, to learn the truth, which was that things weren't what they thought they were. They had already fallen, since when Adam was lonely, Eve was created from Adam's rib, which somehow made her less than him, since she was referred to as his *helper*. She was created when he was asleep, which symbolically means he was unconscious, and he wasn't aware of how she was created. There were also rules in the Garden, which they *had* to follow, or they'd be punished, and that means they weren't free. God was in control, separate from them, and superior. All of which relates to our story of "The Handless Maiden." Why? Because in Western culture, which includes these fairy tales, we are steeped in the consciousness of the Christian story.

There wasn't equality in the Garden between Adam and Eve, or between God and them, and the family in our story were out of the Garden, since they lived in lack, limitation, and poverty consciousness. Since the daughter was sacrificed for wealth, she had to find her value within and reconnect to her inner power, which is God. That's what it means to be in the Garden, walking with God, as Jesus said, "I and my Father are One."

The miller's family lived in poverty, since they had lost contact with true abundance, in which needs are fulfilled easily and effortlessly. This abundance is not money-based, as we can see, because the miller traded his daughter for riches. It's the recovery of the feminine that will return us to true wealth. "The Handless Maiden" story will show us how to resolve this fall, that has actually only happened in consciousness.

The apple and tree represent an awakening in consciousness, and the feminine is related to the tree, which the devil knows. This is where the Maiden's family enters. They are in the toiling stage, having left the Garden, and now live in lack and separation. They don't realize the value of the tree, or the young feminine, as it relates to abundance and wholeness. These are states of consciousness that are not achieved by toiling in the world but must be found within and through the soul. The Maiden's journey will be her attempt to re-enter the Garden of wholeness, where she (the soul), reunites with the masculine (spirit), becoming One, and reaching Christ consciousness.

This expansion on the meaning of the apple tree deepens our understanding of the implications of this tree and the loss of the feminine to us. It relates to the evolution of our consciousness as we journey through life. Life is cyclical: we begin in wholeness, then the ego is created, the fall occurs, and that's the separation, but then (if we are lucky) we make the journey back to an awareness of the ever-present wholeness. We live in the belief of separation and seek to reunite, even though we might not be aware of that desire. Many of the significant stories that we hear are symbolically similar once we move beyond a superficial literal reading, which means that even religious stories can be perceived symbolically as pertaining to the evolution of the soul.

An Obedient Daughter

The father, as one aspect of the masculine, doesn't value the young feminine. Another aspect is the devil, who will give the miller all the money he wants for his daughter. We can read this as the devil essentially saying, "Here, take all of these riches, which is what you want, and give me what you don't want or value." The devil represents an egoic masculine that brings the unconscious bargain, which was made and not realized, into consciousness. Just like in the Garden, the sacrifice of the Maiden had already been made, the devil just brings it to consciousness. He shows just how far the father is willing to go for wealth. Repeatedly, throughout the story, he serves as a catalyst for the daughter's transformation and growth, revealing what's unconscious, just as the serpent did.

The family's poverty consciousness causes the father to make bad decisions. He sacrifices his daughter out of ignorance because he thinks he's giving the devil a worthless apple tree, without realizing the devil really wants his daughter. Even though the father doesn't trade her for money on purpose, he does it unconsciously, which means he's unaware of his motivations. How could he not see that something is amiss? He may not realize what he's done, but the mother immediately and instinctively knows.

The mother, the older feminine, has a certain amount of awareness. Because the deal is so out of balance, she recognizes the devil is behind this transaction. The Maiden's mother is horrified at the sacrifice of their young daughter but is helpless to do anything about it. Since the deal has already been made, it's too late. She's a presence in consciousness, and as such, is evidence that a small remnant of instinctual awareness remains, but she's still powerless to free her daughter from the devil. Or is that the origin of the trace of instinct in the Maiden that keeps her out of the clutches of the devil?

Once the deal is made, the devil tells the miller that he will return in three years to collect what is his. As I've described in earlier chapters, the number three is associated with transformation. It's the third thing that is born out of the union of opposites when we hold the tension of the two. The Maiden needs three years to integrate the implications of this new masculine's emergence into consciousness and to become aware of the truth of her family. She's learning that the masculine that values her, the devil, is another aspect of her own consciousness that is feared by society. She's afraid of him too. The story doesn't elaborate on what the devil's plan was for her, but we sense that whatever it was it would be unpleasant. If he took her to his home in the underworld, she would go into the unconscious.

The good daughter is small, quiet, obedient, and subservient. She's been taught to serve, care for, and sacrifice herself for others. This out-of-balance feminine doesn't stand up for herself, speak up, disturb the peace, listen to her inner knowing, or follow her heart and dreams, because she doesn't think they matter. But the obedient daughter in the psyche is starting to change. The fact that the young feminine has been sacrificed for material gain is now being brought to light.

This may surface in our lives as a growing unwillingness to work just for money, and as the desire for something more meaningful…much more. It can arise as a refusal to follow the old masculine at the expense of the young feminine and as a shift to involve the inner feminine in decisions about what's to be done. What will honor the soul? What feels right? This means opening to a greater consciousness that's unseen and learning to trust it as a source and guide. It means seeing and valuing the feminine, soul, spirit, the cyclical flow of life, and consciousness.

The Rejected Masculine

The anti-Christ, or devil, resides in hell, which is at the center of the earth, underground, unseen, and in a world of fire. The devil is the rejected religious figure associated with sin and the flesh, and the soul resides within the body, which walks upon the earth. In religion, the devil is perceived as the one who tempts the soul to do things that are considered bad. So, he could be blamed for the father's behavior, and yet, we see the daughter being sacrificed repeatedly, in story after story. Often, it's the goddess, in her various disguises, that facilitates the growth of consciousness in the daughter. In this story though, it's the devil who's interested in the feminine—the soul, the body, what's hidden, what's rejected—and ultimately is increasing awareness.

Deferring to the devil is a way to avoid responsibility, as in, "the devil made me do it," which makes a person powerless. In Christianity, he's the reason why good people do things that are deemed bad. He causes bad things to happen to good people as in the Biblical story of Job. But the devil character in a story tests someone to see what's valued more, the material or the spiritual, as with the Maiden's father, or Jesus in the wilderness. We could say the father failed the temptation and Jesus didn't succumb to the devil's antics.

In the psyche, the devil is associated with aspects of the feminine that are also rejected by society. In religion, a female is sometimes perceived as a temptress, and is associated with the flesh, body, soul, darkness, evil, and this world. She's the one to blame for the fall of mankind, which of course is only one outdated interpretation of that story. The devil is unlike Jesus who is traditionally associated with spirit, heaven, light, and good. It's easy to accept credit for the good things we do, but we can hide and project what we perceive to be unworthy aspects of us.

The devil is a projection of what's rejected in us and in society. He is a masculine that is associated with the body, flesh, passion, feeling, sensuality, indulgence, and desire. Spirit is believed to be pure, above it all, apart from the flesh, celibate, and is up, as in heaven, while the devil is conceived of as here on earth, or below. This is an example of the opposites that must be united for something new to emerge, which is an embodied spirituality.

The goddess has been hidden in the unconscious and rejected, like the devil, and the young feminine. She is a divine figure in stories who helps and challenges the heroine as she moves into greater awareness. The role of divine initiator into higher consciousness is filled by the goddess. In this story, the devil is the one to move the heroine forward as he brings the father's ineptitude to consciousness. The devil knows it's time for the daughter to leave home and the old parental consciousness. He's the catalyst for that to happen, and yet, the answer isn't for her to go with him, since he's fear-based like her father. The devil rejects the Maiden's purity, which is why he can't take her when she's clean.

Purification

The daughter is traded for wealth and sacrificed for material gain. True abundance, however, includes the young feminine and doesn't exclude her. Real abundance isn't based on materially-based wealth, but on soul-based wealth. This is lasting fulfillment that doesn't depend on financial circumstances, but the state of the soul.

The young feminine feels the consequences of our actions. She's the internal compass that perceives what's right and wrong. She's empathetic toward others and not immune to them, because she knows that all of life is interconnected. She's not about me, me, me, and more, more, more, but is content and always has *enough* to share. The young feminine knows the deeper meaning of life and understands the rhythms and cycles of the natural world. She isn't afraid of life but embraces all of it.

In the current paradigms of how we live our lives though, many of these qualities of the young feminine are out of reach. These parts of us can get buried and seem unrealistic from a conditioned vantage point. Her abilities can seem impossible to embody and make us feel vulnerable to even consider them, which is why a paradigm shift is required in order to help free her to live as herself in the world. Fortunately, our story will help us get there too.

The Maiden purifies herself during those three years of waiting. She clears the old beliefs that created this situation. She weeps at the implications of being sacrificed by her own father. This emotional purification is represented as an inner cleansing by tears. We cry at the loss of the young feminine in ourselves. We mourn how we sacrificed our feminine for patriarchal values and material gain. When the devil appears, the Maiden has bathed and drawn a circle around herself.

The circle is a symbol of wholeness and a transcendent being. Because the Maiden is now purified of her feelings of not being or having enough, she has discovered an innate sense of wholeness. As such, nothing is missing. *She is and has enough, unlike her father. The fear of the devil and ideas of inadequacy can't touch her in this conscious state of wholeness.* He can't tempt her as he did her father, because she isn't in lack consciousness, which means she's immune to him. She remains stable in the face of his belief that he can take her.

The devil his instructed the miller to not let the Maiden wash, because he can't touch her if she's clean. This is an ongoing purification of the fear of this wounded masculine who thrives on beliefs of inadequacy. There is this sense of her, standing in the circle, still, at peace, calmly waiting for him to arrive. The mind is quiet, when it isn't, this is the tempter. That's the part of us that taunts us and makes us afraid. It's what causes us to do what we don't want to do. Hurry and do something now! This is what's being cleansed and purified. When the mind doesn't control us, we aren't identified with the fear it generates, and it loses its power over us. When her mind is calm, clarity comes, and along with it, the realization that *he has no power over her.* The mind is powerless and can't touch her. *Her* fearful thoughts are losing their power and control over her behavior.

When Jesus was in the desert, and Buddha sat under the Bodhi tree, they were tempted by demons and Satan. These tempters are the mind that comes at us with thoughts in the darkness of night and creates the fears that torment us. The mind doesn't have to control us. Who we truly are is not our thoughts. The mind can't disturb the soul, which shines through when there is inner quiet. When we stop following old beliefs, fears may arise that can challenge us. If we remain still, and witness the feelings and thoughts moving past us like clouds in the sky, and don't identify with them, then we can grow stronger, clearer, and more stable. When we purify ourselves, we aren't tempted by our thoughts or emotions to react to them out of fear.

The second time the devil appears to take her away, the Maiden has cried on her hands, which has cleansed and purified them. He still can't touch her and has no power over her. She witnesses the thoughts that arise without moving toward or away from them. She doesn't resist what comes up or follow it, but watches. *The devil—the mind—comes to take her away from a greater truth and she remains still, standing, unmovable, right where she is. The mind can't knock her off her center, since she has rooted herself in stillness and silence, which is the truth of her being.*

Losing Her Hands

On the second day, since he can't take her again because of her cleaned hands, the devil tells the miller to chop his daughter's hands off. When the miller protests, the devil says that he will take the father if he doesn't comply. There's a bit of wrangling in the psyche between these two masculine energies. The father ends up agreeing to cut off the Maiden's hands because he's afraid of the devil and doesn't want to die. The father consciousness can't stand up to the devil, since the devil has more power in the psyche than the father. As in other tales we've already discussed, we see another situation in which the father can't protect his daughter.

The young feminine vacillates between being rooted in stillness and being caught in the mind's chatter, which is active. The father wouldn't have to cut her hands off, if she was able to hold on to the inner quiet. Her willingness to sacrifice herself, in order to save her father, is something we have seen before. This self-sacrifice means she's in victim consciousness, which stems from a sense of inadequacy. This devil masculine in her own psyche prompts her to sacrifice herself to protect others. It's the devil's idea to cut off her hands, the Maiden agrees, and it's the father's task to do it. The fear-based mind still controls what happens, to some degree, and she's affected by it.

The old consciousness in the family is based in poverty and the devil brings to awareness the extent to which the old masculine consciousness is willing to go for material gain or to protect himself. The father will sell what he can't see—the apple tree and what it represents, which is the daughter and the soul. The old father seeks control. What are we selling of ourselves for material gain? Is the soul being considered or sacrificed?

Fortunately, the feminine isn't entirely sacrificed here, but only her hands. This puts her into a position of being unable to defend and protect herself, or to create. She can't take care of others now, but has to rely on them for her wellbeing, which is receiving instead of sacrificing and giving. The devil's final request leaves her with no choice, other than to depart from the old father and mother consciousness. It doesn't serve her and she must leave it behind. She has an experience of wholeness in order to leave behind the old psychic state, but now her hands are missing, and she isn't "whole."

The Maiden's hands are associated with touch, feeling, sensing, and are a means to connect with others. Hands give her a sense of control and without them, she has to surrender control and learn to trust others. She can't protect and defend herself if she feels threatened. Her family has problems with abundance, receiving, and protection, and is unaware of the true goodness of life. They are afraid, in scarcity consciousness, and don't recognize the natural way of a soul-based abundance. The Maiden is in a situation in which she's at the mercy of others and needs to be taken care of. She's forced into a state of total surrender to life and can't control anything now.

She cries on the stumps when her father chops off her hands. Her tears are over the loss of her parents, who she previously thought of as different than what she now sees. She mourns the realization of her lack of value and their inability to protect her. When the devil arrives on the third day, he still can't touch her, which means she's free. He loses…this round anyway. Her father says he will take care of her, since now he has large amounts of money from sacrificing her, but she refuses his offer.

The Maiden may appear to be a victim of the father and devil, but this is a crucial step to her learning a new way of being in the world. In the past, she was helping, sacrificing, and caring for her parents, but now she absolutely cannot do anything for herself. She is forced to surrender her care and well-being to a higher power. This is the same higher power that cares for the birds and the bees, the flowers and the trees.

She willingly agreed to sacrifice her hands and then leaves the parents' house. In order to embody wholeness, she can't remain in an old state of consciousness in which she's not protected or valued, is exploited for money, and where there's a belief in lack and limitation. She's giving up her old life and old way of perceiving because they are limiting. What's really being sacrificed is the parental consciousness of not enough and inadequacy, in exchange for the possibility of wholeness, freedom, and living in an entirely new way.

What beliefs do we need to leave behind that are limiting? Are we choosing financial security over the heart? Are we afraid to follow the heart because we can't see how we will support ourselves? Are we afraid to surrender control and listen to the still small voice inside because it doesn't feel safe?

Leaving Home

Leaving the parents' house is a type of death that correlates with an expansion in consciousness. The Maiden can't remain a child and live with them for the rest of her life, literally or psychologically. She surrenders control, leaving her home and her parents with her arms tied behind her back. Hands being "tied behind the back" is a saying that means there isn't anything that can be done about the situation. It can't be changed. And so, she departs at sunrise, which symbolizes new awareness and the dawn of a new day.

The Maiden will now have to surrender control in all areas of life. It doesn't mean she does nothing or accepts all circumstances as they are, she just sees how she has sought to control things in the past and stops acting in those ways. She will have to refrain from manipulating situations in order to protect herself and keep from being hurt. The mind *expects* the past to repeat itself, interprets experiences based on what has occurred previously, and then acts accordingly. This is all under the erroneous assumption that it's seeing what's happening accurately.

As she stops telling herself the same old stories from the past, she begins to see with new eyes. This is easier to do in a place that's unfamiliar, but many times even in those situations, the mind searches for a past experience that is similar to the present one, and then assumes they are the same. It will be necessary for her to *look and see* what's actually happening in the moment, which her father didn't do. He thought he knew what was behind the mill, based on his past experience. He didn't take the time to look and see what was there and erroneously assumed he knew.

There can be a resistance to what is, which means accepting the situation as it is, and then surrendering to it. The mind is the part of us that says, "No, this is wrong and shouldn't be this way." When the Maiden opens to the moment and accepts what's happening, a new solution arises, which is to leave. It's as simple as that. A new response to an old pattern comes into consciousness. She realizes that this old way of being—sacrificing the feminine—no longer serves her, and a new response constellates a fresh opportunity. This is the way to break old patterns of behavior. She isn't a victim but stands in her center and responds to what happens. She knows what to do and does it. She leaves and surrenders her fate to Providence, letting nature provide.

The Pear Orchard

The Maiden arrives at a pear orchard in the moonlight, which means the nourishment the feminine needs is in the dark unconscious. She can't reach the orchard because a stream blocks her way. Previously, the Maiden faced her thoughts and feelings, which helped free her from the devil, but now they are a hindrance. The stream of emotion blocks the way to nourishment. This situation is asking for a new response from her. She must let go of the old way of getting caught up in emotion that keeps her from moving forward and being nourished. She must peer beyond these emotions to something deeper.

This orchard is protected, which means that there's an understanding in the psyche now of the fruit trees value. The father didn't see it, but the new conscious masculine in the psyche does. This is a significant change that was preceded by the appearance of the devil. He was a transition from the father to this new masculine, although he had the potential to pull her into the unconscious with him. That didn't happen and now there's the possibility for greater consciousness.

In order to reach the nourishment she needs, the Maiden needs to learn how to move past the emotion associated with the stream, since her way is blocked by it. Emotion purifies but can also derail her if she gets stuck in it. The emotions are fed by the mind. If the mind is quiet, then the emotions are quiet.

The Handless Maiden prays, asks for what she needs, and help arrives. She surrenders to the situation, requests help, and waits for the response. She doesn't, and can't, grasp what she needs, but merely opens to receive. Her prayer is answered by an angel who helps her cross the stream. The Maiden calms her emotions by connecting with a divine feminine angelic presence that represents the spirit within her. This heavenly angel is the opposite of the devil from the underworld. This aspect of her has a non-physical power that transcends the material and assists her in accomplishing tasks without using physical hands.

This is a change in consciousness from the father. The father chops wood with his hands to make money and then he chops off her hands for money. She shifts to a new consciousness by asking and receiving help not from an outer, but an inner source. She receives the pear from the tree of abundance and is nourished. She gets a taste of greater awareness. This feminine angel resides beyond the emotions and thoughts.

In a practical sense, when we face a challenge and can't see how to go forward, we can get caught up in the emotions of frustration, anger, grief, sadness, and feelings of being a victim. When we stop to feel our feelings, we can sometimes experience an intense desire to act and do anything to avoid the discomfort of not knowing what to do. But if we can stay with the intensity of the compulsion to do something, anything, and sit with not knowing, it will pass, and peace (the angel) will come. We can then calmly take action once we know what to do from that place of peace, and easily move forward.

The Maiden's inability to fulfill her need leads to a request for help, which brings the spiritual aspect of her to consciousness. She's learning that this inner assistance is always available. When she gets quiet and asks, then surrenders, she will receive. The key is to not attempt to control what happens, or when, and in reality, the Maiden can't. Her needs can't be met by anything outside herself, nor can she depend on an external source to take care of her. Here we see that she surrenders, with full confidence and knowing that what is asked for will come…and it does, at exactly the right moment.

This is how she learns to trust that the universe is on her side and has her back. It's the beginning of the developing awareness of the union of spirit and soul. The angel works with the human to create in the world. Angels are magical and have an ability to fulfill that which is desired. This aspect of spirit is within us and is what allows us to flow with life. But, since all of this is happening in the orchard at night, it remains in the unconscious. This realization of the inner spirit is important to the embodiment of wholeness, because there isn't anything missing in wholeness, and we always have everything we need.

New Masculine Energy

There is a new masculine energy in the story, which appears as a gardener, who tends the orchard. He *sees* the Maiden and witnesses her eating a pear, but is afraid of her, since she is accompanied by an angel and so he just watches. The Maiden's identity is unclear to him. This masculine watches and cares for the trees and harvests their nourishing fruit. He's curious about the feminine. Who and what is she? She's seen and then she hides. She's still afraid to be seen. Is she concerned that she will be caught nourishing herself? Why? Is there a fear of being selfish? Taking care of herself? Receiving? Not sacrificing.

The next day the king asks the gardener about the missing pear. This king values the trees, which symbolize a connection to the source of creation, generativity, and abundance. He also appreciates what is created enough to know exactly what he has. The pears are numbered in order to keep track of them and to know if something is missing. This contrasts with the father who didn't value the apple tree at all, even though it represents abundance and nourishment. We keep track of what we care about. These trees produce fruit and seeds, which can create so many more trees and fruit that it boggles the mind. They are an infinite source.

When the gardener responds to the king's question about the pear, he explains that the Maiden was in the garden, though he doesn't really know what she is.

The priest accompanies the king to the orchard, and they join the gardener. That makes three new masculine energies indicating a transformation in the masculine. The priest knows about the spirit, the gardener tends the soul and the earth, the king rules over the kingdom and is the primary new masculine energy in the psyche. The king represents the union in the masculine of spirit and soul, since he rules over the priest and gardener. He replaces the devil and the father as the next evolution in consciousness of the masculine energy and represents a glimpse of a united masculine.

Come nightfall, the three men are waiting in the garden to see the Maiden. She comes out when it's dark, and therefore represents an emergence of a new aspect of feminine energy in which she's receiving what she needs. The first encounters happen at night, which means in the unconscious. The priest asks the Maiden what she is. She replies that she's been forsaken, abandoned by the world, by all but God. (If you are uncomfortable with the word God, substitute the Universe, Spirit, the Infinite, Presence, or whatever feels right for you. This isn't about religion, but we see it symbolically, like all aspects of the story.)

The young feminine has been abandoned by the world, but not by God, although it may appear that way in the world if one attributes material wealth to God. Our worldly circumstances are not a barometer of God's pleasure or displeasure. The Maiden has nothing. She relies on the kindness of strangers to meet her needs. If we saw her in the world, we might believe she was abandoned by Spirit, but in fact she isn't. She states that very clearly. She's been deserted by the world. The soul has been forgotten by the world, but not by Spirit, because the world ignores the needs of the soul.

Christianity rejected the devil, soul, and the feminine, often portraying women negatively in the Bible. But here, the Maiden says that although the world has abandoned her, God hasn't. This means the Spirit inside her will never leave her. It's the true source of all things in her life. The king promises that, like God, he will not abandon her. He's the new united masculine that *sees* her, *values* her, and *loves* her. He's committed to her regardless of what the culture and religion believe about her worth.

The king, as the inner masculine, commits to the Handless Maiden and they marry.

Silver Hands

As we learned in the previous stories, this is the wedding of masculine and feminine, spirit and soul, united in the kingdom. This union is a movement into greater consciousness. Heaven on earth is being created. The spirit is being embodied, which means it unites with the soul. This may appear in life as a vision of what's possible, or a momentary direct spiritual experience.

The king has new silver hands made for the Maiden. The new masculine comes up with a way for her to become acquainted with receiving good. It is still somewhat uncomfortable for the heroine to receive, because she doesn't know if what's coming is going to be good or bad, due to her conditioning. The little old man turned out to be the devil, to whom her father sold her. Two different masculine figures, who were initially trusted, turned out to be untrustworthy. They didn't value and protect her, as the young feminine. Now who can she trust?

The hands the king has made are silver, which is a metal associated with the feminine. These hands are not human flesh, but are cold, rigid, and sterile. She can't *feel* with them. They look like hands but don't function as such. They represent the next stage in the emergence of a new receptive feminine consciousness. She begins to learn to receive in a way that isn't felt, it is stiff, awkward, and not natural. It's a transitory period of exploring what's possible. The solution to the missing hands came from the king, the masculine, which means it isn't a true solution, but more of a temporary measure. This is a limited awareness of what it means to receive. It's the first stage in the return of her hands and the integration of a new conception of life.

And how are your needs met? Are they? Is it easy and effortless? Is it a co-creation with spirit in which life is lived in an abundant flow? Do you believe you can have, be, and do anything you want? How are you doing at receiving more good?

The Warrior

Once the honeymoon ends, the warrior is activated. New fears surface that are about uniting the masculine and feminine. This happens with any union, which may start out happy, but then the repressed emotions and unconscious beliefs get pushed, by the relationship, into consciousness. This is when we often start to wonder if we made a mistake, and worry that we don't get along, but it's life helping us and an opportunity to grow. The masculine began as the inept father/devil, evolved into the king/gardener/priest, and now the warrior is coming to consciousness.

When the king goes off to war, it means the loving king is being replaced with the warrior. He's afraid of his feelings, intimacy, the feminine (his wife, symbolically and literally), and being vulnerable. The Maiden, and the feelings she evokes, are perceived as a threat to his masculinity. He doesn't feel safe with her and is afraid she will hurt him, so he pulls away. Love makes him feel vulnerable and exposed. His issues regarding love are constellated by their union in order for him to see them. He isn't conscious of feeling unsafe with her and so reacts unconsciously. His fear of losing or being hurt by her causes him to protect and defend himself. We get activated by those we fall in love with in order to be shown the ways we are afraid of love. Our partners reveal the areas where we withhold and resist love.

More than just romantic relationships are affected by the warrior. It can be seen in all areas of life when it's utilized as a coping mechanism. The fight-or-flight response comes when we are afraid. When we feel threatened, we can become the warrior and fight, or the victim and flee.

When the devil appeared, the father, mother, and daughter all responded as victims. They didn't feel like they could do anything about what happened. Even when the devil wanted the father to chop off the Maiden's hands, the response was to just accept it. They were victims of the devil. But, once her hands were cut off, the Maiden left home. That wasn't a fearful running away, but was an appropriate choice to leave a situation that no longer served her. She could not stay in the old consciousness.

The victim and warrior often go hand in hand. They can be seen in one person who plays one and then the other role. The victim can feel helpless when encountering a warrior and flee. Flight doesn't necessarily mean the person always literally runs away. They can flee in consciousness as well. We see this when someone stays right where they are physically and avoids taking any action. When they encounter a challenge, they feel helpless to change the situation and don't feel strong enough to handle it. A person may prefer one role to the other, say if he's afraid of confrontation and anger, he would choose to flee. If she can't run away, she may choose to fight.

We fight to defend and protect. When feeling challenged, the warrior comes out with fists ready. This can go hand in hand with the flight as well. Choosing to respond with fight and then flight. In either case—warrior or victim—the situation is resisted rather than accepted and felt, and we then miss what the experience is trying to reveal to us. Challenges are to build strength and experiences show us where we still become activated.

The king goes off to war and leaves the Maiden with his mother, who values the Maiden as he does. He wants to be kept informed of how she's doing. He loves her and cares about her wellbeing. Even though the king is in the warrior pattern and is afraid of her, the loving masculine energy is still also present.

The warrior is in both men and women. It can appear when there is a lack of trust, and a belief that the past is going to repeat itself. When we look at what's happening without expectation and not through the eyes of conditioning, we might see something new. We could realize that in fact the past doesn't endlessly repeat itself in the present, but we are merely interpreting it that way.

The mind's preconceived interpretations can be subtle, which can make them difficult to see and shift. We can misinterpret things repeatedly. Erroneous thoughts activate the emotions and then we may spiral out of emotional control. When the emotions are really strong, there can be a sense of helplessness as they emerge. If we can learn to hold steady, remain in the inner calm, not act them out, and just watch them, along with the thoughts, we will see that they come and go. Thoughts and emotions are not even necessarily true, nor are they who we are. We are the still silent presence that witnesses the passing phenomena.

Opening to love and being loved can be difficult if we have been hurt before. Opening to that vulnerability can be scary, but it must be felt in order to transform the warrior We need to be curious about what appears in life, which is essential to not judging and interpreting each experience as a repetition of the past. Life is unfolding and evolving, it isn't stagnant. See what shows up and watch what appears. Ask, "What is being revealed through this experience or encounter?" "Why did I draw this experience to me?"

When the warrior appears in the psyche, there is fear. It shows up in response to a feeling of being unsafe and needing to be protected. What is being protected? The aspect of the personality that feels threatened. A belief or thought, the body, a feeling? Often what we are trying to protect is a sense of self that isn't real. As long as we have the warrior, and the corresponding belief that we have to defend and protect ourselves, we aren't free. We are reacting to what occurs unconsciously and not choosing how to respond creatively to a situation in the moment.

Who are we protecting ourselves from? Often it's anyone and anything we think might be a threat. It can even be the unknown, or not knowing, which means it's not even a *thing*. In our culture, the warrior is often perceived as the path to freedom, except it isn't the way to true freedom. The warrior is always looking for an enemy to defend against. As long as the warrior exists in the psyche, there is fear present.

Unclear Messages

This is beautifully illustrated in the story when the messenger is delivering the letter the mother sent to the king announcing the birth of his son. The messenger falls asleep at the river crossing and the devil changes the message to say the Maiden gave birth to something horrible. The original message is not the message that's received. Something is distorted in the transmission.

This is exactly what happens in the psyche to constellate the warrior. A happy message is sent by the king's mother to the king that his wife has given birth to a healthy baby boy. The messenger falls asleep at the brook, which means he goes unconscious on the way to the king. The brook—emotion—causes the messenger to lose consciousness. (We first saw the brook in the pear orchard and here it appears again.) So, looking at the brook as a symbol, the heroine is being challenged by her emotions, and since the warrior is active in the psyche, she's operating in defensive mode. Instead of connecting with the inner angel, or we could say, going in to connect with the peaceful stillness—which means she would see the message clearly—there is a descent into fear and the devil gets constellated. The devil appears while the messenger sleeps, which means fearful thoughts come into her head about what's being said and activate her emotions.

What is heard, or received, can be completely different from what was said. The filter distorts the message and by the time it reaches the king, it's no longer good news. The changed letter states that the queen has given birth to an abomination. This happens when we assume we know what's being said by another and what's motivating them, but are wrong. We often don't even realize it, and subsequently, don't bother to seek clarity. These misunderstandings between the masculine and feminine in consciousness means things aren't clear. The king tells his mother to care for the Maiden and baby, but the devil changes it at the creek again when the messenger again falls asleep. The changed message says to kill the queen and child. The Maiden doesn't feel loved by the masculine. Why else would he send the message to take care of her, and she hears to kill her? That's not what he said, but what she heard, and what she received. The confusion around giving and receiving clearly show the fears that are still present about receiving good.

Here again, as earlier, we are faced with the result of erroneous beliefs and thoughts that hamper our sight. We can't truly see and receive what is occurring, if we are defensive and protective, anticipating an attack at every turn. We can't be present if we are afraid for our life. This isn't literal, but emotional and from the mind. Even innocent comments are interpreted erroneously, and chaos is created.

The king's mother weeps when she receives the message, which she believes is from the king, that instructs her to kill the young feminine. This is the first time anyone, besides the Maiden herself, has wept for the loss of the feminine. This old woman is wise. She weeps but doesn't collapse into helplessness and agree to what she's being told, like the old parents did. The king's mother protects the young Maiden by sending her into the forest with her child. Both she and the king love the Maiden. But can the Maiden see or receive that yet? No, she doesn't feel safe to open fully, so back into the unconscious she goes.

Instead of killing the queen and child, the king's mother orders a doe to be sacrificed instead. The result of the chaos created by messages erroneously interpreted is the death of the doe, the young wild innocent feminine. In the beginning, it was thought acceptable to sacrifice the feminine, but now it isn't. A doe is killed in her place. A doe is a gentle, peaceful harmless feminine animal. It's the opposite of the warrior, since it's from nature, as opposed to the warrior created by man's mind. This sacrifice results in the queen and child going back into the isolation of the unconscious, because she isn't feeling safe.

The doe's death can also be an integration and infusion of its qualities into the psyche. She needs to become acquainted with its instinctual trusting nature, which is unfamiliar to her and something she really must learn to join with the masculine.

We can also explore our own lives to see how much we are willing and able to trust. We can also determine if we need to sacrifice something in our lives at this time? Something other than ourselves or the feminine?

The idea isn't to eradicate the warrior, to kill him or be killed by him. It's to shift perspectives, from one of defense and protection, to the deer's open curiosity. What am I being shown in this situation? A doe exemplifies curiosity and innocence. Have you ever stood still when encountering a deer? It moves closer and tries to figure out what you are. It flees if it feels threatened, but it responds with openness and curiosity when you are an observer. It can't really protect itself and isn't an aggressive creature. This aspect of the feminine is being brought to consciousness.

Open Curiosity

Open curiosity to what appears will transform the warrior and is the path to freedom. What's going on here now? What is believed about what's happening and is this what's really occurring? What are you being shown? How are you interpreting it?

The mother keeps the eyes and tongue of the doe as proof that the queen and child were killed. These represent sight and taste, what's seen and what's communicated. The king/warrior and his mother have trouble communicating. He's interacting with his mother and not his wife. When he looks at the Maiden and speaks to her, he filters everything through his past experiences with his mother. He's not interacting directly with the Maiden. This can be transformed through the instinctual nature of the doe. Then we can respond to what is conveyed in each situation with open curiosity; instead of being afraid and running away. We can then be open to see and receive what's really being presented. This situation emphasizes what is required to heal the hands, which is the main reason for the story: to learn how to receive again.

The devil would have taken the Maiden back into the underworld, or unconscious, at the beginning of the story if she had ended up with him. Here it's clear that the death of the Maiden is the intention again when the final message is to kill the young feminine in the psyche, but the king's mother won't do it. She sends the Maiden into the "wild forest" with her child strapped to her back. The forest is the realm of the doe. This is a descent into the wild instinctual unconscious as opposed to a death.

When she is sent away, the Maiden prays and an angel appears again. She's connecting once again with her spirit while in the unconscious.

In the Forest

The angel takes the Maiden and child to a cottage with a sign over the door that says, "All are welcome." This is significant because it's in this place of isolation and solitude that the Maiden will discover who she really is so that all *will* be welcome. She will learn to truly receive and allow all experience in without fear or reservation. There won't be any reason to defend and protect herself ever again. She has to bring the young masculine to this place as well so he can be transformed from the warrior to a new masculine.

The angel suckles the Maiden's child. It's in this new space of connection with spirit that the masculine is nourished. The cottage is all white, which illustrates the purity of this inner state of consciousness that's untainted by the world. This is the time when she directly experiences the knowing that she is always safe. There isn't anything in the world that can harm who we really are. The spiritual aspect of us can never be touched or changed by anything in the world. We are and always have been untarnished by our experiences. We go beneath and beyond the thoughts to determine what we really are apart from what we have been conditioned to believe. This creates a new foundation in the stillness and silence of spirit. That ever-present awareness begins to become a greater presence in consciousness. It creates clarity of sight and mind. It restores peace in the psyche. Truths are revealed.

All that appears to us reflects what we have inside of us or what can be transformed by us. We discover we have a power to shape our outer lives through our inner beliefs. When we transcend the warrior consciousness, we embrace the world open-heartedly and fearlessly. We can trust that all we experience is in the service of love and good.

The Maiden lives in the cottage for seven years during which time her hands grow back. What is the significance of the number seven? It took God six days to create something and on the seventh He rested. This is a cycle of creation for a new world. From the ground of the void and darkness all of life sprung forth and God saw that it was good. From nothing, God created everything. He deemed it all good. Heaven and earth are One. The light of heaven shines through everything on the earth.

Then, God created Eden, man and woman in His image, and it was all good. They were not to eat from the Tree of the Knowledge of good and evil, or they would discover death. This means they were not to ingest the thoughts of the mind of duality that judges good and bad or death would ensue. What dies when judgment arises? The ability to reside in heaven on earth, or the Garden of Eden, ends, and one falls out of paradise.

The Fall is merely the life that's created by a mind stuck in fear and judgment.

In the seven days of creation, God illustrates the balance between doing and non-doing, giving and receiving. The separation is created, and it is good. There isn't any judgment between doing and non-doing, giving and receiving; all is good. There isn't any victim or warrior when there isn't any judgment.

Returning King

When the king returns from his time as a warrior, and learns what happened to his wife, he's devastated. He expresses grief over the loss of the feminine and his son, the young masculine. Their death was brought on by the activation of the warrior in the psyche, but they have only gone into the unconscious and aren't really dead. The king's mother sees that he's truly moved by the loss and that he can feel again.

In order to be a warrior, he had to disconnect from his feelings to protect himself. *He had to harden himself to the losses that resulted from his actions to be able to survive what was happening.* Now that he's no longer a warrior, he feels his grief, which means he understands what he's lost, and what he's sacrificed to be a warrior, which was the feminine. His mother then tells him that the Maiden and Child didn't die at the hand of the warrior, but they merely went into the unconscious for safekeeping. The loving king is back, and the warrior is transformed. He wants to feel and love once again. He can't be truly nourished without the feminine soul and begins to search for her and his child.

The number seven appears again, as the king wanders for seven years, which is the time that it takes for him to integrate his feelings and to fully transform from being a warrior. Instead of being still like the Maiden, he wanders around lost, searches dark places, and remains unnourished by the world the entire time. He's in the desert, wasteland, or wilderness. What sustains him? The connection with spirit, which is the result of the young masculine being suckled by the angel. He isn't nourished through consumption of worldly things, and is isolated, like the Maiden, during the seven years he searches. In the world, it appears as though nothing is happening all this time, but the connection between earth and heaven, spirit and soul, are being strengthened. This is a crucial phase of the integration process.

When the couple first united, as I mentioned previously, it appears in our lives as a vision or momentary spiritual experience that usually cannot be sustained. This is when the couple was in the bliss of the honeymoon phase. Then came the fall from that Edenic consciousness, and things changed, as the loving king became a warrior. This would be the end of the visionary, or spiritual, experience for us, and when we would begin to clear whatever keeps us from embodying the glimpse of higher-level consciousness we had. When the king left the warrior consciousness, he wandered for seven years while the Maiden was in isolation. This was the integration phase for them, and for us. During those times we all are more fully clearing any fear that keeps us out of Eden, or the new consciousness.

This may also be evident as a seven-year cycle that plays out in your life. Explore if there are any parallels and if there is a repeating pattern that occurs in this time frame. We can sometimes see how it's not quite a circle that is going around and around in exactly the same way, but is a spiral in which we move into greater consciousness with each turn of the wheel.

While the king is searching, there is a deepening into stillness and silence for the Maiden. She's learning how to listen and hear the still small voice within her. She's uniting the masculine and feminine and embodying wholeness. The king searches for seven years, wandering through the forest without success. Then one day...

Reunion

He comes to a little house in the forest with a sign over the door that says, "All are welcome," and now it's true. The king really is welcome, since he's no longer the warrior and the Maiden has healed her fears. He goes into the house to rest but refuses the food the angel offers to him.

The Maiden taught her son that his father was in heaven, so when the boy sees the king, he doesn't know who he is. This new masculine, like Jesus, has learned that his true Father is in heaven, is spirit, and isn't a man in the physical world. This goes against all we have been taught about our parentage.

We have been conditioned to believe that we are the body and therefore, our parents are the ones who participated in the making of the body. Except, when "we" die, the body is left behind, and "we" leave this world. Who we really are cannot be the body if we leave it here. Our true parents aren't who we have been taught they are. Who we really are is the soul, and our parent's didn't create that, it comes from elsewhere. Therefore, the soul wasn't "born" and we won't ever "die," because it existed before and after the body. The body ages and dies, but *we* don't; we will leave the body and return to where we came from.

The soul's entrance into this world is like putting on a new outfit of clothes. We wear the body while we are here and then leave it when we go. We aren't *born*, but merely enter into physical form through the fetus.

The body is transformed throughout its life, but *we* remain the same ever-present soul.

The Bible verse, "I and my Father in heaven are One," means there isn't any separation between the soul and spirit. The Father is the still silent peace within us. It's not a gendered figure but the title implies it's merely something greater than what we perceive ourselves to be. It existed before the concept of "me" was born, before we collected the identities we know of as "us" in the world. Think of Father, Mother, and Child as merely symbols pointing to something beyond what we know and not literally as they are often interpreted.

The king shows up at the cottage looking like a wild man. He has returned to his instinctual natural self, like the doe. The gentle curious consciousness of this animal has been integrated into his own and he's no longer conditioned by society's beliefs.

When he sees the Maiden and his son, he doesn't think it's really his wife, since she was handless, and this woman isn't. In order to prove her identity, the angel goes into the next room, and retrieves the silver hands. The king is then overjoyed that he has finally found the queen and his son.

In one version of the story, the boy's name is Sorrowful, which indicates the sadness initially born of this union. He's a child born of sadness and grief over the loss of the feminine, and the inability for the masculine and feminine to truly unite the first time they were married. In the end, the king and queen are remarried and live happily. Therefore, this sorrow has been transformed into a true joy that is unaffected by the conditions of the world. They return to the kingdom transformed. They now reside in the kingdom that is right here—heaven on earth.

The Maiden has learned to trust, which enables her to *receive* the love that's inside, and outside, of her. This trust also allowed her to open to the good within her and know that her needs were, and aren't, met by an outer, but an inner Source. Her hands have regrown and are an indication that *her* true nature has been restored. She needed to understand that her good, and care, does not rely on her husband, or parents, but that she is strong, and competent enough, to always stand on her own. Once she became aware of this, the Maiden knew she would *always* be able to take care of herself.

The old masculine was in poverty consciousness and believed wealth had to come from the world of form. He didn't realize that it is actually based on an inner Source, which is love. He, as the warrior, was in defend and protect mode, and couldn't open to love. The new masculine, in contrast, is aware of the value of the tree, generativity, and connection between the above and below, inner and outer, human and Spirit. When he, or she, has access to the tree, there is always abundance available to everyone.

The Maiden can now interact with life naturally, openly, and without fear. All those years of being unable to give were a gift to teach her how to surrender to Source and that it's safe to receive. In the beginning, she gave too much with her parents and was willing to sacrifice herself for her father. The Maiden has learned how to balance giving and receiving. Since she knows she can trust, she's available to all of life and approaches every situation with open curiosity. The Maiden embodies this new state of consciousness, which means she sees and knows that all that happens is for the good.

When we shift into a consciousness of wholeness, we discover that we don't live in the world we have been conditioned to believe we live in. In wholeness, the feminine is equal to the masculine in all ways. The ego, or devil, cannot touch us with any fear-based ideas of inadequacy, since there isn't anything missing, to get, or to lose, in this place of fullness. This is achieved through trust, openness, and an ability to love it all as it is. This is a new world, a higher level of consciousness, and a new paradigm in which the masculine and feminine are united as equals. The result of this union is an ability to access the inner Source and know that all of our needs are always met from within. We can stand on our own and know that our well-being doesn't depend on anyone else.

Our Maiden is now able to live a beautiful life of trust, surrender, love, peace, and joy, which is the kingdom at hand. And so can we...

CHAPTER

Six

Inchelina (Thumbelina):
Finding Wings to Fly

O *nce upon a time a lonely childless woman bought a barley seed for 12 pennies from a witch. She was told to plant the seed in a pot and a tiny baby would grow. The seed grew rapidly into a large red and yellow tulip bud. The woman kissed the tip of the brightly colored flower, it opened, and there was a lovely little girl, who was just an inch long. The woman named her Inchelina.*

The woman set up a little walnut shell bed and bowl of water as a lake for the little girl to play in. She loved listening to Inchelina who sang so beautifully.

One night a big mother toad jumped in through a broken window and took the sleeping Inchelina to be her son's wife. While Inchelina slept, they put her on a waterlily leaf in the middle of the stream and prepared an apartment.

Inchelina awoke in the morning and cried when she realized she was stranded. The mother toad swam out to Inchelina and told her that she was to marry her toad son. They took her walnut bed back to the apartment as Inchelina wept on the lily pad.

The fish all heard the old mother toad's plan and saw Inchelina crying. They felt sorry for her and chewed through the flower stalk that held the lily pad in place. Inchelina was relieved as she sailed away from the toads. She floated for a very long time until a butterfly landed on the leaf. Inchelina removed her waist ribbon, tied one end to the leaf stem, and the other to the butterfly. They merrily flew even faster down the stream. A Maybug saw them, picked Inchelina up, and sat her in a tree. Inchelina was horrified as she watched the butterfly go downstream tied to the leaf. She worried the butterfly might die if it couldn't get free.

The Maybug fed Inchelina honey and decided she was pretty enough to marry. His Maybug friends arrived, and the Maybug women convinced him that she was quite ugly, so he abandoned her at the foot of the tree. Inchelina happily spent the summer and fall alone, but when winter arrived, she couldn't survive on her own. She shivered as she walked through a field but then reached a mouse's hole. She knocked on the door and asked for shelter. The field mouse said she could stay for the winter, if she cleaned, cooked, and told the mouse a story every day.

Inchelina was happy with the mouse. One day the mouse mentioned to Inchelina that their neighbor, the blind mole, was coming to visit. The mouse thought it would be a fine idea for Inchelina and the mole to marry, since he was so rich and could take care of her. When the mole showed up, he told Inchelina how smart and wealthy he was, that he had a big house, and hated the sun and flowers. Inchelina sang to him and he fell in love with her, but kept it hidden.

The mole took Inchelina and the mouse through a new passage he had dug. He told them to ignore the dead bird buried there. Inchelina felt sad when she saw that the bird had probably frozen to death. The mouse and mole made fun of the swallow for singing all summer and then starving when winter came. Inchelina visited the bird that night and put small pieces of cotton under the bird to protect it from the cold. She said goodbye to the bird, put her head on its breast, and heard a heartbeat. The warmth had revived the bird and it was alive.

The next night she returned and the swallow was awake. The bird thanked Inchelina and said he would fly away. Inchelina told the bird it was winter and that he had to wait for spring. She secretly nursed him through the cold months and in spring the swallow asked if she wanted to go with him. She declined and he left.

The mouse helped Inchelina prepare to marry the mole against her wishes. The fall came, which was the time for Inchelina to marry. That would be the end of her life above ground and the beginning of her life underground. She told the mouse she didn't want to marry the mole and the mouse threatened to hurt her if she didn't.

Inchelina went to the opening of the mouse's house to say goodbye to her old life on the day of her wedding. As she stood in the sun, saying farewell, she heard a tweet. The swallow was coming. He asked if she wanted to go with him and she said yes. The swallow flew a long way, with her on his back, to where it was warm and put her on a flower in an old temple ruin.

There was a little king sitting in the flower. When he saw how lovely Inchelina was, he asked if she wanted to be queen of the flowers. They married and she received wings as a gift so she could fly. The king changed her name to Maja and they lived happily ever after.*

Introduction

This story, also known as "Thumbelina," is about finding our way back home. The journey is not only about returning to where we belong, but to

---

* Full story in Manheim's Grimms' Tales for Young and Old.

who we really are, when we have been "abducted." Inchelina is born into a place that doesn't reflect who she is, but she doesn't know that. Her journey takes her through a variety of different situations, with people who are not "her people," until she eventually finds where she belongs. She must learn to act on her behalf, to reclaim her freedom, find her way home, and discover who she really is. Then, once she knows who she is, she can be seen and valued for herself.

The Childless Mother

Many of us have been raised to believe that our happiness depends on something outside of us. The mother in this story wants a tiny child, which she can't give birth to herself, so she asks an old witch for help. The witch tells her it's easy and gives her a magic grain of barley. The mother doesn't know how to create and looks outside herself for help to do so. She doesn't have a child in the usual way, but uses a seed, which she plants in a pot. This will not be a normal child, but something different than herself, since she wasn't born from a grain of barley.

Others cannot tell us how to give birth to that which is within us or provide the seeds for our needs to be met. Our ideas, the answers to our questions, and the seeds of new life all lie within us. We can't ask others what we need to do, who we are, or who to be. This mother hasn't yet discovered who she is and therefore can't create something that comes from herself.

The mother-to-be pays twelve pennies for the seed that will create the child. Twelve is the number of months, zodiac signs, disciples, and is associated with completion. This number suggests the story will have a fulfilling conclusion and the Self will be realized by the heroine. The twelfth Tarot card is the Hangman, which is a card of rebirth. When things are turned upside down, the answers we seek don't come from the mind. This card indicates a time of stasis, when things aren't moving, like when a seed is in the earth and we don't see anything happening, or when a baby is in the womb. The gestation period will be important for our heroine.

When the digits of the number twelve are added together, we get three, which is the number of rebirth as well. When two (such as a couple) unite they create a baby and become a family, which is the third thing that's created. The number three therefore suggests that something new is being born. Three is a magical number that frequently appears in stories to indicate that a transformation is complete.

The father—who normally provides the seed for a child—is missing from the story, and it's offered by a witch instead. This suggests that what is about to be created isn't a normal family in the sense that we are used to. It also implies that something is up regarding the absent father. The masculine provides the energy to move forward and he isn't present at the beginning, it may lead to stasis. This means the inner impetus to evolve, and know when it's time to move on, is compromised.

The Tulip

Often in myths and fairy tales, there is something magical or unusual about a hero or heroine's birth, which is certainly true here. Inchelina is born from a barley seed, which isn't a normal seed that grows barley. It's a barley seed that grows a tulip with a miniature baby inside. The seed is planted in a flowerpot with dark, moist soil, representing the womb of creation. When we plant a seed in the dark, we must wait as the seed matures in a place beyond our awareness. Then, once it sprouts, we nurture it until it blooms into its fullest expression. The stem represents the umbilical cord connecting this child to the earth, which is her true mother and source of nourishment. Inchelina further develops in the heart of a red and yellow tulip until the loving kiss of the surrogate mother opens the petals and she's born.

The red color of the tulip is associated with love, passion, and the blood of life. Spiritual teacher Ambika Wauters describes the qualities associated with the corresponding archetypes of the chakras. Red is the color of the first, root chakra, which is identified with the primary needs of being nurtured, nourished, and relates to safety and security. This chakra has to do with the connection to the earth, being grounded, and the mother or victim archetypes.[35] When the root chakra is balanced, we nurture, nourish, and care for ourselves in ways that allow us to thrive in good health and experience feelings of harmony and wellbeing. If this chakra is out of balance, victim energy is activated, and we can't nourish or take care of ourselves. In victim energy, we tend to give up too easily and we don't know what to do to resolve challenges when they arise. Victims want others to solve their problems and rescue them, like Inchelina's mother did. They don't realize their inner power, and instead project it outwardly onto others. It's fascinating that the tulip is also yellow, since that's the color of the third chakra, which has to do with power.

Yellow is a color of happiness and sunshine, and also the coward. This color is associated with the third chakra, the solar plexus, and with the warrior and servant archetypes.[36] When this chakra is balanced, we embody a healthy warrior archetype and have a strong sense of our own self-worth. This archetype is positive in that life isn't lived as a battle, or seen dualistically, but we are perceived as all being on the same side—without any outer enemies. When this chakra is healthy, we have the strength and courage to stand up for ourselves. We aren't defined by others, nor do we confront them in a combative way, but confidently stand in our power. Whether others agree, or believe as we do, is irrelevant. Our validation and support come from within. When this chakra is out of balance, an unhealthy warrior or servant energy manifests.

If we are operating out of the servant archetype, we tend to take care of others and depend on them for validation and care. Our actions will be determined by what will win us approval and not on what we want or need. When in servant energy, our dreams may not be pursued because we don't feel deserving or worthy of receiving what we want.

The green color of the stem suggests spring, new life, healing, and is also the color of envy. It's associated with the heart chakra and the archetypes of lover or actor.[37] The lover is someone who truly loves, while the actor only pretends to. When this chakra is healthy, we freely express unconditional love for all. This is the center of joy, peace, and contentment with life, knowing that everything is okay and will turn out well.

Inchelina must heal and balance these three areas—root, power, and heart—in order to experience wholeness and live an authentic life. She will learn about nourishment and feeling safe, releasing the victim, transforming unhealthy warrior and servant archetypes, and opening her heart to love.

Inchelina's Mother

Inchelina is born into a home without a father. Her mother wants a child, but not a real one; instead, she's interested in a child that's more like a toy. It's as though this mother wants a baby to play with and not the kind that grows up, leaves home, and becomes her own person. This child serves the mother and keeps her company. She's in a perpetual state of infancy, since she's so tiny and depends on her mother to survive.

This mother doesn't seem concerned with pertinent questions about her child's future. Questions like, "What will happen to her when I'm not here to care for her?" This mother thinks only of herself and her desire for companionship, without considering the implications for Inchelina. Since her "mother" is a human being and not like her, Inchelina won't be aware of her true identity. This mother won't be able to reflect to Inchelina what she is, or who she is, because the mother doesn't know herself.

Inchelina's mother is thinking only of herself when she decides to have a child. She isn't living her own true life and depends on her child to define her. She didn't develop her sense of self apart from her child and needs this baby to make her feel better about herself. The child, in turn, doesn't develop normally because she focuses on the mother's needs and ignores her own. This type of child (and later on as an adult) takes care of others and ignores herself in the same way her mother did.

This child doesn't know herself, or what she desires, since her identity is enmeshed with her mother. She depends on the mother's presence, or someone else, to define her. As an adult, she looks outside herself to determine who she is. If there isn't anyone to tell her what to do, who to be, how to feel, or what is important, she feels lost, confused, and vulnerable. It's difficult for her to make her own decisions, since she has based her existence, responses, and actions on the mother's desires and needs.

The father is irrelevant in this family and would be wounded even if he was present, since the mother is the focus. The girl takes the place of the missing father as a companion to the mother.

Inchelina's mother gives her a superficial name based on her appearance and not on something deeper such as her essence. She is kept on a table by a window and plays in a bowl of water surrounded by a garland of flowers. Inchelina is like a doll. Her life is restricted in terms of what she can do and in her lack of opportunities to interact with others. Although, she seems unaware of the limitations of her situation, as she sings and plays.

The Characters

Now, let's look at the characters as aspects of the heroine. The mother is the part of her that doesn't know who she really is, can't *see* her, and ignores her needs. It's the part of her that wants someone else to come along and make her feel better about herself. The mother will never let Inchelina grow up, go out into the world, and have her own life. This is a part of her that wants to maintain the status quo and keep things as they are because it's safer. The world is perceived as unsafe.

The witch is the other main character who has what the mother doesn't have, but wants. She has the seed for new life and tells the mother how to nurture it to fruition. She's willing to receive something in exchange for what she shares. The witch is different from the mother, but doesn't remain an active character in the story, nor, therefore, is she a continuing presence in the psyche of the heroine. She has a wisdom the mother doesn't possess.

Witches in a story are often perceived negatively, when in reality they are important for new growth. There is a witch, or wise woman, in ourselves that truly knows what the mother doesn't, which is who we are. There is a seed in the psyche that our circumstances conspire to bring to awareness. The witch carries the magic. She has something that appears as one thing but is really something else. The barley seed isn't really a barley seed, but the seed of a new aspect of the self. This suggests that what we perceive as one thing is really something else. Here, that something else is the young feminine soul, which is emerging into the world through beauty.

Inchelina is content at home with her mother and accepts things as they are. She plays in her little world and is protected from the larger world. Are you content with something, just going along with things as they are and not living your truth? This is the time to take stock of your life to make sure you aren't settling. Events will unfold for Inchelina with the intention to reveal the greater truth of who she is. What may appear as victimization is merely an experience intending to awaken her to her truth.

Mother Toad

Inchelina is abducted at night by a mother toad who slips in through a broken window. She and her mother are asleep, which means they aren't awake, or aware, of what's going on, and so fate intervenes to help Inchelina wake up. If they are sleeping, they aren't conscious of their situation and don't realize they've been lulled into a sense of complacency. There isn't any growth happening. All appears as though it's well, but there's something undeveloped, and the truth isn't being lived. The truth wants to be known and the authentic life wants to be lived. It's the nature of life itself desiring expression, just like a planted seed will become the flower it was always meant to be. The acorn will become the oak tree, and you will become who you were always meant to be. But we have to leave the mother's house.

We might say there's neglect in that the broken window is right near Inchelina and that the mother didn't protect her. The mother is wounded, and this safety issue relates to the first chakra. We may not initially know how to protect that which is special within us, our gifts or ourselves, and may expose them to others who are insensitive. It's like having a new baby, painting, cake, pottery, or whatever is meaningful to us, and having someone make a thoughtless comment, which causes us to want to retreat. Then we don't want to share what's special to us because our feelings might get hurt. But we need to learn to feel these feelings and keep going anyway. We want to be thoughtful initially as to whom we reveal ourselves or our gifts. Even as we cultivate discernment though, the key is to persist and keep going forward. Remember, the father is missing, and he represents action and moving forward, so this step might take a bit more effort, or the universe might make it happen for us.

Inchelina has to leave the wounded mother in order to find herself. We can assume her growth would have been limited had she remained on that table for the duration of her life. And so, the mother toad initiates Inchelina's journey from the known to the unknown, from her mother's house to the world beyond, or from the unknown to the known, meaning from not knowing who she really is on her journey to knowing. Regardless of how we perceive it, it's an expansion of consciousness.

The mother toad wants Inchelina to marry her toad son and live in the mud on the banks of the river. It's interesting that Inchelina is abducted and this new life is strangely reminiscent of her old life. She had a bowl of water on the table and now it's the banks of a river; and the mother toad even brought Inchelina's bed. It appears as though nothing has really changed with this move.

The ugly mother and son toad represent that which is "ugly" within us. They are the part of us that ignores what we want when we agree to a life that isn't ours. The mother toad doesn't ask Inchelina if this is what she wants; she just goes ahead with her plan to marry her son and Inchelina. She tells her son to be quiet so he doesn't wake Inchelina up, thus quieting the inner masculine voice that could bring Inchelina some awareness. The mother toad doesn't want Inchelina to know her plan.

This can happen when we agree to something that doesn't honor who we are and we don't realize it's out of alignment. Why don't we know it's wrong for us? Because we might never have asked ourselves what we wanted, since it didn't matter. Many of us can remember a decision we made in the past where we didn't follow our feelings, instincts, or gut reaction, and knew somewhere inside us that the path we were taking wasn't right. We were asleep to our innate guidance and continued forward. Later, often after things didn't work out, we realize we knew all along.

The Toad's Plan

The mother toad doesn't want Inchelina to wake up to the realization that this isn't the path for her. This may occur when a part of us wishes to take a safer path, find an easier way, or stick with what's familiar. The intellect can make suggestions that appear to be right, but when we look more closely, we can see that they aren't in alignment with our heart. Since the mother toad takes Inchelina's bed, it suggests that our heroine isn't really awake yet.

Toads navigate between dry land, mud, and water. They live in the mud, between land and water, and can therefore unite the two elements. This suggests an ability to bring things out of the unconscious and into a concrete form. Ideas from the unknown, intuitively grasped, need to be grounded, made a reality, and lived. The lessons and information Inchelina receives have to be integrated. But this is at the beginning stages, since Inchelina doesn't want to be a toad's wife. The union of the masculine and feminine is what seeks to be realized, but it has to be the right masculine, and this toad isn't it.

The mother toad puts Inchelina on a waterlily in the center of the river, an island without an escape, or so Inchelina believes when she wakes up. She opens her eyes at dawn, which represents a new day and therefore a change. She comes to her senses, but only once she's in what appears to be an impossible situation. When Inchelina realizes she's stranded on a leaf she cries bitterly, activating her victim energy. She doesn't see any way out of her situation and feels helpless.

The mother and son may have been frogs and not toads, since frogs live near water and toads live on dry land. If they are toads, then they aren't in their natural habitat, since they normally live on the water. As such, they emphasize the part of us that is out of our element and is living someplace, or doing something, that isn't in harmony with who we really are. This is echoed by the toad mother's desire to make Inchelina her son's wife. Does the son's desire matter? Doesn't the son want a wife who isn't a toad? It appears as though the mother toad doesn't care because she never asks, just like Inchelina's mother.

The frog is associated with water and emotions. The water here is a river and indicates the necessity for the movement of emotions and flow of energy. Mud unites earth and water, ground and emotions. Frogs represent the possibility of "transformation through water and sound,"[38] meaning emotions and the throat chakra. The throat has to do with speaking up and Inchelina's singing. If the mother and son are frogs, then Inchelina needs to come into harmony with her emotions and integrate them. She needs to flow with events and learn from them.

Overwhelming Emotions

When emotions are overwhelming, we often revert to either the victim or warrior archetypes, which can appear as fight or flight patterns. When our emotions are healthy, we experience what we feel and then let it go. We can see this sometimes in young children who haven't been conditioned yet to repress their feelings. If we feel something and release it, we don't become attached, or mired in emotions, and stuck in the mud. We get "stuck" when we allow a thought or emotion to take us on a downward path. One unpleasant thought leads to another, and another, and another, and these thoughts fuel the emotions. If there is muddy water, say in a dream, it can indicate chaotic emotions, and stillness will allow the water to clear. This can be applied to us in the same manner in which it works for a body of water. Frogs live in the mud, which is also considered a substance of creation.

Water symbolizes emotion and can also be the unconscious, or that of which we are unaware. As we bring unconscious aspects of ourselves to consciousness, we understand more of ourselves. The toad mother ignores the needs of others and acts in her own self-interest. The son serves the mother and does as she wants. When we don't know who we are, and attempt to help others, we aren't always serving them as we believe we are, but can use them to make us feel better about ourselves. The mother toad probably thinks she's doing something nice for her son, since she found him a pretty wife and prepared his apartment for her soon-to-be daughter-in-law. It appears as though she's being altruistic, but in reality no one's desires are being met.

The mother toad, as an aspect of Inchelina, busies herself with activity to avoid her feelings. If the mother toad stops for a moment to think about what she's doing and feels her feelings, then she might realize the situation isn't right. Busyness is one of Inchelina's coping mechanisms to avoid what she really feels.

If upon reading the previous description of the toad mother, we say, "Oh yes, I recognize the mother toad as so-and-so. That's exactly how she treats me," then we might realize we are still projecting that aspect of our consciousness and turn within to own the mother toad in us. That which is outside of us and upsets us, reflects that which is within. This is a time to also explore our activities to see if we are using busyness as a way to avoid our feelings. The healing takes place when we accept these disowned parts of ourselves and transform them. Many of us are taught to avoid this at all costs, but this is what frees us from our fears of the other. The mother toad part of us ignores our needs and feelings and is willing to sacrifice who we are for the comfortable and familiar. We must awaken to the things in our life that don't honor us.

A Creative Solution

When Inchelina's bed is taken to the bridal chamber, the fish realize her predicament. We could also say that Inchelina finally realizes what's happening, and what she's agreeing to. The fish move out of their natural environment, as they poke their heads above the water, to "see" what's going on. This allows them to get a different perspective on the situation. If we get caught in the emotions, then air, as intuition, can help us see a new way through our circumstances. If the emotions take over and stir things up, we can sit quietly to let them settle, then something new may emerge. Inchelina didn't know the fish were in the water, which means something came from the unconscious to help her.

A new perspective can lead to creative solutions. The fish are comfortable in the water, the realm of emotions, which is why they can assist with not getting mired in them. They are able to rise above the emotions, get a different perspective on what's happening, and provide a new answer. The fish represent Inchelina reclaiming some of her power when they chew the stem of the waterlily leaf to set her free. The fact that the fish free her, without Inchelina's knowledge of them, suggests that she's helped by something that is beyond her awareness. In times of need, we can get help from the nonphysical realm. They can assist us in ways we don't even realize. Inchelina won't be able to return to the same state of unconsciousness that she had been in, since the mother toad and son have her bed, which she leaves behind.

The fish is a symbol associated with the Christ, which is the archetypal Self. Help comes from within and without when we are stuck and need assistance. The Self can appear through dream, synchronicity, inspiration, or actual physical manifestations of either information, healing, or resources. Fish also represent "independence, potential and possibilities."[39] They suggest the need to reduce the amount of activities we are involved in, protection, the need to change environments, creativity, breath, sight, and fluidity. We already mentioned the mother toad's busyness as a way of avoiding emotions. Many of the aspects of the fish have already been addressed in the story, except for creativity, breath, and fluidity.

Creativity was initially touched on as something the witch had access to but Inchelina's mother did not, since she couldn't create a child. How capable is Inchelina at creating a life that is in alignment with who she is? We can see that this isn't an area of strength for her at the moment, but then again, she doesn't know who she is yet. She's more of a victim of life than in her power, as the latter would mean being able to create opportunities to be who she is and that honor her. Does she know what she wants to create or how? Not yet, but the witch aspect of her does, so that part of her, the wise woman, still needs to come to consciousness.

Water is also symbolically associated with creativity. Creativity is employed when the fish come up with a solution to Inchelina's dilemma. Creativity implies something new is created from the present circumstances to provide a new path and continue the journey. It might appear as a door that opens, which wasn't seen before.

If Inchelina resists events that appear, then she will "put the brakes on" as she's guided to her healing. If she stays in situations that need to end, she may remain "stuck in the mud." Regardless of what happens or how things appear, she needs to flow with what unfolds and grow through her experiences. Inchelina needs to release what she knows no longer serves her and move on. Rather than falling into a victim role, she must continue to see *through* whatever appears to the lessons they contain. When she discovers the insights into herself and her limitations that these experiences are revealing, then she will be transformed by them and her awareness will expand. All that happens is a gift. She needs to learn to trust life.

The breath can be restricted when we are in situations that are out of alignment with who we are. It can occur when we judge ourselves and our experiences, which evokes a feeling of not being safe. When we feel unsafe, our breath can become shallow and rapid. The breath may also feel constricted when we are too busy. We need to have space and time to relax and to breathe easily. When we are calm and at peace, our breath is gentle and nourishing. This is often when fresh new insights can come to us.

A Taste of Freedom

Once the fish set Inchelina free, she sails down the stream into the unknown. As she travels, she fully enjoys the present moment, the sun, and beauty around her. Soon she encounters a beautiful white butterfly, which is a symbol for the pure soul. Butterflies and moths symbolize transformation from the old and constricting self to something entirely new, unfettered and free.

Inchelina decides to tie the butterfly to the leaf for fun. This act of harnessing something that is free indicates a change. Inchelina doesn't realize the implications of her actions until it's too late, which sounds a bit like her mother. She's attaching her belief in freedom to something or someone else outside herself. Just moments ago, she wasn't free because of the mother toad, and then was freed by the fish, and now is moving forward on the energy of the butterfly. She doesn't yet understand that freedom comes from within.

If the butterfly is an inner aspect of Inchelina, it can mean she has a brief experience of freedom but loses it. It can also suggest the need to harness a new purer energy to move forward. If we don't feel free, then it can lead to incapacitation. Here we see that, for a few moments, she gets a taste of freedom and flow as her journey continues.

What she has attached to, is something that isn't really making her free. It might have been initially perceived as fun but wasn't really. She may have believed her freedom and joy depended on something else, but in the end, that something carried victim consciousness as well. Here she's beginning to unite the air and water, the conscious and unconscious, the butterfly and fish. This is an illustration of the up and down motion that's frequently seen in dream and story as a part of the generation of greater consciousness. First the fish were under water, they severed the link to the mud below the lily pad, then the butterfly and a new link was established to the air.

Inchelina tied her freedom to something she shouldn't have, something outside of herself, because the part of her that was free, isn't now. This could mean believing freedom has to come in a particular way, as though certain outer circumstances must be met in order to experience it. I will be free when [*fill in the blank*] ...when I have more money, time, a partner, a different job, no job, retire, kids grow up, etc. What happens when we attach specific conditions to our belief in freedom, and the situations do change to what we think we want, and we find that we still aren't free? The freedom comes first, not *after* things change. We are in truth always free; despite the way our lives might look.

The Maybug

Inchelina, the part of her that is the butterfly, is momentarily free, but then she loses her freedom because of her own limited belief. She binds the butterfly—puts a harness on it—and then a Maybug grabs her. She may feel uncomfortable, or unsafe, expressing her joy and being free, so she attracts the Maybug to activate what needs to be healed. The one extreme constellates the opposite. The Maybug will reveal what's holding her back. Sometimes these momentary experiences of freedom and joy show us what's possible and are only intended to be temporary, because we can't yet hold that consciousness. We might have beliefs to the contrary that must be cleared to embody freedom. We encounter the experiences we need to heal in order to assist in our movement toward greater consciousness.

Once with the Maybug, Inchelina grieves for the free part of herself that she has lost. She's also afraid the butterfly may starve to death, which would be the result of her actions. There is guilt about what she's done and for not having thought about the implications of her actions. The fears of starving and death relate to nourishment and the first chakra. Inchelina is worried that the free part of her might die and is concerned with getting her needs met, which is seeing the butterfly as an aspect of her own psyche.

If we look at the butterfly as something outside of Inchelina, then she's projecting her fears onto it. Her concern regarding her own nourishment is for a good reason, since her mother didn't teach her how to take care of herself. This is about meeting her need for food and is also about tending the needs of the soul. Inchelina must nourish the aspect of her that's already free, by doing what she loves to do.

What does the soul need? Are you nourishing your soul, and do you know how? How free do you feel? Have you been abducted by anything that doesn't serve who you truly are?

Many of us have experienced the freedom of flight in dreams and know how it feels. We feel expansive, unbound, joyful, and light. It's so effortless to lift off and fly around. When we are free in life, we do what we love and embody our authentic selves. We feel seen, valued, validated, and supported. When we don't feel free, the breath seems restricted, we believe we can't do what we want, have what we want, be who we want, and can't create. We may project this inner voice who restricts our freedom onto those around us. Then we may see others judging what we do, who we are, or what we want.

The Maybug also flies, which means Inchelina has a masculine aspect that can climb to new heights, have a different perspective, and be free. He takes her up into a tree, which is a new environment. Trees symbolize, as we have seen before, the connection between heaven and earth, with roots deep in the dark soil and branches reaching into the sky. Now she experiences the link between the earth and air, intellect and intuition, seen and unseen. We saw the earth with the toads, the air with the butterfly, and now Inchelina lives in a place that connects them both.

These abductions are opportunities for her to see what's happening unconsciously with regard to freedom. What are her unconscious beliefs and feelings about her own freedom? The abductions also reveal the things that take her away from herself—the ways she abandons her dreams, attends to the wishes of others, and ignores her own needs and desires. The Maybug will help her see more of what she believes and then move beyond the limitations. These circumstances mirror her inner beliefs and are situations from which has to learn to free herself.

A Taste of Nectar

The Maybug initially adores her and feeds her honey—the nectar of flowers—which would be her own food, since she was born from a flower. First, with the butterfly, she gets to experience a few moments of freedom and now she gets to taste her own food. As we learned, Inchelina was worried about the butterfly's nourishment, and here she gets exactly what she needs physically. This experience with the Maybug relates to love and the nectar of life associated with the heart chakra. This chakra is sometimes considered a connection point in the body for heaven and earth, or the upper and lower chakras. Is this new masculine loving and committed to Inchelina? Does he stay with her regardless of how challenging things get? Does Inchelina love him back?

We each have inner aspects of ourselves that represent the opposite sex. Masculine energy is solar, about consciousness, taking action, moving out into the world, is logical, rational, and gets things done. When it's healthy, it supports the feminine, responds to her feelings and intuitions, and acts on them. Feminine energy, besides feeling and intuition, is about being, relating, and is lunar, which means it relates to the unconscious. These two energies dance within us and when they relate well, we function in the world with ease and grace. We receive ideas from the feminine based on intuitions or feelings, and the masculine responds to these appropriately. He brings her ideas out into the world, protects and values her.

If the masculine is unhealthy, he devalues the feminine. He (or the inner masculine for a woman) ignores her needs, feelings, and intuitions. A person with an unhealthy masculine is too busy, makes decisions from the head, is overly intellectual, rational, logical, can be angry, irritated, and opinionated. An unhealthy feminine (or the inner feminine for a man) is critical, overly emotional, depressed, lethargic, and unable to act or get things done. These normally go hand in hand, meaning if there is too much masculine energy, then there isn't enough feminine, or vice versa. If one is unhealthy, both are unhealthy. There can be a vacillation between one and the other as well, such as too much action and then none at all. The ideal is for both aspects to be healthy and mutually respectful working in harmony to create a life that's wanted.

Why is this important? Because the intuition knows who we are, what we want, and how to get there. It knows how to create a life that honors all life, as well as our own deepest yearnings, and will be fulfilling. The intuition guide us home—to ourselves, our gifts, love, and joy.

Rejection

When the Maybug's friends appear, they don't approve of Inchelina. The most vocal opponents are two single female Maybugs, who appear to resent the competition. They reject Inchelina because she isn't like them.

These lady Maybugs indicate the need to explore the responses of others and ourselves to that which is different in us and may not fit in. Are we rejecting parts of us, which are considered by society to be different? Is there some part of us that initially pleased us, but when others responded negatively, we hid or rejected it? Maybe while laughing one day, you were told you were being silly, too loud, or should grow up. From that time on you might have been reluctant to laugh freely and tucked that part of you away. Let's say you were excited about a creation, until someone said something critical. As a result, you abandoned the artist, potter, chef, theatrical, or musical part of yourself.

These issues relate to the third chakra, and the servant archetype, who looks to others for validation and doesn't realize her worth. The fact that most of the active characters in the story up to this point have been female is interesting. They are the ones who cause Inchelina the most harm, while the masculine characters are passive and succumb to the ideas of the females who don't value who Inchelina really is. The female characters represent Inchelina's issues with her mother and the feminine. Inchelina feels like she isn't appreciated for herself, and so this aspect of her is critical of her. This is an inner dialogue of self-rejection. One part of her says, "I'm okay," and the other part says, "No you're not."

The female Maybugs can appear in your life when you try to take a stand in some area, and someone criticizes, or rejects you, or what you are doing. It's important to really look inside closely to see if there is any part of you that believes that what's being said is true. It's so easy to dismiss the comments and come up with a seemingly valid reason for their unkind words. An example would be to tell yourself that they are just jealous. This is the time to clear whatever shows up by sitting with the feelings that arise. Repressed feelings of sadness, shame, inadequacy, or whatever they are, can hamper your progress. Now is the time to free yourself of them.

Freedom

The butterfly and fish are associated with Inchelina's freedom, the former refers to the above and the fish to the below. These two aspects of her are beginning to relate in order to unite the opposites in conscious and unconscious, masculine and feminine, air and water. The fish is a symbol of Christ, which set her free when she was with the toads. The Christ, or

Self, which resides in her unconscious, released her from that which was not in alignment with the truth of who she is. Butterflies symbolize the soul, which suggests that her moment with the butterfly was an experience of the joy and freedom associated with the freedom of the soul. The embodiment of the united Christ consciousness is what the entire journey is about. Here we see how the embodiment grows through this weaving back and forth of the seen and unseen, above and below, inner and outer.

The witch, or wise woman, told the mother when she gave her the seed, "This isn't what it appears to be," and then explained how to care for it. Inchelina, as the soul, is the feminine aspect of us. In alchemy and Gnosticism, the feminine is perceived as being captivated by matter and needs to be released or set free. Our souls have been "captured" by the world of form, and as such, we don't know who we really are. We've become identified with the story of ourselves, which we were taught, and lost touch with our true essence—the soul.

When the soul is free, we are spontaneous and flow with life. We do what we love, are creative, love unconditionally, and live in joy. Living from the soul means we know who we are and why we are here. There is an ability to listen to and follow our inner promptings. Since we trust others and life, we can relax and rest into the knowing that we are enough exactly as we are. This enables us to feel loved, accepted, and supported.

Christ, as the fish, was free, although still in the unconscious. The Christ isn't masculine, nor is it Jesus, but is a title that isn't associated with any gender. It's born in consciousness when the time is right for it to make an appearance. Spirit represents that which is transcendent, up, skyward, and masculine, while the feminine soul is thought of as immanent. The Christ is, in the deepest sense, our true selves, healed and whole. In this consciousness, we realize that everything is love, and we are in a state of unity rather than duality. We are transformed from separation into union and true freedom.

Inadequacy

The female Maybugs think Inchelina is competition, which is an idea that is based on lack, judgment, other, separation, a win-lose mentality, and limitation. This idea that we need to compete with others reduces our ability to trust. If we don't trust, say for example, other women, and we are a woman, then we may have trouble trusting or valuing the feminine within us. An inability to trust may originate in early relationships where females had to compete for attention or to get needs met. It can also happen in societies that reject the feminine, believing women have less value than men, which creates a sense of unworthiness. This fosters the idea that we need to compete, and put others down, in order to feel better about ourselves. Women aren't the only ones to feel this way, because I've also discussed this subject with men, who say they have also experienced these feelings. When we believe there isn't enough for everyone, we think we have struggle to get our share of what's available in order for our needs to be met.

We live in a time when ideas of lack pervade our world. There is a scarcity of resources, division between haves and have nots, and a competitive corporate culture that strives for an ever-bigger slice of the pie. What would it be like to live in an abundant state of consciousness and a world in which we are enough, have enough, and there's enough to take care of everyone? Nature is naturally abundant. An example is an apple tree that can produce an endless bounty of fruit and seeds. We are naturally abundant as well.

Up to this point in the story, the characters have said that Inchelina was pretty, but here we see another part of her that believes she's unattractive. Since she just left the ugly mother toad and her son, she should have incorporated their energies, but she hasn't fully accepted and realized this inner belief. She projected the idea of ugliness onto the toads and now she's at the receiving end of that same projection. We all have things within us that are difficult to look at and aren't "pretty." In order to come into wholeness, we must take back our projections—good and bad—so that we may be ourselves and also love others unconditionally. When we truly know who we are, there isn't anything anyone can say to change it.

The Maybug who captured Inchelina finally succumbs to the pressure of his friends and rejects Inchelina. If he could abandon her so easily, because of the opinions of others, then he couldn't have loved her that much. This may mean Inchelina is abandoning some aspect of herself that she believes others don't like. It can also be that she deserts herself when others criticize her. It can feel daunting to reclaim the discarded aspects of us that were unappreciated by others, but we must do it. Our own feelings of jealousy, competitiveness, unworthiness, fear, or ideas of lack and limitation need to be acknowledged and really felt.

We don't need to judge any of these "negative" feelings in ourselves because every single one of them reveals something to us. Jealousy, for example, can serve us by showing us what we want but may believe we can't have. If we see this in ourselves, we can explore what it is we really desire and begin to move toward its fulfillment, rather than projecting those feelings onto others. If we believe we can't have it, then we sit with the feeling that we can't have what we want or need. It's all good.

Love originates in our own hearts and doesn't depend on external circumstances or other people the way many of us have been taught. True unconditional love is for all of us, the good and the so-called bad. When we connect to the Source of love within us, we are undaunted by the opinions and ideas of others. This masculine Maybug part of Inchelina initially nourished her but eventually abandons her when faced with others' criticism. A lack of inner masculine support is reflected as minimal outer masculine support. This can be literal when the men around us, like the Maybug, aren't being supportive. It can appear as Inchelina being unable to engage her own inner masculine energy to move forward, stand up for herself, or to successfully bring her gifts into the world. If the inner masculine is healthy, he sees our beauty and value, and takes the steps necessary to carry our intuitions to completion. He loves us as we are and helps us to stand in our own power fearlessly.

Alone and Free

The Maybug leaves Inchelina on a daisy at the foot of a tree and tells her she's free. She has spent time in the treetop and now returns to the earth. The daisy is symbolically associated with "increasing awareness, creativity, and inner strength."[40] Since the masculine didn't love and support Inchelina, she needs to *look inside herself to find the love and support she doesn't receive from others.* By doing so, she will increase her awareness and grow in inner strength. That which we seek in the world must be discovered within. We also relate daisies with the game, "he loves me, he loves me not." In Inchelina's case, this time it was, "he loves me not." How does she react to this rejection by someone she didn't even like or care about?

Well, Inchelina cried and cried at having been rejected by a Maybug of all things. She didn't handle it very well. It seems her victim energy is activated, and she isn't seeing her own value apart from the opinion of the Maybug. *Our value does not, in any way, depend on the actions or beliefs of others.* Oh, this is so easy to say and yet can be so challenging to live. Many of us have also been conditioned to tie our ideas about ourselves to others' beliefs about us. Life can be difficult if others determine what we feel about ourselves. Someone thinks Inchelina is pretty and she's happy. Someone thinks she's ugly and she feels sad. This rollercoaster can go up and down forever unless we discover our inner truth.

It is easy to see that the female Maybugs had an ulterior motive. They are insecure and feel threatened by Inchelina. This isn't to say that everyone who makes a negative comment is envious or wrong, but merely that we can't assume everyone's motives are good, nor that their perceptions are accurate.

In this case, the Maybugs comment on Inchelina's appearance, which of course is their personal opinions. If they said something about her personality, then she might want to examine it before she rejects it to see if in fact there is some truth in it. If they told her she was irritable, then she needs to take an honest look at her behavior to see if her tone of voice, or her actions, reflect an irritation she isn't aware of. If she reviews her actions carefully, and finds out that she doesn't feel irritation, then she can let it go. But, if she does find any truth in it, she can peer deeper into the irritation and attempt to discern what is causing it. In this case, we might assume that her feelings were hurt by the Maybugs, which she expressed as irritation, instead of standing up for herself.

The Maybug tells Inchelina that she's free when he sets her down. Inchelina isn't free though. Real freedom comes from within and can't be given to us, or taken away, by anyone. Our culture teaches us that freedom comes from money, war, possessions, jobs, family, traveling, being single, married, or the ability to go and do things, but none of that is true. These *things* don't give us freedom even if we think they do.

Our freedom comes when we free ourselves from our old false perceptions of what we believe about the world and ourselves. Freedom arises when we aren't victims of our egoic desires, or of the actions of others. When we fearfully believe we *have* to do something, we aren't free. If we think anything in the world will make us feel good, better, or happy, we aren't free, because then our happiness depends on certain external conditions being met. We aren't free, like Inchelina, if the opinions of others determine our well-being.

When we know who we are and don't define ourselves by, or allow our wellbeing to be determined by others, then we are free. In that consciousness, we know what to do and we do it. The heart is our guide and we embrace all that happens without reservation. Why? Because we know it's all love and is serving us by attempting to set us free in every single encounter. How do we reach this point? By discovering the love within us, a love that has never left and will never leave. Then we can live free of fear.

Is Inchelina free yet? Let's see…

Winter

All in all, she fares pretty well through the summer and fall. Despite being alone, she doesn't revert to the victim, which typically surfaces whenever Inchelina is challenged. She's making the best of her circumstances here and taking care of herself. Inchelina is feeling more competent during this time, but when winter arrives, she falters.

Inchelina doesn't have an *inner fire* to keep her warm enough in the winter, since she almost freezes to death, nor can she provide for herself, since she's starving. She isn't aware of her own soul, gifts, value, or who she really is. She needs someone's help to meet her needs. When things get difficult, and she needs to trust and depend on herself to keep herself going, she can't. There comes a time when we realize that what we are seeking in the world isn't there and we have to look inside to find a connection to a sustaining Source. This Source is always available. It's an inner sense of Self that's unwavering and rock solid dependable.

Winter is associated with the darkness of the unconscious. There isn't anything happening on the surface during this time, but inner changes take place beyond our sight. The inner world is the source of outer changes. As we heal and shift our ideas and perceptions, our lives are transformed.

Snow symbolically indicates that the watery emotions are frozen and are therefore stuck. There's something that Inchelina isn't feeling, and so life will take her to the perfect circumstances in order for her to see what's holding her back. She discovers that she can't take care of herself, now that winter has arrived, and she must ask someone for help. This situation is beyond her abilities, which may seem to be a negative turn of events, but by asking for help, she acknowledges her limitations and her need for others. We can learn to view experiences that challenge us, as opportunities to grow and gather more information about ourselves. There's no need to judge the situation, she just never learned that she needs to prepare for the barren winter months, or how.

When new characters appear in the story, we know that Inchelina needs to cultivate new qualities and learn something about herself that she isn't aware of, in order to move forward on her journey. If Inchelina had been able to survive where she was, she might have remained alone and isolated, disconnected from others and her Source. Therefore, we can see that this is the perfect time for her to engage with others.

When situations arise that reveal ways in which we cannot meet our own needs, they are opportunities for us to learn about our own limitations. Are you aware of, and connected to, an inner Source that can meet all of your needs? The help we get isn't only outer but can also be accessed through bringing an awareness to the Divine Presence within. If you don't already have a connection to something greater, then this is the time to begin to cultivate that relationship. If the idea of a Divine doesn't resonate with you, then you can perceive it as your intuition and explore your ability to access an inner guide.

Into the Unconscious

Inchelina walks shivering, hungry, and cold, until she reaches a hole in the ground. She knocks on the door and it's answered by a small field mouse. Inchelina asks the mouse for a grain of barley, since she needs something familiar as nourishment. Have you ever felt so down that you longed for a small taste of a time or place from the past— a time when you were feeling safe and loved? Inchelina has gone full circle, back to the beginning of her journey, when the barley seed that created her was planted in the soil. She intuitively realizes that by ingesting the grain of barley—like planting a seed—it will remind her of who she is and where she came from. But she may also be returning to a situation like the one she experienced with her mother. The field mouse gives her the barley, which connects her to the witch and her mother.

The barley seed was planted in the soil at the beginning and here Inchelina, created from that seed, goes into the earth. This is a descent into the underworld, as we saw with Psyche. The field mouse agrees to take Inchelina in for the winter; and she symbolically returns to the womb. She goes into the darkness of the unconscious, which is a place of discovery, creation, and rebirth.

The Field Mouse

Inchelina and the field mouse come to an agreement for the winter. The mouse represents another aspect of mother energy that sees Inchelina's value as it relates to her. The mouse believes Inchelina can help her, and in return, offers to share what she has.

One of Inchelina's jobs is to entertain the mouse by telling her stories. This will serve Inchelina as she develops her ability to express herself. The throat is a bridge between mind and body, the intellect and emotions. Cleaning is the other part of the arrangement. It is a grounding activity, which can bring Inchelina fully into the moment and her body. Although, it can also bring up servant energy again, and relate to taking care of, or cleaning up after others.

The servant often takes care of other's needs and ignores her own. In this case, with the mouse, they agree to help each other as an exchange. That means Inchelina has to work in order to get her needs met. Does she believe she has to serve, or fulfill other's needs, to receive what she wants? Do you believe that your support depends on others? Can you take care of yourself and do what you want? Do you believe that life supports you regardless of what you do so that you can follow your heart?

The truth is that life supports us all equally. It's merely our beliefs which limit this possibility.

Initially, Inchelina is happy with the field mouse. She adapts and makes the best of her new situation. Mice represent attention to details, since they are close to the ground. *Details and small steps can help us achieve what we desire.* Sometimes a goal can seem too big and distant, but if we persist in taking even small steps daily, we will reach our destination. This lesson in details is reinforced by Inchelina's activities, since the proper amount of detail makes a story come alive and paying attention to details when cleaning often means a job well done.

Grounding is required to manifest what we want in the world. When Inchelina was in the tree and closest to heaven, she would have been most open to messages from the intuitive realm, which is the place where ideas come from. Once we receive an idea, we "return to earth" to bring the message or gift to others. When we aren't grounded, we may have lots of ideas, but can't take the steps required to make them a reality. This can happen for a variety of reasons, one of which is that the idea seems beyond our reach. It may be bigger than who we think we are or more than we believe we deserve. Mouse energy can help to break a goal down into manageable steps and complete them in order to share what's been received.

When the Maybug dropped Inchelina on the daisy, she grew in her ability to relate to the physical world and learned to take care of herself, to a certain degree. Although, she didn't feel safe in the world alone, nor did she realize that she could depend on herself to provide what she needed to survive. She still perceived herself as a victim of circumstances, which is why she must go back into the unconscious in order to learn what she is capable of and to understand how life works. When winter arrived, and she came face-to-face with her limitations, fate guided her to a new place. This situation arose so she might heal those limitations and grow more fully into her truth.

The Rich Mole

Soon after Inchelina arrives, the field mouse announces the arrival of a new masculine energy. Her neighbor, the mole, is coming to visit. He has an ability to easily manifest material abundance, but he's blind. He can't see her, or see where to go, since he's disconnected from intuition—a feminine way of knowing. This can occur when the focus is on the material world and intellect. The benefit of not having sight is that it provides an opportunity to connect more deeply to and develop other senses. When we can't see where we are going, we open to other ways of knowing. When we can't see anything manifesting, we have to depend on other senses to discern that which is occurring out of sight. We have to trust things are happening even when we can't see it.

When we're unable to see, value can't be based on appearances, which was the case with the Maybugs. In order to develop an appreciation for the "other," we have to understand that value comes from sensing something deeper than looks or superficial qualities. Inchelina has been valued, up to this point, because she's pretty. Throughout the story there's been a focus on either her beauty, or, from the Maybugs perspective, her lack of it, and now the new masculine can't see. Others have judged her based on her appearance and Inchelina's self-worth and sense of identity has been influenced by them.

The mouse and the mole are in the unconscious, so they should offer a different viewpoint. This means they will value her based on something other than looks, and we already know what the mouse wants. In exchange for getting her basic needs met, Inchelina will clean and tell the mouse stories. We aren't clear yet as to what the mole's motives are.

If the mole can't *see* her, we do know that he also can't *see* or value her for who she truly is. As a part of her, this will be another masculine who doesn't honor her truth. This means some part of her is unaware of her needs and wants, which was evident from her winter experience above ground. He's a shadow masculine and only perceives her value as it relates to him, instead of for her. He won't be able to see her as independent from himself, and won't recognize her needs and desires, or her talents and gifts, unless they relate to or benefit him.

What's underground is like what's under water, which means these energies are unseen, out of sight, and in the unconscious. Inchelina needs to bring them into awareness. She must realize that her inner masculine doesn't respond to her, know or understand her. On the other hand, he does know how to manifest what's needed. He's also developed the senses that allow him to navigate the dark terrain of the unconscious and is proficient at tunneling through it. Although, he can't see well above ground, he has mobility underground. The mole and mouse both value Inchelina for how she can meet their needs, but then she needs them right now too.

We may find ourselves in relationship with someone who is more competent in one area than we are, like Inchelina and the mole. Instead of feeing inadequate, we can view it as an opportunity to learn from the person we have drawn into our lives. When winter came, Inchelina didn't know how to take care of herself, then life brings her someone who has the exact skill she needs to discover in herself.

The field mouse tells Inchelina that the mole is a good match for her, since he can provide materially, which is exactly what she needs to learn. We know she's deficient in this area. She was freezing when winter came, and this mole has a wonderful fur coat.

All of the mother characters are wounded in that they aren't connected to love and the heart. They are preoccupied with the material world and ignore the inner world, which is the domain of the feminine. This may also appear in life as not having time for the feminine, because attending to material needs takes up most of our time. The field mouse doesn't see Inchelina's power and competence, since she thinks Inchelina needs the mole to provide a comfortable life for her and to take care of her. It's really

Inchelina that believes she needs someone else to help her meet her needs, since she was the one who knocked on the mouse's door.

Although, we may have material abundance, we want to explore whether we give ourselves the things we *really* want and need? Is the soul, and the feminine, being cared for? Do we feel we can do whatever we want and are supported by life? Do we have to struggle and work hard to get our needs met? Are we in balance with activity and rest? Does the desire for material security take precedence over the heart's wishes? Is life easier with a partner?

We may feel overwhelmed by the requirements of life when we are alone. The field mouse erroneously believes that those of this world are responsible for our care. What the mouse doesn't realize is that the healing and integration of the inner masculine and feminine is what determines our wellbeing. Our support comes from a Source beyond our egoic selves and the material world.

Fear of Love

After meeting the blind mole, Inchelina immediately knows that she doesn't want to marry him, since he's a mole. Now, she's doing exactly what was done to her. This is another perfect example of how life shows us what we need to heal. Remember how distraught Inchelina was by the Maybug's rejection of her? This is the same as Inchelina not wanting to marry the ugly toad, nor the mole, based on who they are on the surface. She doesn't know anything about the mole. It doesn't necessarily mean she will like him, or that he's the right partner for her, but she doesn't even take the time to know him first. We want to be aware of any tendency to judge, since our judgment and rejection of others, means we are judging and rejecting parts of ourselves.

Initial impressions can be important and must be attended to, especially if it's our intuition speaking, but we need to be aware if it's judgment. If it is judgment, we want to dispel that tendency in order to approach what we encounter with open curiosity and not reject things at first sight. The mole is in her life for a reason and her judgment may keep her from seeing why he's appeared.

The mole is rich. He's successful in the material world, but not with matters of the heart. He dislikes the sun and flowers, which is significant, since Inchelina comes from, or was born in, a flower and loves the sun. Her true home would be among the flowers and in the sun, both of which he rejects. Remember, he can't see her.

The mole falls in love with Inchelina when she sings but hides his affection. Because he never learned to express his love, he represses his emotions. This stifling of love indicates Inchelina cannot openly love and accept all of herself. This part of her needs to be transformed. We need to be willing to be vulnerable, to love and embrace ourselves and others, regardless of their reactions. We may resist sharing our love with others due to their unworthiness or our own fear of rejection, but eventually we must move beyond that and understand that *the flow of love has nothing to do with the other person and everything to do with expressing our deeper truth.* This resistance to love could hamper Inchelina's progression to her true home, but we can be sure that life will send something to help her see and work through this.

We want to love ourselves fully, and love others, despite any unkindness on their part. Their behavior isn't a reflection of who we are, nor does it determine our worth, or wellbeing, although it can reveal our unconscious beliefs to us. We are worthy of love regardless of what others think or how they act. Their responses are based on their own conditioning and not on our value.

Digging in the Dark

The mole helps Inchelina to dig through the darkness of the unconscious. He spends most of his time in tunnels and isn't afraid of the dark. His energy helps Inchelina fearlessly unearth a part of herself that was buried. Our dreams may reveal unknown parts of us that need to be brought to light.

As the mouse, Inchelina, and the mole traverse a dark passageway between the mole's hole and the mouse's, the mole carries the light to reveal something new and shed light on that which is in the unconscious. He dug the passage and holds the light, despite being unable to see. As they walk, they encounter a dead swallow. The mole opens a hole to the surface so the light outside can shine down on the bird. Obviously, this character has a lot to do with navigating and illuminating the darkness, and what's in it.

The mole may represent someone who appears to be blind to who we are, but is actually helping us to see what's in our unconscious. They are shedding light on what we weren't aware of. What's being revealed now even though this character might be challenging us?

This is a wonderful example of how transformations occur. It appears as winter on the surface, with nothing going on, but here we can see how much is unfolding and happening underground. This is a time of significant growth for Inchelina, and this is where most of Inchelina's story takes place. Everything up until now has been relatively brief as far as her interactions are concerned. The biggest changes are taking place underground, or on the inside.

The mole lights the unconscious and helps Inchelina to see what qualities still need to be developed. This light is about knowing a greater truth than that of the world and being comfortable in the dark of the unconscious. He's not in balance though, because he rejects the light of the physical world and prefers the dark underground. There will be a time when Inchelina has to move out of the underworld and return to the above world of light, but it's not time yet. She still must learn to not be afraid of the dark, the unknown, that which is unseen, being alone, or the fallowness of winter.

The Dead Swallow

A *swallow* is associated with the sun, summer, and brings warmth.[41] The mouse, Inchelina, and mole assume the swallow froze to death, just like Inchelina almost did, which connects her with the bird. The swallow is frozen, wounded, and hidden in the unconscious. When a part of us gets lost or frozen in the past, it's hidden from consciousness. If we were wounded in childhood, and an emotion wasn't expressed, we might say it was frozen. The bird can also apply to a talent or gift that went into the unconscious because it wasn't valued. Another possibility is that the bird is connected with freedom, since the bird can fly. This frozen aspect that the swallow represents is in the darkness of the womb—the earth—and coming to consciousness. The group *sees* it as they go through the passage.

An old Native American legend[42] says the swallow stole light from the sun and brought it to earth, linking it to the mole (and Lucifer) in this story as a bringer of light. In the Middle Ages, there was the belief that the swallow knew of a magical stone or herb (celandine) that could restore eyesight, again connecting the bird symbolically with the mole. The swallow relates to communication, protection of the home, and spends more time in the air than on the ground, thus offering a new wider perspective and a new *vision*. He's the complement to Inchelina, the mole, and the mouse, since they are underground. But the bird, an aspect of Inchelina, is frozen. The swallow also assists in rising above the mundane aspects of life to solve problems.[43]

The swallow's wider vision contrasts with the detail-oriented view of the mouse. In many ways, the swallow energy balances that of the mouse and mole, so Inchelina won't get mired in the details associated with life, or stuck in the unconscious, and help her to remain aware of the bigger picture. The swallow's appearance suggests this aspect of Inchelina is ready to be recognized, healed, and integrated into consciousness. It has to be thawed and brought back to life.

If the underworld is associated with the dark, soul, and the moon, then the swallow represents the sun and sky, spirit, freedom. Inchelina is the soul that's in the unconscious and needs to be brought into consciousness. The introduction of the swallow means the opposite is coming to consciousness so the two can be integrated. The sun and masculine with the moon and feminine.

In the legend mentioned above, the swallow stole light from the sun and brought it to earth, which symbolizes the source of light and warmth in the body. He represents the connection to the light and warmth of Source within us. The light is in the unconscious, since the swallow and mole are underground. Inchelina isn't connected with her own inner light, since she almost froze when she was alone, as the cold weather came. This is what sent her to the mouse's home and the unconscious, in the first place. It's exactly where she needs to be in order to learn what she needs to be free, and to bring the swallow to consciousness.

The mole and mouse ignore the dead swallow because they don't value it, but something in Inchelina is moved. Remember, as parts of Inchelina, the presence of the mole and mouse suggest that she doesn't fully see or value this aspect of herself yet. Since the swallow is in the mole's new passageway, it's the mole's qualities that Inchelina needed in order to find the swallow. The swallow is between the mouse's house, which represents the feminine and body, while the mole's house would symbolize the masculine and intellect, or head. The area between the body and head is the neck, which means the frozen swallow indicates a block in the throat and therefore, expression. At some point, Inchelina learned she wasn't safe to express herself.

She can't freely express who she is, what she feels, or wants. Inchelina isn't living in a place that honors her, which can be symbolic or literal. Her life doesn't reflect her needs, desires, and loves. But, the beauty of life is that it wants us to live in full authenticity and will bring us what we need to see and feel, so that we may realize our true selves. We just need to open our eyes to see what we are looking for, and to recognize the places that we are still being inauthentic.

Inchelina secretly weaves a blanket and stuffs cotton beneath the bird to protect it from the cold ground. She's privately exploring, and becoming familiar with the sparrow, which is a new aspect of herself. Inchelina does this in secret, hiding her actions from those parts of her that might reject it, meaning the mole and mouse. This means she needs to remain hyper-vigilant for any comments from others inside or outside of her, and clear these beliefs if they arise. This is the first time she freely takes care of something other than herself with no expectation of return.

Awakening

Inchelina nurses what's frozen and rejected. Instead of ignoring this part of her, like the others have, she accepts, embraces, and nurtures it. This indicates movement away from being a victim and toward empowerment.

Sometimes we have to *fully accept what's happening* before we see any change. When Inchelina grieves for this frozen part of her, she thaws it out and brings it back to life, which tears can do. The warmth she expresses for the bird, or the part that was free at one time but doesn't feel free now, changes things. Her faith is rekindled when she realizes the swallow's *heart* is still beating. There is still life in this part of her she thought was dead. The aspect of her that carries the light, can express, sing, and fly is breathing. It isn't going to remain frozen in the unconscious forever.

Inchelina is initially afraid of the swallow. The part of her that she has reawakened is much bigger than she is. Symbolically, the swallow carries an expanded vision of who she is and what's possible for her, which is beyond her current ideas. Is it safe to open to something she really wants and take a chance believing she might be able to have it? Can she let go of disappointment? Inchelina is afraid of the possibilities associated with opening to this part of her, but fortunately rises to the occasion and finds the courage to just take the next step. This opening relates to the heart.

When the swallow opens his eyes, he says he will fly away. Inchelina tells him it isn't the right time because it's still winter. Her comment reflects what she's learned about the rhythm of life and knowing when it's the right time, and it isn't now. The swallow needs to stay in the darkness of the earth until spring. He needs time for his wings and his heart to mend. Inchelina's comment suggests that we don't want to emerge too soon. We may feel vulnerable in the beginning of a big shift and want to be strong, ready, and clear, when we share ourselves and our gifts. The conditions must be right. If we go out too soon and encounter the displeasure of others, or remain unseen, then we might go back into hiding. Since the mole and mouse don't like the swallow, Inchelina is wise not to tell them it's alive. Before we have a solid foundation in a new level of consciousness, we need to be careful who we share our dreams with and avoid telling those who won't support and encourage us, like the moles and field mice in our lives. We also, once again, have to pay attention to the mouse and mole parts of ourselves that may reject things before we even get a chance to go out the door.

Spring Departure

Fortunately, the swallow takes Inchelina's advice and waits until spring. As he finally prepares to depart, he offers to take Inchelina with him, but she isn't ready to leave the comfort of her current situation. She perceives it as a safe and predictable place. The memory of the cold winter is still too fresh for her to risk leaving the safety of the mole and mouse, whom she knows will take care of her. Remember, these are also parts of her, so this indicates that there is a conflict between the part of her that wants to go back into the world, and the part of her that's afraid to.

If Inchelina does go with the swallow, then she will be on her own again. Currently, she's ignoring her own needs for the mouse, which is the part of her that says to stay put and play it safe. Inchelina doesn't want the mouse to be sad and lonely and is willing to sacrifice the part of her that desires freedom. This is also Inchelina's projection of her own fear of being alone, which may also cause her to stay. She doesn't feel safe or trust enough yet to follow her dreams and believe she will be supported. Inchelina isn't sure her needs will be met if she leaves. And so, she says goodbye to the swallow.

Are you comfortable being alone? Do you believe you can provide abundantly for yourself as you do what you love and live the life of your dreams? If not, dive deeper and explore the feelings that come up. It's important here to make sure you aren't taking care of others, coaching others into the life of their dreams, while ignoring the deeper call to free yourself. This isn't just freedom that comes with money, but a freedom that comes from believing we can have what we want and need and follow our hearts. When we understand there isn't an outer authority who takes care of us, or tells us what we can and can't, should or shouldn't, do, then we are truly ready to fly.

The mouse thinks that it's best for Inchelina to marry the mole. Her decision to stay where she is means she's remaining with the part of her that ignores what she wants, needs, and can't see her, or acknowledge who she truly is. It's the aspect of her that doesn't think she can't *have* what she wants and needs, or be free. The belief is that it's not possible for her to follow her dreams. She's choosing to not go out in the sunshine and fly away, which means she will stay underground, and hidden in the unconscious. She'll take care of the mouse and mole, and the mole will provide for her, which resembles her original home. The mole and mouse are the parts of Inchelina that reject what she loves, and so, she requires more time to heal. There doesn't need to be any judgment if we aren't ready yet either. We can accept what we feel and allow ourselves to be present with our fears, or resistance.

The blind mole isn't interested in Inchelina's needs. He wants a companion, someone to take care of him and keep his loneliness at bay. There's a disconnection between the masculine and feminine, since the mouse and mole have two separate homes underground. This is like the head and the heart/body separated by the neck, which we discussed previously. The passageway was blocked by the swallow—representing freedom and expression—and here we see that Inchelina isn't ready to speak up for herself yet, nor take action on her own behalf, in order to make her dreams come true.

However, now that the swallow is leaving, the passageway is going to be clear. This frees Inchelina to begin expressing what she wants and needs.

Summer Arrives

Inchelina spends the summer underground preparing for her marriage, which means she's going along with the plan, despite what it means for her future. She's ignoring her own feelings. But, when it comes to within four weeks of her wedding date, she *finally* speaks up. Her throat chakra is now clear, and she tells the mouse she doesn't want to marry the mole. The mouse, who wants to remain in the dark and is comfortable there, tells Inchelina it's the path of safety and financial security.

We can look at what we are doing and if we are making choices based on safety and security for ourselves or others. Are your decisions based on love and the heart, or what's practical and will supposedly provide what you need? Do you feel you have to sacrifice what you want for others? Do you sacrifice what you want for a belief that you can't have what you really want? Or a belief in needing to be practical, responsible, conservative, etc. This is the time to explore how we feel about support, what's possible, and the world we live in. Do you believe life will support you as you follow your heart? Or do you believe that you must compromise or wait?

The mouse threatens to harm Inchelina if she doesn't listen. If she does what she wants, she will get hurt, and won't be safe. This is why Inchelina didn't leave with the swallow to begin with. She didn't want to freeze to death. The mouse represents the out-of-balance feminine, who appears repeatedly throughout the story, ignoring Inchelina's needs and desires, and is also out of touch with the natural laws of abundance. This is a positive step for Inchelina to speak up and challenge this part of herself. She must confront this pattern of sacrificing herself to care for others and believing her security is at issue. Her choice is between the path of love or fear, safety, and security.

Inchelina will reconnect with the original Mother, the earth, and goddess energy. She needs to forgive the mothers for ignoring her needs. She has been unable to experience abundance, because the Mother is in the unconscious and she doesn't know the generosity of the natural state of life. This isn't about money and material things, but all of Inchelina's needs being met, and feeling sustained by a larger, loving, supportive energy. Inchelina must connect with the love and abundance within herself.

What does it mean to truly live in abundance with all of our needs met, if we aren't referring to an excess of material possessions? What nourishes the soul and creates peace? Is it following the heart? Being in nature? Creating? Living free of fear? Simplicity?

Inchelina is living within the limitations she's created for herself in order to remain safe. She can't go outside, beyond the entrance to the mouse's hole, because *Inchelina believes she isn't free to leave.* There will always be practical reasons why we think we can't do what we want to do. There is always someone, or some reason, but the reality is that what prevents us from being free is our fear and conditioning. If you immediately think "this isn't true" for you, "This doesn't apply to me because in *my* situation_____ (fill in the blank)," then it may be helpful to sit with any resistance to change that comes up.

As the wedding draws near, Inchelina goes to the entrance of the mouse's hole, which is the boundary—the edge of where she's allowed to go. She says goodbye to what she loves, the warmth of the sun and living a conscious life above ground. If she stays underground, it means *she's choosing* to live unconsciously, to not follow her dreams, and is ignoring her needs and desires. As she stands in the doorway to say her final farewells to freedom, the sun, the sky, and the flowers, she hears something...

It's the swallow.

Flight to Freedom

Inchelina cries as she tells the swallow about her impending marriage to the mole. These tears heal and cleanse the old wound. She now **sees** *if she stays where she is, she's choosing a life that isn't free. The swallow speaks the truth of what Inchelina needs and she finally realizes what she wants and has to do.* Life is offering her another chance to live consciously and Inchelina chooses flight, life, and freedom.

This is the time to act and take advantage of opportunities that present themselves. We can take the swallow up on his offer to ride away from a situation that doesn't honor us by paying attention to opportunities that present themselves. We don't want to make excuses as to why we can't make changes, because we can begin right where we are. We don't need to wait any longer for the money to come, the move to take place, to find the right space, or any other seemingly plausible reason. The time to challenge the old assumptions that we can't have what we want is *now.* Change the mantra from "I can't," to "I can" and look for those opening doors. See where you are more closely and open to what options are being presented to you right where you are. Freedom is knocking on the door, believe in it, take the steps, and flap those wings. It may feel odd and unfamiliar when the new birdie starts to fly, but just keep flapping. When we decide, make up our minds, and pay attention to those details that will take us where we want to go, we will step out of the old and into the new.

The flight to freedom isn't always smooth, warm, and easy, and Inchelina gets cold along the way. But now she can snuggle up to the warmth of the swallow, the inner sun, and fly away from the coldness of winter, of the old life, and into the summer of the new. Using the gifts we have been given to keep us warm and to keep us going, we must stay the course and follow the guidance of our inner light. We have to believe in our abilities and ourselves, and also understand that we are supported. When we trust life and our ability to fly, we are free. As Inchelina follows her heart, life becomes more beautiful.

A Gift of Wings

When they reach their destination, the temple ruins—a spiritual place— the swallow gives Inchelina the freedom to choose the flower where she will live. The white of the flowers is a spiritual color associated with marriage, cleansing, baptism, and purity. Inchelina intuitively chooses a flower with a king on it. He instantly recognizes her; he *sees her* and her beauty. The heart of the masculine is healed and he knows she's his queen. This masculine is open and expresses what he wants, which indicates that Inchelina has healed her masculine side to be able to now attract this king. He offers her a crown, suggesting that she has also healed her connection to the divine Source. This occurs because she finally heard and followed spirit calling her home to her Self.

In addition to the king, the little flower angels also value and acknowledge Inchelina as they offer her even more gifts. They *see* her and know who she really is. They recognize her as one of their own. The universe is abundant and delights in providing for us generously, when we are able to open to accept what we desire, and more. Now the gifts come directly to Inchelina and she doesn't have to depend on the mole, mouse, king, or anyone else for her wellbeing. Since Inchelina was born to a human, she didn't know who she was, but now she does.

Inchelina receives a gift of wings from the angels, because that is who and what she really is. She didn't know and wasn't able to become her full and true self, until she recognized that she was a fairy and then was able to receive her own wings. Those wings mean that she has integrated the sparrow and butterfly energies, and accepted them as an integral aspect of herself. Inchelina can now fly on her own and doesn't need to depend on anyone else to take her where she wants to go. She discovers she isn't of the material world. The transparency of the king and the angels indicates these beings are spiritual, which is why they reside in a temple—a sacred place.

The king renames Inchelina, since her old name was based on her appearance and doesn't serve her. He gives her the beautiful name of Maja to honor who she is. Maj and Maya were names of the deity that presided over May Eve celebrations. "The festival celebrated her virgin or "flower" aspect, harbinger of fruit to come."[44] This suggests she's cleared the conditioning and returned to the purity of her Self.

Here, the word "virgin" isn't a reference to sexuality, but to an independent woman. This is someone who is able to stand on her own and is whole and complete in herself. She knows how to take care of herself, provide for her needs, and is free in every way.

And now I wonder dear reader... who you really are? Do you have your wings and are you flying free? Are you living your dreams? Is your world a sacred place? Did you choose love like Inchelina did? Do you feel supported by life? If not, there's still time to follow your heart and fly to a place where you belong.

Seven

Brier Rose (Sleeping Beauty): Including What's Been Rejected

*O*nce upon a time, there was a king and queen who longed for a child. As the queen sat in her bath one day, a frog crawled out of the water, and told her they would have a baby girl within a year. The king was so delighted when his beautiful daughter was born that he decided to celebrate. He invited everyone in the kingdom, including the wise women, so that they could bless his new child. There were thirteen wise women, but the king only had twelve plates, so one of them had to be excluded.

The celebration was lovely, and at the end, the wise women took turns blessing the child. The eleventh one spoke and then the thirteenth woman burst into the room to get revenge for not being invited. She said the princess would prick her finger on a spindle when she was fifteen and die. The horrified guests, king, and queen watched as she stormed out of the castle. The twelfth wise woman still had her wish, and although she couldn't undo the spell, she could ease it. She said the princess wouldn't die, but instead would sleep for a hundred years.

The king had every spindle in the entire kingdom destroyed to protect his daughter. Then, on the day that she turned fifteen, the king and queen just happened to be away. The princess spent the entire day exploring all of the rooms in the palace. She climbed the stairs to a tower and discovered a tiny door with a rusty key in it, which she turned. When she opened the door, she saw an old woman who sat spinning flax. The princess asked what the spindle was, because she hadn't ever seen one before, and accidentally pricked her finger on it. She fell into a deep sleep and the entire palace fell asleep with her, including the king and queen who had returned home.

A brier hedge grew up around the entire castle to protect it from the occasional curious prince who had heard the story of the beautiful sleeping princess. Each one, intent on finding her, would try to get through the briers, but got caught in them and died.

Then one day, another prince heard the story from an old man and said that he would try to find the princess. A hundred years had passed and so when this prince approached the hedges, they parted, and he passed easily through. He saw that everyone in the entire castle was asleep. When he came to the tower stairs, he climbed them and walked through the little door. There he saw the beautiful princess asleep beside the spinning wheel. He bent over and kissed her lovely face. She opened her eyes and the entire castle awakened with her.

They married and lived happily ever after.*

---

* Full story in Manheim's Grimms' Tales for Young and Old.

Introduction

The story of "Brier Rose" is more familiarly known as "Sleeping Beauty." This story's focus is on what is being excluded, which in this case, is the thirteenth wise woman. She becomes quite irate when the king doesn't invite her to the celebration. She wants revenge for not being valued and takes her anger out on his daughter, since that's what he values most. Symbolically, this wise woman represents the excluded part of Brier Rose, which is deemed unacceptable to the culture, family, and as a result, to herself. The qualities of the thirteenth wise woman need to be reclaimed and integrated by the heroine, and us, to experience wholeness.

The question this story poses is, "What's excluded because it is perceived as being unacceptable?"

The Couple's Longing

This is the story of another king and queen who can't generate new life, which means they live in a wasteland. Stuck in an old story, it's as though they are in a repeating loop that they can't seem to get out of. This couple doesn't understand the cycles of life, which means they can't produce a child. If they aren't able to create something new, it may be because they cannot sustain the effort to reach completion. The result of this is stagnation and a lack of renewal. The king and queen *long for what they don't have and believe that attaining it will fulfill them.*

We see this desire for a child repeatedly in fairy tales. The couple who wants a baby, which they believe will make them feel happy, fulfilled, and whole. This is the literal view, but when we look at it symbolically, this longing represents the search for what's missing in consciousness. The characters are living an old state of awareness that needs to be transformed and a new energy is required in order to facilitate that transformation. We can perceive the new energy as the baby.

In the world, this inability to create new life may appear as having trouble manifesting. This means projects never quite make it to completion. We have books that never get written and published, paintings that are half painted or remain unseen, gardens that don't get planted. We are too busy to learn new things and our dreams are never fulfilled. There may be a lack of inspiration, or the dream and capacity to begin is there, but the patience to sustain the desire falters, causing it to sputter and die.

Longing can lead to greater resilience, if there is patience in the waiting for fulfillment. In our culture, we tend to want immediate results. If we don't get what we want right away or when we think we should, we can miss what *does* show up or might believe there's some reason why we can't have what we want and give up. For the king and queen, it's the child they desire, and they do remain patiently persistent.

We can have desires, but we don't want to believe we will only be happy when they are fulfilled. Our happiness is here now and doesn't depend on the fulfillment of anything. We are often conditioned by society, parents, and others to believe that when we get what we want we will be happy, but that isn't true happiness. Our true nature is happiness. We want to move toward that for fulfillment and not objects of the world. The king and queen believe something is missing from their lives—in this case it's a child—which they believe will somehow make their lives better.

This longing for something outer, when fulfilled, can lead to short-term happiness. The circumstance or item may then appear to be the answer to our prayers for greater joy, but when our wellbeing is based on certain conditions being met, then we aren't free. As we said above, this desire on the part of the king and queen for a child is a literal interpretation of the story, when what they really want is an inner experience of wholeness.

The thwarting of an outer desire can lead to the search for a deeper inner-based happiness. If we see this child as representing the soul—that which is missing when the focus is on the material world—then what the parents really want is an awareness of their own soul. The couple may realize that all of their riches don't make them feel happy or satisfied, and then look to see what *is* missing. They think the longing is for a child, but the soul is what they truly desire, although they don't realize that's what they are searching for.

The Frog's Message

The queen is in the bath when she notices a frog crawling out of the water. In fairy tales, the frog is usually associated with the prince, who is often under the spell of an evil witch or fairy. A frog is comfortable with water, which we know is a symbol associated with emotion. Since the queen is in the bathtub, which means a cleansing is taking place and the emotions are being contained. The frog emerges from the water, which indicates that there it is necessary to move out of the emotion in order to generate new life. *The couple needs to stop wallowing in their longing and disappointment about the past so they can move forward.*

If we get stuck in our emotions, stagnation occurs, and then we can't move forward. We can't seem to do what's necessary to fulfill our desires or find a true and lasting inner happiness, because the emotions feel overwhelming. Since the queen is just sitting in the water, it suggests that this is a factor in their inability to create a child. The feminine is in the emotions and needs help getting out. It's like we said above, about a story— or pattern—repeating endlessly and causing certain emotions to arise, and we can't seem to get out of the loop. We want to be aware of the stories we are telling ourselves, or what we believe about our current situation, then sit with what we feel. Let's say you have a financial situation that you keep trying to resolve but can't. When we sit with the emotions activated by the situation, and focus on the physical sensations in the body, and not the narrative in the head, then the emotions should settle and pass. If we reach a state of peace, then the answers about how to proceed often become obvious, and the situation changes.

The frog shows up, essentially as the young masculine, to demonstrate how to get out of the emotions. When he does climb out of the water, he shows the queen that the way to new life is to separate herself from the repeating cycle of emotion. She now has a new perspective. The queen knows that the emotions are separate from her. They can come and go, rise and fall, as she remains the witness, and doesn't get mired in them. When the emotions flow and we don't get caught up in them, they cleanse us, and we can move on. The cleansing is complete for the king and queen, which means they can prepare for the arrival of something new—a baby.

The frog, child, king, and queen make the number four, which is about wholeness. This is an indication that this path is about achieving wholeness—a state of consciousness in which nothing is missing, needs to be fixed, added, or taken away. Acceptance of what is will be the key to embodying wholeness and is the way to move forward.

The king and queen wait for a year as their anticipation and desire build. They know they are going to get what they want, which helps them to maintain a consciousness of trust. The queen practices not getting caught in emotion as she sits in stillness. She waits, which is a time of inactivity and receptivity to inspiration, as she remains open to receive the seed of new life. Allowing whatever arises to come without resisting it or getting drawn into it, she learns to listen within and be at ease with her feelings, especially her sense of longing. There is a knowing and acceptance that life unfolds perfectly, which helps her to allow what is, to be as it is, and remain at peace.

We are longing for something unknown, searching for what's missing, and trying to fill an emptiness that can never be filled with things of the world. What we are looking for is the soul, the young feminine that's been absent from the culture and from many of us personally. We often don't recognize what we really want because it's been ignored for so long; we don't even know that is what's lost. It was devalued, and as such, went into hiding, or the unconscious. We're trying to fill our longing with the wrong things, which creates a greater and greater desire in all of us for what's missing. When it does emerge, we will value it even more.

A Baby is Born

The king and queen rejoice at the birth of their beautiful daughter. We will feel as thrilled as the king does when the feminine soul returns, is seen, and experienced within us and our culture. Instead of rejecting things associated with the feminine and soul, we will value them, recognize their beauty and all that they contain. We will understand that this is what has been making us search endlessly, blindly wandering, lost and uncertain, on a quest we weren't aware we were even on.

As we discussed in the previous tales, some of the qualities associated with the feminine are presence, being, beauty, nature, instinct, the body, feeling and emotion, empathy, darkness, power, and connectedness. The ability to wait, be still, and to be content is feminine. In the quiet that often appears in fairy tales as a period of waiting, any repressed feelings and emotions will rise to the surface to be felt. As they are experienced, witnessed and accepted, we grow stronger and more stable. Sometimes, we feel afraid of this darkness—the unknown—because we aren't familiar with the inner world as much as the outer. Most of us were conditioned to believe that extraversion and the outer life matters more than the inner world.

In the story, once the queen gives birth to the baby, we don't hear any more about her, except in passing. She receives the message that the child will come and then gives birth to her. The queen represents one facet of the feminine, the silent mother, who isn't a main character in the story. The king invites other aspects of the feminine, the wise women, to celebrate the birth of the young feminine. The mother steps back and the wise women step forward.

Wise Women

These wise women are in tune with life and in harmony with nature. They *know*, and remember, especially what the mother doesn't, since they are aware of cycles—birth, life, death, and rebirth; winter, spring, summer, and fall. During her time of waiting, the queen prepares the way for the emergence of these deeper aspects of feminine wisdom and the child. *The wise women appear when the new young feminine is born. Wisdom emerges into conscious awareness as the soul arrives.*

Only twelve wise women are invited by the king to the celebration, because he only has twelve plates, which means a thirteenth woman is excluded. Initially, life was not enough without a child, and now there aren't enough plates. Someone is being left out and something is being ignored. We will have to see which wise woman is not included to discern what's being rejected.

The king allows the wise women associated with *good* feminine qualities to come to the celebration. These wise women take turns bestowing their gifts on the princess. The ones mentioned in the story are beauty, wealth, and virtue, but what are the rest? What other gifts come from the feminine? The story tells us, "Everything a person could wish for in this world."[45]

Except that, we know one wise woman is being shut out, so what is the king omitting?

All attention is on the wise women as they bestow their gifts, when suddenly the thirteenth wise woman barges into the celebration. She's so enraged that she angrily puts a curse of death on the baby. She proclaims to the crowd, "When she is fifteen, the princess will prick her finger on a spindle and fall down dead."[46] The curse will come to pass as the princess reaches a critical transition point in her life. This is when a girl shifts away from childhood and toward adulthood. When she is to emerge into the world as a young woman, she will die instead, and remain in the unconscious. This repeats the king and queen's old pattern in which things aren't successfully brought out into the world. They have an issue with generativity, and now the story is clearly illustrating why.

Whatever it is that kept the king and queen from successful creation in the past must be healed in order to achieve wholeness and freedom.

At this point, it is clear that the thirteenth wise woman is actually the key to generativity and life, for the king and queen. Thirteen is a number associated with the feminine, fertility, the goddess, and moon cycles, since that's the number of full moons in a year. There is fear associated with thirteen, and it's considered by some to be unlucky. This superstition around the number has persisted for centuries.

If the king had his way, the thirteenth wise woman would remain unseen, and in the unconscious. But she won't have it; if she's not invited to the party, she's going to get revenge. She isn't happy with being excluded and is going to speak up about it. She's the aspect of the feminine that carries the anger at not feeling seen, included, or valued. Her action is referred to as an "evil spell," but the only way the fullness of the rejected feminine can come to consciousness is by looking within and letting her come to the party as well, even though she doesn't fit in, and we might not like what she has to say. The thirteenth wise woman is the rejected feminine that has a voice and is willing to speak up.

The twelfth wise woman, since she hasn't blessed the child yet, changes the spell of the thirteenth. The princess will only fall asleep for a hundred years and won't die. If the young girl died, the feminine and soul wouldn't be embodied and lived in the world. This softening of the spell by the twelfth wise woman means the princess will spend more time in the unconscious, looking inward, then reawaken and emerge from her sleep. This is going to take some amount of patience.

We want to see if there is a part of us that puts the brakes on things before we bring them into the world. We can look at our challenging emotions and see what we feel about them. Are we free to feel whatever we feel, seemingly good or bad? Do we play the role of the good and project, repress, reject, and ignore anything we deem as negative, such as anger, or any other qualities or talents? It' important to come to terms with all of the rejected aspects of ourselves before going out into the world.

The princess will have to integrate the qualities of the excluded angry feminine and rejected wise woman in order to wake up. This represents what's referred to as the dark feminine. It's Psyche's deceitful sisters and the angry, vengeful, Aphrodite who wanted to kill Psyche. We saw this darkness in Beauty's manipulative sisters, in "Beauty and the Beast," who wanted her to stay at home overlong so the Beast would kill her. It's the witch in "Hansel and Gretel," who eats children. It's the powerful feminine who is jealous, destructive, and frustrated, from being excluded and isolated for such a long time. What does she want? What's she demanding? She wants to be included and have a place at the table.

Fate Intervenes

The father wants to protect his daughter, but he can't. He attempts this by inviting only the twelve wise women, but the one he omits curses the princess. Then, once she has been cursed, he attempts to protect her by having all the spindles in the kingdom removed. He thinks he can keep her safe this way, but this is beyond his reach. Fate is intervening. The thirteenth wise woman is more powerful than he is. Surprise. What does he believe he's protecting her from? Herself? The truth of herself? Or, is he trying to protect himself?

Are we trying to protect, hide, avoid, or eliminate something critical? Some perceived sense of self that would be upset by the inclusion of that which has been isolated and walled off? Do you know of any emotions, work, or talent, that wants to be invited to the party and included?

Fate cannot be manipulated, even by a well-meaning father. The spindle and spinning are associated with the goddess and the weaving of fate. This situation was inevitable, and the interaction with the goddess was necessary, in order to create greater consciousness. Women who use the spindle know how to create. They sit and spin. Fate wounds the princess and then heals her as well. This wound means she will fall asleep to the world—descend into the unconscious for a period of time—and experience the depth of the thirteenth wise woman's exclusion and isolation, before she emerges into the world.

The princess embodies all the qualities that make her loveable, kind, generous, and virtuous. What's missing are the so-called dark qualities such as anger, jealousy, and selfishness, which are often associated with the evil stepsisters, evil stepmother, or wicked witch, but here they are associated with the excluded thirteenth wise woman. The princess is a "good girl" and in order to come into wholeness she will need to experience the "negative" qualities of the excluded wise woman.

Isn't it interesting that on her fifteenth birthday the king and queen aren't at home? He did all he could to protect her, and then on the fateful day, he isn't there. She wanders through the castle alone, which represents the psyche, with her gaze turned within. Exploring out of the way places, she discovers an unfamiliar small door with a rusty key. The room is unknown, unused, overlooked, and contains something that hasn't been seen before.

She turns the rusty key, opens the door, and sees an old woman in the room spinning flax. The princess is enchanted by the spinning spindle, as she should be. Fate is calling her. We often judge what happens as good or bad, but this experience is what will transform her. She's meeting a hidden part of herself that has been cast off and locked away in a tower, alone, isolated, and rejected. It's the necessary wound to release her fully from the old family pattern of an inability to create. This old woman knows how to take raw materials and create something of value. Our challenges are intended to set us free.

Falling Asleep

As soon as the princess touches the spindle, she pricks her finger and falls asleep. Not only does *she* fall asleep, but the whole castle falls asleep. This isn't part of the wise woman's spell, but we can see that if the young feminine isn't fully integrated or awake, then nothing happens. Everything is affected by her state. When she sleeps, everyone sleeps. She's in a death-like sleep, or unconscious to the outer world. This is a sleep from which she can't awaken, until the appointed hour.

Brier Rose pricks her finger on the center post of the spindle. That means she touches the still point around which everything revolves, the center of that which is rotating. She falls asleep to the world because she opens to that still silence within her. When she's focused on this inner space, nothing happens in the world. All is still outside, which reflects the inner stillness.

There's a perfection in the timing of the unfolding that we need to learn to trust. If what we desire hasn't yet come to fruition, there may be a deeper reason why. In this story, there are two things happening during this isolation. One is getting to know the thirteenth wise woman and the second is being in the stillness. The princess remains in the room with the wise woman for a long, long time. They become acquainted, familiar, and the princess comes to know the rejected feminine. She learns of the woman who wasn't good, or virtuous, and wouldn't accept exclusion in the end. This wise woman holds a power that we need to help us speak up, create, and ultimately, emerge into the world, otherwise we can't do it in a healthy and balanced way.

The princess turns her gaze within and discovers something she hasn't seen before. She must witness within herself the angry, vengeful, frustrated feelings of helplessness, hopelessness, disappointment, and loss. The parts of her that feel ignored, unvalued, inadequate, unworthy, unloved, and rejected. She will also discover aspects of herself that were isolated, either from her own gaze, or hidden from the world's. These unconscious parts of her, in conjunction with her feelings, are being brought to consciousness. The depth of emotions here can be *daunting*, but she must witness, and feel them, to be free. And it goes without saying, she doesn't want to get mired in them, like her mother did in the past.

When these emotions are brought to consciousness, they can feel very powerful indeed. Their intensity does diminish over time though, as they are integrated. When we sit in stillness and look into ourselves, and allow our feelings to be, regardless of what appears, we *see* what others didn't want to. We witness what the king excluded from the celebration and feel whatever we feel without judging it. We welcome that which was ignored, unseen, not valued by others, and accept all of it.

This is the process of embracing all of ourselves—that which is loved by the culture, and that which is despised by it. We can let go of being "good," doing what others want, being who others want us to be, and sacrificing ourselves for the needs of others. Fearlessly, we may then embody who we truly are. The death-like sleep symbolizes the death of the old pattern of being "good"—all light and no dark.

If we have wanted to be perceived as all-good, then we need to look at how willing we are to let go of that old role in order to fully become ourselves? The extent to which we are invested in that pattern of behavior will determine how free we allow ourselves to be.

A Brier Hedge

An impenetrable brier hedge grows up around the castle, or the psyche, as the princess sleeps. That which is innocent is protected while no one is conscious, aware, or able to protect her. She is vulnerable. The hedge may appear as our being defensive when we don't feel safe. This keeps others out and away, at a safe distance, for the moment. The princess is isolated by conditions beyond her control.

When we perceive our situation as isolating, and feel unable to change it, we can sit with it to see why we are where we are. Then we want to full accept what is happening. It may feel uncomfortable because of the emotion that gets activated when feeling helpless to change what's occurring. What are the current circumstances showing us? Is the space that has been created here to help us to deepen into a learning we have recently acquired? Or, to embody some new way of being?

If the princess had emerged into the world as a good girl at fifteen, then she wouldn't have been able to remain true to herself. It wouldn't have felt safe. Brier Rose would have been who and what her father wanted her to be, and what he thought was acceptable. Those were the limitations imposed on her from her childhood circumstances. She might have believed, like him, that she needed to control events to be safe. Staying true to her calling may have proved to be a challenge and she would have been swayed by the beliefs of others. Sometimes our path can take us down roads the culture considers unorthodox. This may be something as simple as taking a creative path or speaking out in ways that aren't validated by society.

In order to transform the culture in which we live, we may have to challenge current paradigms and choose to live differently. We don't want to do this from the ego and charge into the world as a rebellious warrior, like the thirteenth wise woman, with a chip on her shoulder. If we wish to live authentically and follow our hearts, then we must be fearless in following an inner voice that's free of egoic desire. This is what's happening for Brier Rose. She's learning to listen and gathering the strength to follow her own calling.

As she sleeps, the princess transforms the belief that she needs to defend herself from those who ignore, can't see, or don't value her. This is a time for her to learn to relax, feel safe, and let go of control. She can *surrender* to the spinning of fate and *know* that she doesn't need to interfere, but that all is unfolding for her benefit and her greatest good. Brier Rose's true inner joy is arising with ever greater frequency. This is a happiness that isn't contingent on things being a certain way in the outer world, but surfaces spontaneously, regardless of circumstances, because she's undefended.

The king tried to control the fate of the princess and keep her safe. He wanted to protect her from what he thought was bad, but he couldn't. Her father wanted her to be a "good" girl, but that's not her path. She must accept and surrender to a sleep in which she learns to allow and receive whatever shows up. Then, her response will be intuitive and not from the intellect or judgment. She doesn't have to protect herself from what appears, since it all arrives for her to grow in consciousness. Brier Rose emerges from the old patterns fear, anger, and outdated beliefs.

Awakening

As the princess is sleeping and encountering challenges on her inner journey, the frog from the mother's bath at the beginning of the story is transforming into a prince. It hasn't been an easy process for either of them. The masculine attempted many times to enter the castle but couldn't. This is an indication that there have been many failed attempts to unite and emerge. Each time the masculine attempts to penetrate the brier hedge, he is evolving in her consciousness. This new masculine must learn not to judge experiences as good or bad, in order to protect and defend, or avoid and exclude, like her father did. He's must be able to fearlessly face whatever arises—in every situation—in order to clearly see what needs to be done, and then act. All the princes who try to reach the princess are combined in consciousness, to represent one masculine energy, who won't give up and continues to try to enter the castle.

Then one day, an old man tells the story of a sleeping princess called Brier Rose to a prince. Her name suggests an integration of the rose's beauty—her "good" qualities—with the thorns—that which is perceived as "bad." The old man warns the prince that many other young men have died trying to get through the thorny hedges, but the prince doesn't care about the others. He's courageous. He isn't afraid of the possibility of death because he knows the only way to live is *with* the feminine. He'll take his chances and attempt to penetrate the protective barrier, to awaken the princess.

Many princes have died trying to get in because a defensive stance prevents anything from coming in or going out. People can't get in and gifts can't be shared with the world. The princes have been unable to get through the hedge, because the princess didn't feel safe. Therefore, the union of the masculine and feminine couldn't happen, either inside or outside.

The fearlessness of this prince parts the briers, which means the princess now feels safe. The hedges open as he approaches, and he easily passes through. This means there has been a transformation in consciousness and the princess isn't afraid of challenges, judgments of others, or the emotions of those around her. This masculine energy is decisive and goes forward with determination. The king thought he had to protect the princess from the angry wise woman, by attempting to control the situation, and isolate Brier Rose to keep her from harm. This new prince isn't afraid, since the princess has faced and integrated the wise woman.

We can bring to consciousness all the emotions that are activated by feeling ignored, unvalued, or excluded. As we witness these feelings and accept them as our own, whatever we ignored, didn't value, or excluded is now included, valued, and seen. If we accept all of ourselves, and don't care what others think about who we are and what we do, then we are immune to the actions and beliefs of others, knowing they don't determine our worth. We can freely speak up for ourselves and don't need to remain silent, passive, or "good," anymore.

The love and acceptance we seek from others must come from within us. All that appears around us reflects our inner state of consciousness. If we change inside, then the outer changes. When we believe differently, we experience differently, or it doesn't bother us. There isn't anything to defend or protect, which makes us immune to the opinions of others. When we give ourselves the freedom to live authentically, and don't give our power away, then we are truly free.

At this point in the tale, the princess feels safe enough to open herself to the masculine. The prince wanders around the castle until he finds her and then kisses Brier Rose. The new masculine in the psyche awakens the feminine with a kiss that lets her know that the time for slumbering has come to an end. She allows the masculine in, which means she feels ready to take action on her own behalf, leave the castle, and feel safe in the world as herself. The feminine energy has an inner orientation and when the masculine energy arrives, it's time to emerge. Brier Rose can now step beyond the confines of the castle and into the world as a powerful and fully integrated soul.

When the soul awakens to her true identity, the entire court is brought to life and becomes aware of the innate wholeness. She's accepted the rejected and excluded parts of her and now is free to be herself. The wisdom of life is understood and therefore there is peace, joy, and trust. *This* is how they lived happily ever after.

CHAPTER

Eight

Hansel and Gretel: Searching for Lost Treasure

*O*nce upon a time, there was a little boy named Hansel
and a little girl called Gretel. They lived near a forest
with their woodcutter father and stepmother. They were so
poor that there wasn't enough food for the children. One
night after the children had gone to bed, the stepmother
told the father that they should take the children deep into
the forest and leave them there. After much convincing,
the father agreed. Their parents didn't realize the children
were awake and could hear them. When their father and
stepmother fell asleep, Hansel went outside and collected
the pebbles that were shining in the moonlight.

In the morning, they all went to the forest. Hansel quietly dropped the pebbles as they walked without the parents noticing what he was doing. Their stepmother saw Hansel was looking back at the house as they walk away and asked what he's doing. He told her that he was saying goodbye to his kitten. Once they reach the forest, the father told the children to gather wood, which they put in a pile and lit. The parents said the children should rest by the fire and they would return for them later. When the children woke up it was dark and the fire had gone out. Gretel started to cry, but Hansel calmed her when he said that as soon as the moon came up, they would follow the pebbles home. They made it home before sunrise. Their stepmother was upset, but their father was relieved.

Eventually, it came to pass once again that the family didn't have enough food. The stepmother suggested that this time they lead the children more deeply into the forest and leave them there. The father was finally persuaded after much discussion. The children were once again awake and overheard their parents' conversation. Hansel said he would go out and get pebbles again, without realizing the stepmother locked the door. Gretel cried and Hansel told her they would find another way.

In the morning, the stepmother gave the children small pieces of bread to put in their pockets. Hansel crumbled his and secretly threw the crumbs down as they walked. The father asked Hansel what he was doing, since he noticed Hansel was looking back at the house. Hansel said he was saying goodbye to his pigeon. The family walked deep into the forest, made a big fire and again, the parents told the children to rest. When they woke up it was dark. Hansel said that they would follow the crumbs once the moon rose. They started out in the moonlight, but the birds had eaten the crumbs. They only had Gretel's small piece of bread and some berries they found to eat. They wandered until they were exhausted and fell asleep.

On the third day in the forest they saw a white bird sitting on a branch singing. The bird stopped singing and flew a little way. They followed it to a small house made of bread, cake, and confectionary. Hansel ate a bit of the roof and Gretel took a piece of the window. As they ate a voice inside the house asked who they were and they answered, "the heavenly child." The children continued eating as an old woman came out of the house. They were frightened but the old woman told them not to worry. She took them inside, gave them a nice meal, and clean beds to sleep in. They thought they were in heaven.

The old woman was actually a wicked witch whose house was designed to entice children. Any who happened find her house were killed, cooked, and eaten. The next morning while they slept, the witch grabbed Hansel and took him out to a shed with a door of iron bars. He yelled, but no one was around to hear him. The witch went inside and woke Gretel. She told her to get water and cook for her brother, to fatten him up for the witch to eat. Gretel cried, but did as she was told.

Hansel received the best food and Gretel got scraps. The witch went out every day to see if Hansel was fat enough to cook. But she couldn't see well, so when she told him to hold out his finger, he stuck out a scrawny twig. She eventually became impatient and decided to cook him the next day anyway.

In the morning, the witch told Gretel to get water and light the fire. She said they would make bread first. They went to the oven outside and the witch told Gretel to get in to see if it was hot enough. Gretel knew the witch planned to cook her and told the witch she didn't know how. When the witch stuck her head in to show Gretel how, Gretel gave her a push, closed the oven door, and locked it. The witched burned to death.

Gretel ran to the shed and let Hansel out. They danced and hugged and were so happy. The witch was dead, which meant it was safe to go back into the house. They found boxes of jewels, which they stuffed into their pockets, and then walked until they came to a lake. Hansel wondered how they would cross it, but Gretel saw a duck and asked it for a ride. They were carried to the other side one at a time.

Once on the other side, they walked until they figured out where they were, and eventually saw their house. They ran home, rushed inside and jumped into their father's arms. He was alone, since their stepmother died while they were *gone. Gretel showed her father the jewels in her apron and Hansel emptied his pockets. They lived happily ever after.*

Introduction

The negative older feminine in the psyche appears in this story as two women: the stepmother and the witch. Their state of consciousness keeps the family from thriving and living in abundance, because there is a fear of not enough. The father, who is the partner of the stepmother, is weak, ineffective, and doesn't stand up to her.

Believing they don't have enough to eat, the stepmother thinks the solution is to abandon the children, while the witch wants to eat them. These women and the father are the reason for this wasteland in which there is inadequate nourishment. The healthy feminine is critical to the emergence of the gifts into the world. She needs to learn that she is enough and has enough in order to be fully free. The masculine also needs to learn to stand up to the unhealthy feminine and follow the lead of the young intuitive feminine so they can find the way home.

Between Worlds

Hansel and Gretel live at the edge of a forest, which is a transitional place "between" worlds—the conscious and unconscious. The forest is a symbol of the unconscious. As human beings, we are also a link between the conscious and unconscious, the above and below, as well as the inner outer. We embody and can bring the union of the spirit and the soul to consciousness. The ability to miraculously bring unconscious gifts to consciousness, and then give them form, is ours alone. The children are symbols of the gifts of the unconscious that generate new life, and which need to be nourished, tended, and cared for.

This family is in lack consciousness, which is demonstrated by the stepmother. She doesn't want to feed the children because she doesn't feel like they have enough food for all of them. The children represent her own gifts, which she doesn't see or value, and neither does the culture. Her beliefs stem from her conditioning, which in turn is reflected, and

---

 Full story in Manheim's *Grimms' Tales for Young and Old.*

reinforced, by her experience. She didn't learn to value her gifts and so she doesn't hesitate to dispose of them herself. Since they weren't validated, they go back into the unconscious from whence they came.

When we feel overtired and so busy that we don't have the time, energy, or desire to nourish our children, meaning gifts of the soul, then the stepmother is active in consciousness. We feel like they are just another drain on our energy and don't even want them. In this situation, it's difficult to see their value and may cast them aside because there are more pressing things to take care of. Or so we might think.

In order to perpetuate the old pattern of poverty consciousness, the stepmother knows that she and the father must get rid of the children. She tells her husband that he might as well construct their coffins if he intends to let Hansel and Gretel stay. This shows us the stepmother's perspective: it's either the children or the parents who will survive, but they both can't live in consciousness together. This is actually true, it's either a new state of consciousness or the old. They are too different to coexist.

The old consciousness is one of famine and poverty, which can result from too much masculine energy. There's an imbalance of too much head and not enough heart, which results in inadequacy and a disconnection from the innate and natural state of abundance. This imbalance creates, and is the result of, a fear of needs not being met. We know this as "survival mode," which means the parents must work tirelessly just to make ends meet. Then there isn't any extra time, energy, nor is there the inclination to do more than only what must be done to survive.

In this situation, the feminine is unhealthy, while the masculine is passive and wounded. He can't, or won't, stand up to the stepmother's insatiable sense of inadequacy. They need to keep all they have for themselves. There isn't enough to go around, or enough to feed that which is youthful and vital. Here the masculine is incapable of quieting the voice of a feminine consumed with "not enough." She has a hunger that can't be filled and a thirst that can't be quenched. Her ceaseless striving to try to be enough, get enough, and have enough is exhausting for herself, and for anyone around her. She doesn't see or value the inner gifts that come from the Self, but believes the world of form and outer takes precedence over the inner. The emptiness she feels can't be satisfied because there isn't ever enough to fill it. Isn't it amazing how often we see similar themes in these stories?

These children, as symbols of the soul and spirit, represent inner wisdom, creativity, the ability to thrive and play, see magic, be content and happy with the sweetness and abundance of life. The gift of being in the moment and being present to life as it unfolds is a natural aspect of the child. They contain peace, love, wisdom, joy, and a fresh state of consciousness that approaches life with new eyes untainted by the past.

Hansel and Gretel together represent the union of the masculine and feminine. This is the way the opposites contained in the Self can appear in a fairy tale. The boy and girl unite as wholeness. *In the wholeness of the Self, nothing is missing. It includes everything and all needs are met.* This is the answer to "not enough" consciousness; it's not an outer change we need, but an inner one. We can look at the story to see how to reach a wholeness in which our needs are always met.

Into the Forest

The stepmother convinces the father to abandon Hansel and Gretel in the forest. She's afraid there isn't enough food for all of them and that they will all starve if the children stay. The old feminine wants to desert the gifts of the psyche, which means that they will go back into the unconscious. These children, or gifts, evoke feelings of inadequacy for her, and require too much time, energy, or effort. An example of this state of consciousness would be if she baked a loaf of bread with the intention of giving it to someone, but the end product didn't meet her standards, and so she scrapped the idea, possibly even throwing it away.

This abandonment is agreed to when the passive masculine in consciousness doesn't object, and goes along with, her belief that she must do "other things." Her actions are a distraction from taking action to change her life, which would get them out of poverty consciousness. If he was healthy, then she would have the thought to let's say, clean, instead of writing her book, and he would protest. He would be another voice in consciousness that would speak up and say, "No I'm not going to keep doing the same old thing!" In ourselves, we perpetuate the old patterns that are based on the values of the culture and our parents, by ignoring the parts of us that are generative and represent new life.

Hansel overhears his parents as they plan to abandon them in the forest. He sneaks outside in the moonlight and picks up stones that look like silver coins. Both silver and the moon are symbols associated with the feminine. The moon is the light shining in the dark, or the light in the unconscious, which illuminates the stones. This is the beginning of bringing something to conscious awareness. Hansel—the masculine—believes he can find his way out of the forest—the unconscious—by dropping the stones, which is a logical solution that comes from the intellect.

As the family leaves their home in the morning, Hansel secretly drops a trail of stones. The stepmother notices him pausing to look back at the house and asks why. He tells her he's looking at a kitten on the roof. This kitten is white and represents the purity of the young feminine. It's an animal that is earth-based, agile, and independent. He tries to maintain contact with this new young feminine energy as he leaves. The old woman can't see it because she can't see what she doesn't value.

When the parents build a fire for the children in the forest, they demonstrate how to create warmth and light in the unconscious. It isn't a sustaining fire however, and it goes out while the children sleep. The parents don't have the ability to create a fire that stays lit. The sustaining fire is one that would stay lit for as long as is needed.

When the children wake up, the moon is full, representing the fullness and wholeness associated with the feminine. The circle is a symbol of wholeness and the divine. This is the light in the dark that illuminates the stones. *The light of wholeness that can guide them home.* But in this case, they return to their parent's house of inadequacy, which means they aren't ready to leave that old state of consciousness yet. Hansel left a trail of stones in order to not get lost if they need to return to the old way of being. The children are abandoned in the unconscious, but find their way back, and resurface.

It's as though there were two options here. One was to return to the old state of consciousness which was one of "not enough." The other possibility was to remain in the light of the feminine state of wholeness. That would have been the new consciousness, but the children aren't ready for that yet. They still must go back to the old parental poverty consciousness.

We may decide that we will act on our dreams, say to write a book, but then, after a few chapters, we get busy, stick it in a drawer, and forget about it. This means that the child is being returned to the unconscious, where it came from. If one day, we find it, and resume working on it, then the child has found its way back into consciousness.

If we are afraid to leave the old consciousness behind, we may keep an escape route back to the past open until we are certain the new path will work out. This may look like working with our gifts but stopping just short of a full commitment. Our ability to move forward might be hampered by choosing to stay at an old job that doesn't give us the time we need to create a new life or holding onto friends that don't support our dreams. If we keep the old paths open, then we might retreat to what felt safe, when our insecurities or fears rise up.

Abandon the Children

The stepmother is quite irritated when the children return. They remain at home for a period of time, until the poverty consciousness gets to be too much for her, and she convinces the father once again to abandon them in the forest. The children are terrified when they overhear their parent's conversation. They are being rejected again and going back into the unconscious.

Hansel, the young masculine, comes up with a solution based on the past and what worked before, but the stepmother isn't going to let that happen again. She locks the door so he can't go out to get the stones. The door has closed to that and the past can't be repeated. Hansel doesn't have access to the wisdom in the psyche but relies on the intellect and reason. Sometimes that's effective and sometimes it isn't. In the morning, the stepmother gives the children morsels of bread. Hansel decides to leave a trail of crumbs from the house to the forest.

As they walk to the forest, the father asks Hansel why he keeps peering back at the house, to which he responds that his pigeon is saying goodbye. The pigeon is associated with the dove, which is the bird of the goddess and peace. Birds symbolize the connection between heaven and earth. They are messengers that deliver communications between gods and humans. This is Hansel turning back, to connect inside with a divine feminine and instinctual energy. With the kitten, the first time, it was an earth-based instinct and now it's a bird with an instinctual air orientation. A bird can navigate with a wider perspective, but doves are also connected to the earth.

Hansel, the new male aspect of the divine child, sees what the stepmother can't. When he says he's looking back at the pigeon, a new valued aspect of the feminine, she can't see it. *We need new eyes to see something new.* We can't depend on the old fear-based eyes to view the world, because that seeing is rooted in the past consciousness and beliefs. If there is lack, it's what is expected, and the abundance that's present can be overlooked. A new vision, a more expansive way of seeing is being called forth by this experience. A greater truth is coming into consciousness. What is it?

A new feminine is surfacing, since the old one is based on an erroneous belief. As the kitten, this feminine is independent and agile. She knows when to play, work, and rest. This feminine with the bird qualities isn't earth-bound and materially-oriented but is free of the fetters of a mundane life associated with conditioning. She's cared for by a Source that is beyond the material. All the bird requires to live is provided by nature. This is so foreign to our way of living and perception of the way the world works. Imagine the life of a bird. They sing with such joy when they wake up in the morning. They chatter animatedly, fly free, eat when hungry, and build nests with what is available. Birds live in harmony with nature and live in a world where there's enough for all, which is in stark contrast to the stepmother. Birds don't struggle to live. Nor do they hoard, or fear that there isn't enough to meet their needs. The parents aren't aware of the natural abundance of life.

This time, the parents build a big fire and leave the children even deeper in the forest than before. Again, they can only light a fire that warms temporarily. The gifts of the heart are being brought to consciousness and worked with. This is the second time a fire is kindled and goes out. In life, this appears as us working with our gifts for a period of time, but then our attention drifts. We get distracted by the world, lose confidence, or just don't trust. This fire refers to the heart and passion, which can nourish, but which this family can't access, since they are starving. They nourish themselves with a small amount of bread and warm themselves by the fire, but neither lasts. The heart connection can't be sustained.

The children haven't ever been to this part of the forest, which means they are exploring a new aspect of the unconscious. *Something new could happen in this moment*, but the children can't remain conscious and fall asleep. If they fall asleep, they go unconscious. They've been triggered by a familiar situation and revert to reacting with an old response. They need something new to arise out of consciousness.

A New Way

When the children wake up, it's dark. They wait for the moon to rise, but then realize they can't see the breadcrumbs Hansel put down for a trail. In the perfectly beautiful unfolding of the story, we see that the pigeon watched them leave the house, it watched Hansel drop the bread crumbs, and then ate them so the children can't return home. The old woman locked the door and then the pigeon ate the trail back to the old consciousness. That path isn't an option anymore and they are forced to look for a new way.

Hansel's idea doesn't work this time, or does it? Does he even have a choice in the matter, or is bird of the goddess doing this to prevent them from returning to an old way of life that's no longer suitable? The intellect can't figure out how to get them back to where they were, and the children remain in the unconscious. During this phase, it may appear to the outer world as though nothing is happening, because all of the work is taking place in the unconscious. This time, when the children try to return, they can't find their way home, and get lost. Or so they believe...

The children can't return to their home and now something new needs to happen to transform this situation. First, they must accept the feeling of being lost and not knowing what to do to resolve the situation. They are in an unfamiliar part of the forest—the unconscious—which indicates something will arise in consciousness to assist in the expansion of awareness. This can appear in a dream or in life.

Why do the gifts, or the new state of consciousness, keep landing back in the unconscious? What's remaining hidden and out of sight? What's preventing the authentic life?

The bird, associated with the goddess, guides the children to the exact situation they need. She closes the old door so they don't regress or look back, but only forward, or inward. If all the characters in the story are parts of the heroine, which would be Gretel, then the dove is another aspect of her, as much as the stepmother. The implication of this is that *the guidance comes from within*. Who locked the door? The stepmother. Who ate the breadcrumbs? The dove or the goddess within or without. The next transformation of consciousness is underway.

There can be sadness and grief when an old life ends, but *the old way of being must be released for something new to arise*. The family, patterns, and beliefs, as well as familial, ancestral, and cultural conditioning must be transformed if they don't serve us anymore, or support where we are heading. *We relate to others based on shared beliefs and understandings. When we let go of old beliefs, it changes how we relate.* Letting go of old beliefs can sometimes mean we have to release the people who are associated with those outdated ideas. This is a big shift. If you have related to others based on, let's say, victim consciousness, but then you open to another way of being, and don't want to remain in that state of consciousness, then you may no longer feel as close to those who are still in the old patterns. They may not be able to relate to you either, which may cause temporary feelings of anger, isolation, and loneliness as the energy shifts.

When we break out of fear-based views, we may worry that we will be rejected by others. If they begin to abandon us, we might be tempted to return to the old ways to win their approval, but we need to remain committed to the new path even if it's uncomfortable. When we understand that *we have what we need, will be provided for, are supported, and are not alone*, these concerns are alleviated.

But, at the moment, the children are still lost in the forest. They wander for three days and are afraid that they may perish from hunger and fatigue, just like the stepmother, which suggests that she is still alive in their consciousness. If the children remain in the forest, which again is the unconscious, then they face the possibility of dying there. At this moment though, something needs to come to consciousness, and we need to see what's preventing the emergence of these gifts into the world.

The number three is associated with transformation and the birth of something that transcends an old conflict, or duality. A symbol can appear in a dream, as a vision, or in life, to unite the opposites and be a harbinger of the new revelation. The new symbol that appears to Hansel and Gretel is a bird.

The Witch

The song of a beautiful snow-white bird leads them to a little house made of bread, cake, and sugar. It's the pure and free soul, the goddess, the witch, the inner wisdom guiding them forward to the next experience required for greater consciousness. Of course, this can be an inner or outer experience. The children eat pieces of the sweet house the witch created. When she asks who's nibbling on the house, the children reply that it's the "heavenly child," which is the Self. This child comes from heaven to earth, to unite the two.

She entices the children into the house with a meal and warm bed to sleep in. But let's be clear, the witch intends to devour the children, just as she's done many times before. The pattern is an old one in which she is caught in duality and judgment. The things that can bring new life are consumed—pushed back into the unconscious. Why? Because they, or she, isn't ever good enough.

Bringing her gifts into the world never felt like an option for this feminine—witch and stepmother—since she learned early on that it wasn't safe to do so. The witch and stepmother are two aspects of the same old feminine consciousness. They both want the children dead and gone. If the witch allows the new life out, she will be entirely different, which makes her feel vulnerable. She can't be herself because she got the message that she, and her gifts, are inadequate. The father doesn't challenge that consciousness or protect the children from the stepmother, and so this feminine hides who she really is, which means it's in the unconscious. It didn't feel safe for the stepmother/witch to shine and allow her Self to emerge, so she killed off that which is vulnerable and innocent to protect it from the rejection of others, by rejecting it herself first.

Both the victim and defensive aggressor consciousness must be released. The witch doesn't *trust life*. It's a challenge for her to *let the fullness of her Self shine*, because it makes her feel vulnerable. She needs to *approach all of life with an open curious awareness and surrender control*. Instead of closing down, she must open up and ask, "*What's showing up now? What do I need to see?*" and allow herself to sink into her rejected feelings and feel whatever comes up. She must descend from her head into the body and feel what she's been avoiding.

What does she need to see and feel? She must sit and feel her sadness and grief about being rejected, unloved, unvalued, abandoned, and inadequate, to be with it in a way that hasn't happened before now. Despite her history she could then embrace the idea that she's enough, has enough, and that her gifts are enough. This is an entirely new perspective for her. If she opens to the presence of abundance consciousness, then she may realize that the cup of her life is already filled to overflowing.

When she can listen to her inner wisdom, trust her knowing, her feelings, and the unfolding of her life, she will see that it serves her. The key is to accept all that appears without judgment or resistance. All the characters in the story are aspects of the heroine, so what is there for her to be afraid of?

Capture

The witch has an uncanny sense of smell and knew the children were coming when they were still a mile away. She's aware of such things, since she's devoured all the children who came this way before Hansel and Gretel. This is a familiar pattern of destruction and the way it unfolds may appear as a repeating set of circumstances. The witch illustrates how things end up back in the unconscious. She draws the children to the house with sweets, charms them inside with an offer of a warm meal and bed, and then eats them. She's as hungry and unsatisfied as the stepmother.

What does this look like in real life? We remember one day that we were writing a book, which we tucked into a drawer months—or years—ago, and we retrieve it. We resume working on it, then after a period of time, we get distracted by life *again*, put it back in the drawer *again*, and forget about it *again*. Then we remember it one day, take it out, work on it for a time, and put it back in the drawer when we get busy. This exact cycle can go on replaying for a long time without us even realizing we are in a repetitive pattern. Once we notice the pattern and bring it to consciousness, then we can begin to challenge it and not just unconsciously allow the gifts to return to the unconscious. If the book, gift, or you, don't get out into the world, then the witch has symbolically eaten the child.

This feminine consciousness—as the witch and stepmother—has an instinctual ability to *know what's coming*. This is what the children haven't been able to successfully do before, since they were always consumed by the witch in the past. They weren't ever able to sense her intentions and became her victims because of it. Previously, they fell for the stepmother and witch's tricks, since they all died. Hansel and Gretel must sniff out the witch's plan before she snares them in her trap. They saw what the parents were up to initially but couldn't get out of the unconscious on their own the second time.

Hansel gets trapped by the witch and the young masculine loses his freedom, which means the heroine must sit with the feeling of not being free. All three of them are in the unconscious—the forest—and the masculine is caged, which means nothing is going to happen in the world. This is an inner transformation of consciousness and no amount of outer action is going to change anything.

Normally, Hansel is the one who provides the solutions, but he's unavailable. He can't come up with an answer, either through the intellect, or action, because that's not the way to break this pattern. If action is taken out in the world, then the witch remains alive in the unconscious. If the intellect is utilized, then it won't be a new solution, since it's based on knowledge and previous experience. The intellect and action might have worked in certain circumstances in the past, but in this particular situation the children had always been devoured. This time needs to be different.

Gretel—the new young feminine in consciousness—must devise a plan that's entirely new by accessing a deeper wisdom. Until this point, Hansel has been the one in charge, but *now that the masculine is forced into inactivity, Gretel must come up with the answers herself.* She represents a new feminine wisdom, an intuition and instinct that hasn't been accessed before. She would be the embodiment of the kitten and dove, which Hansel brought to consciousness earlier, and now, also the witch's gift of knowing.

Intending to fatten him up, the witch feeds Hansel, and starves Gretel. She values the masculine and believes he provides the nourishment. Right? Most of us have been conditioned to believe that we need to take care of the masculine first and tend to the outer world. We must be responsible, take action, and do our work, if we want to eat and get our needs me. If there's enough time and energy, then we can attend to the feminine. The witch pays attention to the masculine and ignores the feminine. She doesn't feed Gretel because she doesn't value the young feminine, except as a servant to take care of her needs, wants, and wishes. She doesn't understand how critical the feminine and the inner world are to life.

Another aspect of feeding the masculine and starving the feminine is when the witch exploits the fruits of the feminine for financial gain. This happens, for example, when she uses the inner gifts with the primary focus of making money and loses the good feelings that she once received from them. It's when a painter ends up painting what sells and feels like a machine churning out products, instead of getting joy from her painting. This is taking the food from the psyche to feed the masculine. The witch forgets, doesn't care, or isn't aware, of the soul, and feels like she has no other choice than to do what she's doing to survive.

There are two important aspects of the inner world that the witch doesn't realize are integral to a good life. One is that inner beliefs shape the outer world. The second is that taking care of Gretel—the young feminine that represents the soul—is critical to our wellbeing. What that means for each of us can be different, but there are activities that tend to the feminine. The soul can be honored through meditation, being, gardening, anything creative, contemplation, spending time in nature, music, or dance, just to name a few. When we do these kinds of things and do what we love, it impacts our lives, our sense of peace, and makes us feel we are *living* our lives. These activities open us to a sense of meaningfulness, a depth of joy, and awaken our passion. They plant us in an embodied way into the realm of the soul.

The witch also doesn't understand that the inner world defines the outer. She carries an old feminine consciousness that's based on outdated beliefs that the outer world must be taken care of first. These ideas regarding the world and how it works must be transformed. The stepmother and witch live in a poverty consciousness and don't realize that the new feminine carries a consciousness of abundance, which is grounded in love, value, enoughness, and support. In this consciousness everything is enough, our needs are met, and we have access to an endless supply of ideas to create a life we love.

Hansel tricks the witch to buy time. He holds out a stick to her when she comes to feel his finger to determine if he's fat enough to eat. She's tricked because she can't see. She can't see what is right in front of her. She doesn't recognize the value of the inner feminine, which is the only place to feel that sense of enoughness and truly satisfy her hunger. Eventually, she gets impatient and no longer cares if Hansel is fat enough; she's going to eat him anyway.

What do we need to see? What's right in front of us that we don't believe has value? Or, that we have been told doesn't have value, but really does? It relates to the soul, the feminine, and abundance. What are the intuition, synchronicities, and dreams saying?

The witch tells Gretel she's going to eat Hansel, which activates victim consciousness in Gretel. She feels grief over the possibility of loss and is frightened. Gretel gets the water to cook with and weeps. The water symbolizes emotion and the unconscious. Tears are a purification by water and this grief cleanses the heart. Then, because she allowed her feelings to flow, there's a shift in consciousness from the victim to the opposite— empowerment—as a fire is built in the oven. When fire is used to cook, it symbolizes a purification and transformation. It can appear as anger, desire, or passion, which can be an energy that compels her to act and burns away anything that hampers her progress. This flame of the heart is being stoked for the third time in the story, which means a transformation is immanent.

Freedom and the Feminine

When the witch tries to trick Gretel into climbing in the oven to cook her, Gretel *knows* what's happening. This time, she *sees* what is going on and tricks the witch instead. Gretel senses the truth behind the witch's actions and knows she's up to no good. She tells the witch she doesn't know how to get into the oven and asks the witch to show her. The witch, unaware of Gretel's intent, shows her how to climb into the oven. Gretel gives a great heave, pushes her in, and closes the door. The witch burns to death. She's transformed by the fire of the heart, which finally frees the children.

Fire can be anger, which helps Gretel to stop being a victim, to see what isn't right, and then act appropriately. She can now see how the witch isn't serving them by keeping them in the unconscious or killing off what can save them. The witch is the aspect of Gretel that has been sacrificing the young feminine and her gifts, fearing that others would see her inadequacy. Gretel must come to realize that *she and her gifts have value, in and of themselves, and that she's enough as she is.* She must *feel* this inside of herself. The fear of being seen and in the world is transformed as it's repeatedly challenged. Gretel has to sit with the fear to feel it and then continually take steps to move out of her comfort zone.

Gretel finally stands up for herself when she pushes the witch into the oven. The old self-sabotaging patterns of hiding herself, or abandoning her gifts, are no longer acceptable. There's something inside of her, a feistiness, that rises up as she recognizes the value of her gifts and herself. She won't stand by and allow her gifts, or herself, to be devoured by the witch, sacrificed, or devalued by others, ever again. And that is that. It happened to the other children, but she won't be the victim this time, of herself, or anyone else.

Gretel is the one who frees them. She utilizes the fire to cook and transform the witch/stepmother in consciousness. This is the voice—inside or outside—that has said nothing is ever enough and believed the heart couldn't be followed because of some inadequacy, in one area or another. *It's during a time of inactivity, forced or chosen, that the witch is transformed by the heart through stillness, introspection, and taking the time to do what we love to do.*

We witness the witch as she's transformed and come to see that she's not a "mean" witch, she's just afraid, and contains the gift of knowing. We can have compassion for her—this part of ourselves—that's scared. She's not the enemy; she's merely afraid of being hurt again, like she was in the past. But the past is over, and now it's a new day. She can't go on forever expecting the old to endlessly recur, but instead, must open to new possibilities for greater good to appear in her life. We don't need to trample over her on the way out the door but can be gentle and kind to her, and the frightened inner child. She kept us safe until we were strong enough to emerge and stand on our own two legs. In this phase of deep change, it's helpful to watch for any form of protest that arises from within and keep going forward anyway.

During this time in the unconscious, we sit in stillness and watch what arises. We can see the witch as she tries to trick us into distraction, activity, and doing things her way, the old way of hiding, and not valuing the soul's gifts. If instead, we do what we love, and what feeds the soul, she will be transformed. We can witness whatever feelings and thoughts arise, allow them to come, and accept them. If we feel sadness and grief, we can give ourselves the space to breathe, weep, and mourn. When anger surfaces, as we challenge the witch, we watch it get stirred up, let it pass, and resume what we were doing. We will discover that we are more than these transient emotions as a deep foundation of stability is created within us.

Despite the past rejection of the witch and stepmother, a deeper sense of value is found within. The undernourishment of the past is transformed when abundance is realized. It's not just a material abundance, but the inherent abundance of life. It's knowing we are enough, our gifts have value, and the world is a lovely place without the fearful witch and stepmother active in the psyche.

A foundational stillness comes and is established as the ground which we stand. This is the presence that's always there regardless of any life circumstances. It's an inner awareness that knows what to do in each situation. In this consciousness, there isn't any valuing of one thing over another, as all things are perceived as equal and as having value. Every experience is met with an open-hearted curiosity and acceptance.

The beauty of all of our experiences is seen.

Gretel frees Hansel. The story says that now Hansel and Gretel don't have anything to be afraid of, since the witch is dead. She represents the part of them that was afraid and has been transformed. The children go back into the witch's house and discover a treasure trove of pearls and precious stones. It was there all along and available to them, they just had to awaken to a new consciousness to see it. Since the witch, who inspired fear, is dead, the treasures of the psyche can safely be carried out into the world.

Our fears are often of that which is perceived as being out in the world, but we can see from the story that the only thing to be afraid of was the inner witch and stepmother. They were the ones who were frightened by the idea of freedom, while the father stood passively by and didn't confront them. Meanwhile, the witch was the gatekeeper—with access to the bounty of the psyche.

Upon seeing the treasure, Hansel and Gretel fill their pockets with the precious stones. Then they leave the house, and walk along for a few hours, until they come to a lake. Hansel asks Gretel how they will cross it, which is a change, because, in the past, he had the answers, but now he knows that she does. Gretel says the white duck will assist them if she requests help. She comes up with the solution and demonstrates how all of nature, and the entire seen and unseen world, supports this emergence into wholeness. Unusual synchronicities can occur as the transformation to be ourselves, and bring our gifts into the world, unfolds.

The duck has the ability to fly and navigate the water. As such, it symbolizes the union of spirit and soul—the conscious and unconscious—which are united as one. In a consciousness of wholeness, there aren't any divisions between the spirit or soul, as they are one interconnected seamless reality. Nor are there any judgements of anything as good or bad, since all is perceived as in the service of love and the good, like we saw with the witch.

In response to Gretel's request, the duck comes to ferry them across the water. Hansel suggests they both get on the duck, but Gretel realizes they are too heavy, and so they ride separately. She has learned how to listen and follow her inner *knowing* about what to do in each situation, even if it is unfamiliar. Hansel and Gretel easily find their way home, since this is the right time for them. The witch may have prevented the return home in the past, but now the transformation is complete, and the healing has occurred. In this state of consciousness, there is a sense of freedom as the authentic self is lived.

When Hansel and Gretel reach the house, they discover that their stepmother has died. She and the witch were connected, since they perished together. Their deaths transformed the father, which means that now he's free to act without the influence of the old feminine consciousness. This leads us to the story's, and our, destination—an embodiment of home consciousness. The longing for home—a place of safety, security, love, peace, abundance, and a sense of being enough—is often sought without even realizing the presence of that desire. We can sometimes mistakenly search for it in the world, but here we are shown, by Hansel and Gretel, that what we are searching for is within us. The inability to satisfy this longing outside of us, can lead us to the inner home, of being and presence that is who we truly are.

The family doesn't have to worry about anything anymore and they live happily.

Epilogue

Happily Ever After

*T*he question I hear most frequently about fairy tales, after, "Why is the passive princess always waiting to be rescued by the prince?", is "What happens after they get married?" The stories say they lived happily ever after, but that's not real life. However, as you are quite familiar with by now, that's a literal perspective on the story.

When we perceive the fairy tales symbolically, we notice that the stories have common themes. The soul has been conditioned to identify itself in relation to the material world and forgets who it truly is. It then desires fulfillment through the outer, because that's what it believes will fill the emptiness. A sense of momentary wellbeing may arise when certain conditions are met, otherwise, there are varying degrees of suffering. The suffering serves a purpose initially, when it causes the soul to search for a *lasting* inner peace and happiness instead of the temporary fulfillment of the world. The search begins in the world, but for some, eventually turns inward.

Imagine living in a world where we sit with the discomfort of emotions, instead of running from them, because they have value and reveal more of ourselves to us. A world in which we learn that we aren't only bodies and minds, but souls who have a purpose. Life would be about becoming more and more authentic and that all events happen to assist us in the expansion of our consciousness. We are taught to embrace and value the inner world of imagination, dreams, and their stories. It could be a life in which we understand who we are, why we are here, and perceive our role in the greater cosmic unfolding.

We might imagine this new world as one in which everything has a meaning and purpose that is knowable to us. Where we live in harmony with nature and understand the cycles of expansion and contraction, building up and falling apart, within ourselves and in the world. We approach all that's unknown with a fearless, open curiosity and love unconditionally. The stories of our families are no longer repeating from one generation to the next, like the inevitability of inherited DNA, but seen as evolving and transforming into greater possibility through a conscious engagement with life. It is a place where differences and uniqueness are perceived as having value and as adding something to the emerging wholeness.

Without a shadow of a doubt, we know that freedom and happiness must be found inside first, and then the world around us transforms to reflect that consciousness. It is a world in which happily ever after isn't an absurd fantasy at the end of a fairy tale, but the life we live when we shed the old conditioned story about ourselves and the world. It doesn't mean that we don't have any challenges, but that our experiences show up to teach us and help us grow into a newer and more expanded version of ourselves.

In this new world, we are living outside of the storied patterns we see in fairy tales, which means we are embodied souls that are open to, and one with, spirit, rooted in the inner stillness, and guided by it. We create a fresh abundant life in each moment, with the inner source of wisdom offering new gifts of ideas, talents, and spontaneous insights. Every day is approached as the unknown and met with clear eyes that don't peer through the glasses of yesterday, but through the fullness of the present moment. We embrace the freedom inherent in life, experience the joy of being, and are excited about what's coming. It's a world where our feet are firmly planted on the earth and our hearts are living in heaven. That's a happily ever after for the soul.

Acknowledgments

*I*t was an interesting journey to bring this book out into the world. At times, like the characters in the fairy tales, I was uncertain if I was ever going to bring it to full fruition. Unlike my first book, this one had its own rhythm and flow, and I learned much about life and trust through the creation process. I felt like the characters were my companions as I wrote and their experiences were mirrored in my life, which enabled me to understand their stories more deeply and have compassion for all of them. I felt new emotions for characters that I hadn't felt in the past as I learned more about why they were the way they were. The outer and inner journey with these stories has been fascinating. I would like to thank many of those who have been instrumental in the unfolding of my story.

My dreams have been a constant companion and have helped me, as much as the stories have, to reach new ways of perceiving life. I appreciate the wisdom of the dream source and am immensely grateful for the support of this constant companion. Sophia (Wisdom) made herself known to me years ago during meditation. She has appeared in various ways over the years and helped me to see her as a guiding presence. She is the divine feminine for me and her divine masculine counterpart has also been active in my life.

Close friends have been fundamental to my ability to remain on a path that has felt lonely and unclear at times. They have exhibited great kindness and patience as I endlessly talk about the fairy tale characters as though they are living friends. Teresa Schact has been a loving supportive soul sister to me since third grade. She has been there through all of the ups and downs of life and believed in me even when I lost faith in myself. I can't imagine my world or what my life would have been without her. Wendi Hill, coach extraordinaire, has been an invaluable guide and friend. She's been there at key times with a thoughtful open heart and loving arms. Soul sister and brother Karuna Mae and Ramprashad have pushed the envelope with me spiritually and materially. Their presence has been a comfort and makes me smile. I gratefully acknowledge Karuna's invaluable assistance in the editing process. Mytrae Meliana has been a wonderful and encouraging friend through our personal transformative journeys.

There were people that I met at various times in my life who were instrumental in seeing things in me that I couldn't see in myself. Mr. Blumenthal, Dr. Charlotte Zales, Dr. Thomas Legere, Alexander Hromlich, and Rev Wayne Sauder were a few of those angels. My cohort and our years at Pacifica will always hold a special place in my heart. The professors at Pacifica, with their vision and ideals, have been inspirational. I acknowledge those whose names I don't know but have seen the evidence of their hands at different times in my life.

I see the people who help make this book a reality as partners in its creation. Their paths inextricably intertwined with this for their own reasons. I thank them for assisting in the birth of this book into the world. A special mention to Sandy Draper for her patience and editing services and Mark Quinn for reviewing earlier versions of this book.

I would like to mention Ana Strandquest, Lisa Hunter, and Catherine Cook all of whom I remember with love and fondness. And finally, love and deep gratitude to Darrall Huber for believing in me and my work, even when he didn't understand what I was doing.

Appendix

Initiatory Qualities

Beauty—Seeing the true deeper beauty of life, nature, and the world, in oneself and others.

Blessing—Understanding that everything is a blessing, even those things that don't appear as such are trusted, knowing that in the end they will be revealed to be so. An innate desire to bless others and be generous of heart.

Creativity—Expressing what wants to emerge. Bringing what's fresh and new to awareness. Sharing it with others. Seeing the inherently creative nature of all life.

Discernment—Discerning projections, what belongs to us and what doesn't, when to stay and when to move on. What needs to be followed and what needs to be transformed. What serves and what doesn't. Knowing how to maintain balance and how to make adjustments when out of balance.

Freedom—Discovering inner freedom and being free. Realizing true freedom can never be given or taken away. No one can be restricted unless they agree to it on some level. Being willing and courageous enough to live freely. The truth will make you free. Being willing to hear the truth and live it.

Joy—Being in that place of joyfulness that arises from, and is based, deep within. It doesn't depend on life circumstances but is the true nature that arises spontaneously at the beauty of life.

Light—Allowing one's light to shine in the world as a beacon that leads the way to truth and as an inspiration to others. Seeing and honoring the light in self and others. Being fearlessly willing to embrace the so-called darkness, until we discover the light within it.

Love—Living courageously with an open and curious heart, not defensively protecting self or others. Loving everyone and all situations unconditionally. Receiving and giving love freely. Understanding that all is love, even though it may be difficult to see.

Patience—Understanding timing, and the rhythm of the journey. Knowing when to act and when to wait, if things are in the incubation stage, or are being integrated. Being able to sit in the stillness and patiently know the right moment will arise. An awareness of where you are in the process of transformation. Being able to change course if you are wrong. Not allowing the mind to take over and try to "figure it out," because when it can't "understand," it may lapse into fear.

Peace—Remaining stable in the face of all circumstances. Having unshakable faith. A foundation based in grace and stillness. Emanating an aura of peace that calms others.

Power—Learning to stand in your own power. Reclaiming projections from people and institutions. Stepping beyond warrior and victim roles, as well as allegiances to historic ways of being and believing. Being powerful not from the ego and fear but embodying a power that's based in the heart.

Trust—Learning to trust the process of life and its unfolding. Trust that there's a higher plan and a greater wisdom organizing the events in your life. Understanding that all is well and perfect as it is in this moment, seen or unseen.

Understanding—Opening oneself to greater understanding, meaning, and the wisdom inherent in the unfolding and experience of life.

Wisdom—Knowing that comes from beyond the intellect. A guiding force that is greater than day-to-day consciousness. Wisdom grows from reflecting, integrating, and living the lessons that are learned. It's felt in the body, trusted, and acted on.

Endnotes

1   See Jean Houston, *The Search for the Beloved: Journeys in Mythology and Sacred Psychology* (New York: Jeremy P. Tarcher/Putnam, 1987); Marie-Louise Von Franz, *The Golden Ass of Apuleius: The Liberation of the Feminine in Man* (Boston: Shambala Publications, Inc., 2001); Erich Neumann, *Amor and Psyche: The Psychic Development of the Feminine* (Princeton: Princeton University Press, 1956); Murray Stein and Lionel Corbett, *Psyche's Stories: Modern Jungian Interpretations of Fairy Tales* (Williamette: Chiron, 1993).

2   Houston, The Search for the Beloved, 151,

3   Suzanne Schaup, *Sophia: Aspects of the Divine Feminine Past & Present* (York Beach: Nicholas-Hays, Inc., 1997).

4   www.surlalunefairytales.com

5   Robert A. Johnson, *The Fisher King & the Handless Maiden: Understanding the Wounded Feeling Function in Masculine and Feminine Psychology* (San Francisco: HarperSanFrancisco, 1993), 57.

6   Marion K. Woodman, Kate Danson, Mary Hamilton, and Rita Greer Allen, *Leaving My Father's House: A Journey to Conscious Femininity* (Boston: Shambala Publications, Inc., 1992), 24.

7   Carl G. Jung, *C. G. Jung on Nature, Technology, and Modern Life*, ed. Meredith Sabini (Berkeley: North Atlantic Books, 2008), 1.

8   Ibid, 91.

9   Madame Leprince De Beaumont, *Beauty and the Beast*, trans. P. H. Muir (New York: Alfred A. Knopf, 1968), 4.

10 Jung, Jung on Nature, xi.

11 Ibid, 15.

12 Hans Biedermann, *Dictionary of Symbolism: Cultural Icons & the Meanings Behind Them*, trans. by J. Hulbert (New York: Penguin Books, 1989), 289.

13 Barbara Walker, *The Woman's Dictionary of Symbols and Sacred Objects* (New York: Harper Collins Publishers, 1988), 13.

14 Erich Neumann, *The Great Mother: An Analysis of the Archetype*, trans. by Ralph Manheim (Princeton: Princeton University Press, 1963), 5.

15 Leprince De Beaumont, *Beauty and the Beast*, 18.

16 Jung, Jung on Nature, 18.

17 Ibid, 73.

18 Leprince De Beaumont, *Beauty and the Beast*, 26.

19 Edward F. Edinger, *Ego and Archetype* (Boston: Shambala Publications, Inc., 1972), 150.

20 Ibid.

21 Leprince De Beaumont, *Beauty and the Beast*, 46-7.
22 Carl G. Jung, *Memories, Dreams, and Reflections* (New York: Vintage Books, 1963), 388.
23 Ibid, 17.
24 Robin Robertson, *Jungian Archetypes: Jung, Godel, and the History of Archetypes* (York Beach: Samuel Wiser, 1995), 191.
25 Ibid.
26 Barbara Walker, *The Woman's Encyclopedia of Myths and Secrets* (San Francisco: Harper San Francisco, 1983), s.v. "Witch."
27 Clarissa Pinkola Estes, *Women Who Run with the Wolves: Myths and Stories of the Wild Woman Archetype* (New York: Vintage Books, 1963), 388.
28 Sally Nichols, *Jung and Tarot: An Archetypal Journey* (York Beach: Samuel Wiser, 1980), 284.
29 Mary Esther Harding, *Woman's Mysteries: Ancient and Modern* (Boston: Shambala Publications, Inc., 1971), 129.
30 Edward F. Edinger, *Anatomy of the Psyche: Alchemical Symbolism in Psychotherapy* (La Salle: Open Court, 1985), 18.
31 Harding, Woman's Mysteries, 129.
32 Edinger, Anatomy, 10.
33 Ibid, 11.
34 C. G. Jung, *Alchemical Studies*, trans. by R. F. C. Hull (Princeton: Princeton University Press, 1967).
35 Ambika Wauters, *Chakras and their Archetypes: Uniting Energy Awareness and Spiritual Growth* (Toronto: Crossing Press, 1997).
36 Ibid.
37 Ibid.
38 Ted Andrews, *Animal Speak: The Spiritual and Magical Powers of Creatures Great & Small* (St. Paul: Llewellyn Publications, 1999), s.v. "Frogs."
39 Ted Andrews, *Animal Wise: The Spirit Language and Signs of Nature* (Jackson: Dragonhawk Publishing, 1999), 359.
40 Andrews, Animal Speak, 49.
41 Ibid, s.v. "Swallow."
42 Ibid.
43 Ibid.
44 Walker, The Woman's Dictionary, 186.
45 Jakob L. K. Grimm, and Wilhelm K. Grimm, *Grimms' Tales for Young and Old: The Complete Stories*, trans. by R. Manheim (New York: Anchor Books, 1977), 175.
46 Ibid.

Bibliography

Andrews, Ted. 1999. *Animal Speak: The Spiritual and Magical Powers of Creatures Great & Small*. St. Paul: Llewellyn Publications.

—. 1999. *Animal-Wise: The Spirit Language & Signs of Nature*. Jackson: Dragonhawsk.

Apuleius, Lucius. 2012. *The Golden Asse*. Translated by W. Adlington. Amazon Digital Services, LLC.

Biedermann, Hans. 1989. *Dictionary of Symbolism: Cultural Icons & the Meanings Behind Them*. Translated by J. Hulbert. New York: Penguin Books.

De Villeneuve, Madame. n.d. *Beauty and the Beast*. Translated by J. R. Planche. U.K.: Pook Press.

Edinger, Edward F. 1985. *Anatomy of the Psyche: Alchemical Symbolism in Psychotherapy*. La Salle: Open Court.

—. 1972. *Ego and Archetype*. Boston: Shambala Publications, Inc.

Estes, Clarissa Pinkola. 1992. *Women Who Run with the Wolves: Myths and Stories of the Wild Woman Archetype*. New York: Ballantine Books.

Grimm, Jakob L. K., and Wilhelm K. Grimm. 1977. *Grimms' Tales for Young and Old: The Complete Stories*. Translated by R. Manheim. New York: Anchor Books.

Harding, Mary Esther. 1971. *Woman's Mysteries: Ancient and Modern*. Boston: Shambala Publications, Inc.

Houston, Jean. 1987. *The Search for the Beloved: Journeys in Mythology and Sacred Psychology*. New York: Jeremy P. Tarcher/Putnam.

Johnson, Robert A. 1993. *The Fisher King & The Handless Maiden: Understanding the Wounded Feeling Function in Masculine and Feminine Psychology*. San Francisco: Harper San Francisco.

Jung, C. G. 1967. *Alchemical Studies*. Translated by R. F. C. Hull. Princeton: Princeton University Press.

Jung, Carl G. 2008. *Jung on Nature, Technology, and Modern Life*. Edited by Meredith Sabini. Berkeley: North Atlantic Books.

—. 1963. *Memories, Dreams, and Reflections*. New York: Vintage Books.

Leprince De Beaumont, Madame. 1968. *Beauty and the Beast*. Translated by P. H. Muir. New York: Alfred A. Knopf.

Neumann, Erich. 1956. *Amor and Psyche: The Psychic Development of the Feminine*. Princeton: Princeton University Press.

—. 1963. *The Great Mother: An Analysis of the Archetype*. Princeton: Princeton University Press.

Nichols, Sally. 1980. *Jung and Tarot: An Archetypal Journey*. York Beach: Samuel Wiser, Inc.

Robertson, Robin. 1995. *Jungian Archetypes: Jung, Godel, and the History of Archetypes*. York Beach: Nicholas-Hays, Inc.

Schaup, Suzanne. 1997. *Sophia: Aspects of the Divine Feminine Past & Present*. York Beach: Nicholas-Hays, Inc.

Stein, Murray, and Lionel Corbett. 1993. *Psyche's Stories: Modern Jungian Interpretations of Fairy Tales*. Williamette: Chiron Publications.

von Franz, Marie- Loise. 1956. *The Golden Ass of Apuleius: The Liberation of The Feminine in Man*. Princeton: Princeton University Press.

Walker, Barbara. 1988. *The Woman's Dictionary of Symbols and Sacred Objects*. New York: Harper Collins Publishers.

—. 1983. *The Woman's Encyclopedia of Myths and Secrets*. San Francisco: Harper San Francisco.

Wauters, Ambika. 1997. *Chakras and their Archetypes: Uniting Energy Awareness and Spiritual Growth*. Toronto: Crossing Press.

Woodman, Marion, K. Danson, M. Hamilton, and R. G. Allen. 1992. *Leaving My Father's House: A Journey to Conscious Femininity*. Boston: Shambala Publications, Inc.

www.surlalunefairytales.com. n.d.

Index

defined, xxxv
knife as symbol of, 22
of location, 60, 78
of longing, 88
as male quality, 7, 129, 134, 137–138
of motives, 40
sorting and, 30–31, 123, 125
without sight, 198
dishonesty, 18–19
distractions, 39–40
divine feminine, xxx–xxxiii, 6–10,
38, 42–44, 116, 151–152, 219,
236–237. *See also* Aphrodite;
mother; wise women
does (deer), 165–166, 170
doubling, 18, 118, 141
doves and pigeons, 134, 141–142,
234–236
dreams, 14–15, 28, 71–72, 78–80, 87,
115, 123–124, 129–130, 138,
205–206
duality. *See* opposites
ducks, 244

eagles, 37–38
Eden. *See* Garden of Eden
Edinger, Edward, 71–72, 116
ego, xvii–xviii, 5–6, 23, 37, 44, 71–72,
87, 107–108, 135, 222. *See also*
devil
The Emerald Tablet, 125
emergence, 62, 104, 134, 140, 150,
159–160, 217, 230, 237, 244
emotions, 53. *See also* tears
bringing to consciousness, 221–222
challenging, 133, 162–164, 183–
185, 218
fluctuations in, 34
moon as symbol of, 116
"negative," 192–193

repressed, 28–29, 52–54, 161, 190,
201–202
response to, 74, 98–99, 123–125,
135–136, 157–158
romantic relationships and, 14–15
sitting with, 26, 28, 35, 115–116,
158, 190, 193, 208, 215, 239,
242, 245. *See also* witnessing
snow as symbol of, 195
water as symbol of, 27, 32, 60, 214–
215, 241
witnessing, 19, 28, 33–37, 40–41,
98, 100, 135, 153, 215, 221,
224, 243
empowerment, xxxiv, 95–96, 133–136
enlightenment, 10, 16, 142
enough/being enough, 7, 69, 77, 86,
96, 103, 119, 131, 138–139. *See
also* wholeness
Eros. *See also* Psyche and Eros
awakening Psyche, 44
meaning, 5
Psyche's search for, 26–27
role of, xxxii
escape, 32, 95–96, 135, 233
Estes, Clarissa Pinkola, 88
Eve, xxx–xxxi, 86, 147–148
exclusion, 211–225. *See also* Brier
Rose (Sleeping Beauty)
extraverts, 56

fairy tales, xxxi–xxxiii, 114–115, 121,
245–246
family. *See also individual family
members; individual stories*
in Beauty and the Beast, 56–57
caring for, 79, 118, 122–123, 150.
See also sacrifice; servant
archetype
new identity and, 134
normal, 176–177

intellect, 51, 56–58, 95–96, 105, 109, 182, 233–234, 236, 239

introverts, 56

intuition, 42–43, 92–93, 105, 109, 134, 184, 188–189, 198, 200, 240–241

invitations, 129–130

isolation, 72, 93–95, 98, 102–104, 107–109, 220

jealousy, 16–17, 23, 51, 77–78, 192–193, 219

Jesus, 10, 107, 116, 148, 153. *See also* Christ archetype

joy, 108, 170–171, 178, 187–188, 191, 222, 235, 249

judgment, 89, 126, 142, 167, 200, 238

Jung, Carl, xxiii, 55, 67–68, 85, 114

kairos, 114

kings, 129–130, 159, 168–169, 209–210, 213

kittens, 233

knives, 22–23

lack consciousness. *See* poverty consciousness

light, 21–23, 36, 60–61, 67, 115–116, 167, 201–204, 232–233, 249

lilies, 186

Lilith, xxx

limiting beliefs, 14–15, 37, 50, 76, 87, 141, 155–156, 187–188, 196–198, 207–208

longing, 106–107, 213–214

lost treasure, 227–244. *See also* Hansel and Gretel

love. *See also* Aphrodite; Eros
abandonment by, 7–9, 27
divine, 115–116
as energy, 90

fear of, 161, 163, 200–201
freedom and, 191, 193, 195
inner masculine, love of, 50, 80–81, 141–142
nourishment from, 188–189
opening to, 170–171, 207, 250
power of, 21–23, 38, 108–109
rose as symbol of, 59
value of, 64

Maj/Maja/Maya, 210

manifestation, 31, 67–68, 134, 197–199, 213–214

marriage, xviii, xxxi, 6, 24, 44, 51, 160, 209. *See also* weddings

marriage of Cupid and Psyches. *See* Psyche and Eros

Mary, 59

masculine. *See also individual characters*
blind masculine, 105–106
energy, 189
masculine-feminine balance, xxxiii–xxxiv, 7, 51, 95
new, 13–15, 158–160. *See also* prince archetype
old masculine consciousness. *See* father archetype
rejected, 151–152

maybugs, 187–195

merchants, 57

messages, 163–165, 214–216

mice, 196–198

missing feminine, 50–52

mole, 198–202

moon, 7, 52, 115–116, 147, 203, 232–233

mother archetype. *See also* parents
absent mother, 50, 52, 59, 127, 129
childless mother, 176–177

death of good mother, 111–142. *See also* Ashputtle

field mouse, 197

helpless, 150

Inchelina's, 178–180

insatiable, 99

king's mother, 164–165

Mother, 52–53, 207–208

mother toad, 180–183

negative mother complex, 85–87

silent, 217

stepmother, 118–119, 121, 127, 230–231, 234, 237–238

wounded mother, 121, 181, 199

nature, rhythms of, 55, 57–58, 91–92, 94, 152

nectar, 188–189

negative mother complex, 85–87

neglect, 8–9, 29, 181

Neumann, Erich, 62

new feminine. *See* daughter archetype

nigredo/blackening, 120

not enough. *See* inadequacy

not helping others, 39–40

nourishment, 61, 86, 157, 187–189, 230–231, 240

numbers

one, 78

three. *See* three

four, 110, 215

seven, 167–168

twelve, 176–177

thirteen, 217–218

obedient daughter, 149–151

oil, 23, 25, 27

old beliefs/patterns

about self, 135–136

abundance and, 76–77, 231–232

death of, 221, 223, 236–237

family beliefs, 100–101, 153–157

generativity, 217–218

protection, need for, 97–98

one, 78

open curiosity, 89, 101, 125, 165–166, 171, 200, 246

opposites

Ashputtle's sisters, 118

black and white, 118

confronting, 85

docile and aggressive, 33

duality, xiii, xvii, 34–35, 85–86, 118, 124, 142, 148, 167, 191, 237

enough/not enough, 131. *See also* enough/being enough

inner and outer, 22, 35–36, 39, 104–105, 114, 125, 134–135, 138, 171, 191

large tasks and small details, 30–31, 37, 130–131, 197, 203, 209

Psyche's sisters, 18

separation of, 125–126. *See also* separation

silver and gold, 133

union of, 37, 135–137, 150, 152, 190, 192, 231–232, 237

Oracle of Apollo, 10–11

outer world

devaluation of feminine, xxxiii

dreams and, xxvi, 98

inner world and, 13, 19, 24, 43, 64, 68–69

material success, 61

not-enoughness and, 40

perceptions of, 52–54, 57–58, 76–77

sense of self from, 11, 85–89, 102–103, 105, 125–126, 132, 214, 220, 236, 240–241

Pan, 26, 32

purity of, 151–152
soul and, 6–7, 36, 134–137, 244
tower and, 92, 101–102
spring, 43, 178, 205–206
stepmother archetype, 118–119, 121, 230–231, 234, 237–238
stepsisters, 118–119
storms, 59–62
summer, 207–208
sun, 7, 32, 34–35, 116, 200–203, 208–209
surrender, 71–72, 222–223
swallow, 202–204, 208–209

tears, 60, 109, 126–127, 130–131, 153, 155, 164, 204, 208, 241
third chakra, 178, 190
thirteen, 217–218
three, 41, 74, 101, 129–130, 138, 150, 176–178, 237. See also Trinity
throat chakra, 183, 203–204, 207
Thumbelina, 173–210. See also Inchelina
toads, 180–183
tower, 38–39, 92–93, 220
transcendent center, xxvii, 85, 104, 109–110, 138–139, 142
transformation, 25–26, 81, 145–146
transitions, 14–16, 72, 217
treasure, searching for lost, 227–244. See also Hansel and Gretel
trees, 126–128, 136–137, 171
apple trees, 147–149
pear trees, 157–158
Trinity, 101–102, 104, 110, 134. See also Christianity
true bride, 141–142
trust
lack of, 162
in life, 17, 20, 22, 129, 146, 185, 250
in masculine, 160

in others, 29, 75, 155, 165, 191–192
in Self, 80, 170–171, 209, 238
in timing of unfolding, 41, 54, 220
in universe, 67, 107–108, 151, 158, 167
truth, 64–66, 72–77, 140–142, 249
tulips, 177–178
twelve, 176–177

ugliness, 181, 192
unclear messages, 163–165
unconsciousness, xix, 8–9, 71, 86, 196, 201–202, 230–232. See also repression
underground, 199, 201–202
understanding, 7, 20, 29, 39, 90, 104, 120, 140, 149, 157, 250
underworld, 35, 38–44, 118–119, 150, 166, 196. See also unconsciousness
union-separation-reunion
reunion. See reunion
separation. See separation
union, 6, 35–36, 81, 85, 130, 133–136, 158–161, 182, 232, 244
union of opposites. See opposites
uniting soul with God of Love, 1–45. See also Psyche and Eros
unity consciousness, 86, 191
the unseen, 8, 17, 22–23, 39, 114–115, 127–128, 133, 146

Venus, 116. See also Aphrodite
Vestal Virgins, 115
victim consciousness
Ashputtle, 117, 131–132
Handless Maiden, 154, 161–162
Hansel and Gretel, 238
Inchelina, 177–178, 183, 186, 193–194

About the Author

Author photo by Andy Johanson

*P*amela S. Alexander, PhD, earned a doctorate in depth psychology from Pacifica Graduate Institute. She is a poet, author, artist, dreamworker, and personal/spiritual growth advocate on a passionate lifelong mission to expand people's consciousness and help them reach greater heights. Currently, she leverages an embodied, compassionate approach to assist her clients in tapping into the infinite wisdom within their own transformational dreamscapes. This method evolved over twenty years as she explored the dreams of her clients and herself. Whether it's a self-development course, poetry book, or fairytale, she utilizes the power of words to instill a message of healing, love, hope, and total-life transformation.

Pamela's affinity for the written word began with poetic expression, which resulted in the publication of her book *Psyche's Poetry: Beauty to Awaken the Soul*. Her interest in story interpretation was inspired by a symbolic exploration in graduate school of "Snow White and Rose Red." From there, she went on a journey to see the Wizard of Oz with Dorothy and friends, and before she knew it, she was fascinated with symbolism, which she views as the language of the soul.

Her spiritual journey began at the age of thirty with an awakening, which she refers to as a direct encounter with the void. At the same time, a series of dreams revealed unknown gifts in the arts. The primary focus of her work is around the soul, symbolism, and the emergence of the feminine.

Outside of penning poetry and dreamwork, Pamela can be found either hiking, XC skiing, or cycling. However, her avid interest in all things spiritual and psychological takes center stage.

To find out more about Pamela S. Alexander's work with dreams and her creativity, feel free to visit her official website at www.WisdomOfTheSwan.com.

Printed in the United States
By Bookmasters